the agitator

in american society

SOCIAL SCIENCE SOLVED.

THE MODERN ARCHIMEDES. "*Eureka! Eureka!*"

"Constant Vigilance" (committee) "is the price of Liberty" in San Francisco.

From *Harper's Weekly*, Vol. 24 (April 10, 1880), 225. The caption reads, "SOCIAL SCIENCE SOLVED. THE MODERN ARCHIMEDES. '*Eureka! Eureka!*' 'Constant Vigilance' (committee) 'is the price of Liberty' in San Francisco." Thomas Nast's hostile cartoon concerning Kearneyism and the "New Constitution" of California exaggerates both the violence of the period and Kearney's influence on the California Constitution of 1879–1880. Most agitations are viewed by outsiders as a threat to established institutions. In practice they have tended to modify but not destroy these institutions.

charles w. lomas

the agitator
in american society

prentice-hall, inc.
englewood cliffs, new jersey

PRENTICE-HALL INTERNATIONAL, INC., *London*
PRENTICE-HALL OF AUSTRALIA, PTY. LTD., *Sydney*
PRENTICE-HALL OF CANADA, LTD., *Toronto*
PRENTICE-HALL OF INDIA PRIVATE LTD., *New Delhi*
PRENTICE-HALL OF JAPAN, INC., *Tokyo*

Library of Congress Catalog Card Number: 68–15352

Printed in the United States of America

Current printing (last number):
10 9 8 7 6 5 4 3 2 1

preface

The collection of speeches presented here is representative of important aspects of agitation in the United States over the last eighty years. Agitational speaking is by its nature ephemeral; it is usually extemporaneous, often impromptu. Frequently it is preserved only by the accidental presence of an interested newspaper reporter, by the special interest of a propagandistic journal, or by the hostile pen of a police reporter. In a few cases, the speakers themselves have preserved the speeches in pamphlet form. In the contemporary world, the tape recorder has given access to accurate texts in a few public archives and scattered private collections. None of the speeches in this book may be found in the usual anthologies. In a sense they are speeches that no one except myself has thought worth preserving in an easily accessible form.

Anyone who has studied agitational speaking will think of other speeches which ought to have been included—those of the women's rights and temperance movements, for example. Some contemporary speeches have been deliberately excluded, such as Martin Luther King's "I Have a Dream," which is readily available in other sources. Some may question the omission of Wendell Phillips, the idol of late nineteenth-century radicals. Regional specialists may wonder at the absence of Burnette Haskell or Joe Buchanan or Mary (Yellin') Lease. Obviously, limitations of space require the exclusion of many speeches which might well have been used.

In the selection of those to be included I have been guided to some extent by the practical consideration of availability. For older speeches, this involved access to obscure sources, such as anarchist newspapers and rare political pamphlets. In the case of recent speeches, availability has sometimes required many weeks and months of correspondence. Some speakers withheld texts I wished to use because they were syntactically imperfect, or because the audience was an "in-group" and the materials in the speech were not for publication, or because they were in doubt about the good will of the editor of the collection.

A second criterion was the representative quality of the speeches themselves. The section on civil rights is a case in point. It would have been easy to limit this section to "Negro rights," but such a limitation would do violence to the long history of the civil rights movement. Similarly in the section on socialism, four speakers were selected representing diverse elements of the socialist movement. Obviously others might have been substituted, particularly for Henry George and Big Bill Haywood, but each of the four does represent a distinct phase of the movement.

Finally, consideration was given to the accuracy of the text. With recorded speeches, the only problem was to prevent the authors of the speeches from revising the texts. All speeches presented here from recordings are exactly as delivered. With older speeches, accuracy is a greater problem. Stenographic reports are clearly the best, unless there is evidence that the speaker spoke from manuscript. Where differences in such reports exist, collations have been made to secure as complete and accurate a text as possible. Where choice was necessary, explanations are given in the introduction or footnotes.

In the introduction I have drawn at length from material I have published in *Speech Monographs*, the *Quarterly Journal of Speech*, and *Western Speech*. For permission to use these materials I am indebted to the Speech Association of America and the Western Speech Association.

C.W.L.

contents

the agitator

in american society

introduction

In the quiet decade of the 1950's, many thought agitation a lost art in America. Professors who had been educated or who had taught in the exciting atmosphere of the 1930's, felt that the present students were apathetic. They seemed uninterested in public affairs, and wanted only secure jobs and comfortable homes in the suburbs. Similarly, the nonacademic citizen thought the Supreme Court edict to end segregation in the public schools was necessary, but he was happy that the qualifying phrase, "with all deliberate speed," had been added. Vigor in industry and business and high wages camouflaged pockets of poverty in remote rural areas and in the hearts of American cities. The prosperous could easily believe that poverty had been abolished; the voiceless poor were sunk in hopeless apathy.

But Americans soon forgot the humdrum decade of the average man in the more exciting, even alarming, climate of the 1960's. Many students became activists: they demanded previously undreamed of personal liberty, and participated vigorously in protest and reform movements. A spontaneous mood of anarchy appeared among many young people, most of whom had never heard of Pierre Proudhoun, the originator of the term, or his proud dictum, "Whoever lays his hand on me to govern me is a usurper and a tyrant." At the same time, in both South and North, the shuffling Uncle Tom, who was liked by the white man because "he knew his place," was supplanted by civil rights militants who demanded a "place in the sun." As the 1960's drew to a close, the articulate leaders of the radical youth, the culturally deprived, and the economically poor sought not merely modifications of policy, but also sweeping changes in long established value systems.

Thoughtful men are disturbed by intellectual and moral apathy, for a highly stable society often conceals gross abuses behind a facade of prosperity. A quiet period may well be one of decay. As Wendell Phillips said in his Phi Beta Kappa address at Harvard in 1881, "Parties and sects laden with the burden of securing their own success cannot afford to risk new ideas."[1] But in any society there are also those who are disturbed by periods of ferment and dissent. These people see more than the aberrant actions of a few long-haired, bearded young radicals, or the refusal of strange black men to behave like members of an inferior race. It is not merely the remote threat to property or personal safety that they fear, however credible it might be made by riots in Watts or Detroit, or the disruption of academic life in Berkeley; they are equally alarmed by the threat to destroy comfortable patterns of thought, a process distasteful to most people of mature years.

It is nearly impossible for a contemporary observer of any agitational movement to study it objectively. To some, perhaps to most, it seems to be irrelevant nonsense; to others it is a threat, even a plot, to destroy all they cherish; to those who are actively involved, it becomes a sacred cause. None of these opinions encourages intelligent analysis. It is therefore valuable to observe agitation in a historical context and study its rhetoric after the passions that provoked it have subsided. The perspective provided by such an analysis may make it possible to look at contemporary agitation with new objectivity.

Some Definitions

Agitation may be defined as *a persistent and uncompromising statement and restatement of grievances through all available communication channels, with the aim of creating public opinion favorable to a change in some condition.* Agitation may be *rhetorical*, relying on the written or spoken word for its effect. Such agitation operates most successfully in an open society characterized by free speech and press, but the agitator may use these tools secretly or in defiance of suppression where their use is forbidden. Agitation may also be *activist*, using deeds rather than words. In a totalitarian society activist protest is usually sudden and violent, and is often unaccompanied by rhetorical protest until the activist is brought to trial. The trial itself then becomes a platform for rhetorical statement. In an open society violence is less common; activist agitation is more likely to take the form of nonviolent protest, civil disobedience, parades, sit-ins, underground railroads, and the like. But the line between violent and nonviolent activism is thin. Police violence, justified or not, quickly breeds counterviolence; and the Student Non-

[1]Wendell Phillips, *The Scholar in a Republic: Address at the Centennial Anniversary of the Phi Beta Kappa of Harvard College, June 30, 1881*, Boston, 1881, p. 21.

violent Coordinating Committee is easily and suddenly converted to the philosophy of "black power."

Agitations may also be classified in terms of their desired ends. *Specific short range* agitations are those in which the agitators seek immediate and attainable goals that could be granted by those in authority without any major change in the nature of society. Such agitations were successfully carried out under the leadership of Dr. Martin Luther King in the Montgomery bus strike and in numerous local efforts to integrate lunch counters and other public facilities in the South. The method of these agitations was primarily activist, but rhetorical agitation by Martin Luther King and others played an important part in sustaining the morale of the protestors.

Specific long range agitations are directed against entrenched conditions unsatisfactory to the agitators and their audiences. They are incapable of quick solution. In some cases the changes proposed by the agitators would do serious damage to some other segment of society; in others a long period of re-education must precede acceptance; or economic and political conditions may make the change inadvisable at the moment. It may even be true that though the grievance is genuine enough, the solution is in reality worse than the protested condition. Such agitations bring the question sharply to attention and begin a long period of discussion and debate from which a workable and fair solution may eventually emerge. The Anti-Corn Law League in Great Britain in the 1830's and 1840's conducted a campaign of this nature, and we will examine this movement in more detail in the next chapter. Many phases of the Civil Rights movement may properly belong in this classification, but it is difficult to tell without the perspective of time.

Revolutionary agitations are directed not so much against specific grievances as against the social order itself. As used here, however, the term does not necessarily imply revolution by force. Revolutionary agitations seek to change the balance of power from one group to another. In both Britain and the United States, successive peaceful agitations have continuously enlarged the electorate from the limited property-centered representation of the eighteenth century to the "one man, one vote" concept of the twentieth century. In the next chapter we will examine the British Chartist phase of this agitation. The abolition movement was essentially revolutionary in purpose, as were various anarchist and socialist agitations in the late nineteenth and early twentieth centuries. The demand of students at Berkeley and other university campuses for freedom from restraint is a more recent example of revolutionary agitation.

Finally, *counteragitations* or *diversionary agitations* are designed to direct attention away from unpleasant social problems by creating or magnifying threats to society from outside. Thus Hitler united and enslaved the German people by promoting the myth of the international

Jew, and politicians of all nations and all periods of history have used the adventure of foreign wars to silence domestic discontent. In contemporary domestic politics, leaders of the right wing seek a consensus by exciting fear of the "extremist left," and leaders of the left structure their coalitions by painting lurid pictures of the dangers from the "extremist right." Although these latter examples are not always full blown agitations, they have much in common with agitational activity. In Chapter 2, we will examine the secessionist movement in the South prior to the Civil War, a good example of this type of agitation.

Specific agitations, whatever their outcome, usually benefit society by calling attention to sore spots in the social order and demanding that solutions be found. It is only occasionally that the solutions proposed by the agitators are adopted, but the ensuing discussion and debate bring forth alternative solutions, and eventually measures are adopted which remedy the original evils.

The benefit to be derived from revolutionary agitations is less clear. Because they tend to polarize sentiment, debate on the issues is usually less intelligent, and less good will is shown by the contending parties. Nevertheless if society has become stagnant, if the majority of the people no longer benefit from the existing order, radical agitation is perhaps necessary to secure change. Unfortunately many successful revolutionary agitations bring excesses and evils no better than those of the old order. If channels of communication are left open, these mistakes may be remedied through the normal processes of persuasion and debate; if they are not, the stage is set for a new revolutionary agitation when the errors of the old are discovered.

Counteragitations seldom bring an increase in public welfare. They are more concerned with power than with ideas or ideals. They tend to repress rather than stimulate public discussion. Instead of encouraging solutions based on the widest possible public good, they try to impose solutions in the interest of entrenched groups. Instead of exposing social ills, they conceal them and prevent action until explosive forces have been built up and violent action results.

Agitation and Freedom of Speech

The concept of agitation is often associated with that of freedom of speech, debate, or discussion, but the meaning given to these terms or to the broader concept of liberty varies so widely that some review of varying interpretations is needed. In the Anglo-American tradition, the concepts have varied from the narrow feudal conception of the Magna Charta (liberty for feudal lords only) to the contemporary legal concept that only a "clear and present danger" can justify curbs on the exercise of freedom of speech. Although there have been numerous setbacks, the idea of liberty of speech has been consistently enlarged, if not in each

generation, then at least in each century. The seventeenth century won
freedom of expression for members of Parliament; the eighteenth saw
the growth of local self-government in America; the nineteenth in
both Britain and the United States saw the platform win the extension
of the franchise and the development of a system by which popular pressure could be put upon legislative bodies.

For better or worse, this growth has been so consistent that even the
most conservative leaders have had to accept the principle of free discussion. Often, however, major qualifications have been added by de-
fenders of the status quo. The case for freedom in the full sense was
stated in the seventeenth century by John Milton in his *Aeropagitica,* a
protest against Parliamentary action restricting the freedom of speech
legislators claimed for themselves. "Though all the winds of doctrine
were let loose to play upon the earth, so Truth be in the field, we do
ingloriously, by licensing and prohibiting, to misdoubt her strength.
Let her and Falsehood grapple: who ever knew Truth put to the worse
in a free and open encounter?" More succinctly Thomas Watson, a younger contemporary of Milton, made the same point: "Whoever is afraid
of submitting any question, civil or religious, to the test of free discussion, is more in love with his own opinion than with truth."[2] Others paid
lip service to the idea, but so hedged it about with moral or religious
sanctions as to make it meaningless. Jonathan Edwards, for example,
believed that "True liberty consists only in the power of doing what
we ought to will, and in not being constrained to do what we ought not
to will."[3] It was a satisfying definition for the New England theocracy.
Oliver Goldsmith advised his readers to use speech sparingly, for "he
who best knows how to keep his necessities private, is the most likely
person to have them redressed."[4]

To an intelligent and dedicated agitator like Wendell Phillips defini-
tions like the last quoted ones were pernicious nonsense. Educated men
should lead agitations and give them intelligent direction, he declared
in his Phi Beta Kappa address at Harvard College.

> Trust the people—the wise and the ignorant, the good and the bad
> —with the gravest questions, and in the end you educate the race. At
> the same time you secure, not perfect institutions, not necessarily good
> ones, but the best institutions possible while human nature is the basis
> and the only material to build with. Men are educated and the State
> uplifted by allowing all—everyone—to broach all their mistakes and
> advocate all their errors. The community that will not protect its most
> ignorant and unpopular member in the free utterance of his opinion,
> no matter how false or hateful, is only a gang of slaves![5]

[2]Tryon Edwards, ed., *The New Dictionary of Thoughts,* rev. by C. N. Catrevas
and Jonathan Edwards, New York, 1934, pp. 135–36.
[3]*Ibid.,* p. 336.
[4]*The Bee,* No. 3, October 29, 1759.
[5]*Scholar in a Republic,* p. 16.

The doctrine is utopian and disorderly, and Americans have held to it uncertainly; but in the main it has been the dominant belief in American society, and it has served to prevent the static condition in which change can come only when intolerable conditions breed violence.

Suggested Reading

Wendell Phillips' Phi Beta Kappa Address is printed in many collections of speeches as an example of his rhetorical method. On the dilemma of freedom of speech for all in a democratic society, see Robert M. O'Neil, *Free Speech: Responsible Communication under Law*, New York, 1966. See also George P. Rice, Jr., *Law for the Public Speaker*, Boston, 1958. John Stuart Mill's *On Liberty* is a classic presentation of the case for freedom of speech, and is available in many sources. A recent statement of the issue from political sources may be found in a speech by J. William Fulbright entitled, "The Higher Patriotism," delivered April 21, 1966, and printed in Tristam Coffin, *Senator Fulbright: Portrait of a Public Philosopher*, New York, 1966.

chapter 2

the nature of agitation

At the height of the San Francisco anti-Chinese riots of 1877 the *San Francisco Chronicle* was printing daily stories on the assaulting of Chinese houseboys, the burning of washhouses, and the public threats of mayhem and murder.[1] At the bottom of one such story and in identical type and form, this item appeared:

The Riot and Its Cause

People do not become riotous when a good digestion and an even temperament is kept, but when biliousness, that dread destroyer of a proper digestion and a peaceful mind is tolerated. The once peaceful man is ready for violence. Dr. Van Dyke's Anti-bilious Cure removes it all.[2]

It is a temptation to agree here with the assumption that agitators may be so easily explained. But the problem is somewhat more complex than this. The agitator is always with us, speaking to whoever will listen —a fact which anyone may confirm by a visit to his local equivalent of "Bughouse Square" or the "Spit and Argue Club." However, when large audiences have responded to agitation, more often than not they have been too ill fed to be bilious and too aware of social injustice to be calmed by the application of a patent remedy.

[1] Some of the materials of this chapter have appeared in similar form in journal articles. See Charles W. Lomas, "The Agitator in American Politics," *Western Speech*, XXIV (Spring, 1960), 76–83; "The Rhetoric of Demogoguery," *Western Speech*, XXV (Summer, 1961), 160–68.
[2] *San Francisco Chronicle*, July 27, 1877.

Preconditions

Neither rhetorical nor activist agitations can hope to succeed even partially unless social and political conditions are favorable to the initiation and growth of the movement. There must be clear evidence of *injustice or apparent injustice* deeply affecting the well being of those who compose the audience. On the part of the established ruling group (what civil rights agitators call the "power structure") there must be massive *resistance to change.* This resistance may be motivated by high principles, by apathy, by self-interest, or by fear—it makes little difference to the agitator and his audience. Finally there must be an *available channel of communication* between the agitator and his audience. If speech and press are free, this is easily attained; in a totalitarian system, the act of speaking or writing may itself be a revolutionary act. Even in an open society, the successful gathering of great mass meetings may be regarded as a threat, and may result in repressive action motivated by fear. All three of these qualities are illustrated in the inception and development of agitational movements in Great Britain and the United States. Although all the speeches contained in this book are from American sources, the conditions motivating agitators are similar in Britain and the United States.

A classic example of agitation emerged in the United Kingdom in the late 1830's and continued for many years. Because many of the men involved in these agitations emigrated to the United States and were involved in American agitations in the 1870's and 1880's, these movements have more than historical interest for American society. The Anti-Corn Law League and Chartism developed as two separate and competing agitation movements, although the cause of unrest was the same for both. The former was primarily an economic movement, aimed at the redress of a specific injustice; the latter was a political movement, designed to change the whole political base of power and make subsequent economic and social change inevitable.

William Cobbett, a leading British reformer in the early years of the nineteenth century, once remarked, "I defy you to agitate a fellow with a full stomach." And so it was with the Chartist and Anti-Corn Law League agitators. "It was the pressure of economic distress, irregular employment, low wages and high prices, not enthusiasm for political reform on its own account, which drove the working classes at intervals throughout the first half of the nineteenth century to support the sweeping political schemes of Cobbett and his like," as one student of the period indicates.[3] Wages were consistently depressed after the end of the Napoleonic wars, and the prices of oatmeal and potatoes, the

[3]Donald Read, "The Social and Economic Background of Peterloo," *Transactions of the Lancashire and Cheshire Antiquarian Society,* LXIV (1954), 2.

only staple foods factory workers could buy at all, were higher than they had been in 1810. Meanwhile the cost of wheat and other grains (*corn* is the generic term in Britain) was kept artificially high by tariffs and quotas intended to protect the income of the great landowners. Farm workers, however, did not benefit. In the village of Tolpuddle, Dorsetshire, in 1830 agricultural wages were nine shillings a week. In succeeding years reductions were made to seven shillings, and in 1834, employers announced that they would reduce the wage to six shillings. In most cases this was even less than the inadequate factory wage, and cottage industry, with which farm workers once supplemented their income, had been destroyed by the factory system.[4] It was this economic crisis faced by workers that caused Joseph Rayner Stephens to tell a Manchester Chartist rally in 1838, "This question of universal suffrage is a knife-and-fork question, a bread and cheese question."[5] The problems of the workers were further complicated by the new poor law of 1834, which abolished outdoor relief and herded needy families into prison-like workhouses where husbands were separated from wives, and parents from children. Often the only way the family could stay together was to send the small children to the factories, where they were worked without protection of factory laws twelve to fourteen hours a day.[6]

Throughout this period there was massive resistance to change of any kind. Although the Parliamentary Reform Act of 1832 improved the geographical distribution of seats in Parliament and disfranchised many rotten boroughs, it gave the vote to few workers, and in some cases actually reduced the number of voters in poorer segments of the population. In 1824 the act forbidding labor unions was repealed, but a decade later, six farm laborers at Tolpuddle were sentenced to the severe punishment of seven years banishment to a penal colony for taking an "unlawful oath" not to reveal the membership or proceedings of their union.[7] Union actions to raise wages were uniformly defeated by employers. Many workers whose fathers had been staunch conservatives accepted appeals to militant action as the only solution to otherwise insoluble problems.

At the heart of the issue was the inability of workers to control or even to influence the action of members of Parliament. Though the issues were economic, the belief was widespread that no lasting relief could be obtained from a Parliament dominated by landed interests and a few wealthy manufacturers. Those who called themselves Chartists believed that only a radical shift of power through universal suffrage, frequent

[4] *The Story of the Dorchester Labourers*, Trades Union Congress, London, 1957, *passim*.

[5] *Manchester Guardian*, September 26, 1838. Quoted by Read (see note 3, p. 8).

[6] Henry Jephson, *The Platform: Its Rise and Progress*, Vol. II, New York, 1891, pp. 152–53.

[7] *Dorchester Labourers*, pp. 2–3.

elections, and the secret ballot could ensure legislation in the interest of all the people. On the issues of wages and prices, progress might be made by separating interests of the landed proprietors from those of the factory owners on the question of duties and quotas on imported food, but Chartists refused to participate in agitation toward this end.

It was not difficult to assemble a crowd in nineteenth-century England. There were many densely populated areas, and almost anyone who had a proposal for change seemed to offer something better than the drabness and deprivation of everyday existence. And since hunger and squalor are powerful weapons in the hands of a skillful agitator, public meetings in the 1830's did not lack for speakers. Even where suffering was not acute, the inherent dullness of the factory towns made the speeches of the radicals a welcome diversion. It is true that there were deterrents to free speech. Although there was no pre-censorship, post-censorship in the form of criminal prosecution was frequent enough to weed out those who were not dedicated to the cause or who did not feel that the hope of personal power outweighed the dangers they encountered. But laws governing what might be said at public meetings were vaguely worded, and hundreds of meetings were held without disruption even though nearly all the leaders of Chartism were committed to jail at some time in their careers for inflammatory utterances.

It is evident, then, that the 1830's provided suitable conditions for agitation. The grievances were great; there was intense resistance to change; and audiences were available and receptive to bold speakers. Moreover there were many men willing and able to launch agitations.

The Speaker

The success of any agitation is dependent not only upon the social conditions prevailing at the time, but on the nature of the men who emerge as spokesmen for the cause. Kenneth Burke's writings have popularized the term *identification* to describe the relationship established among speaker, audience, and cause during a rhetorical act. Although the concept is as old as the Greeks who first developed rhetoric, Burke has endowed the idea with almost mystical properties, which, metaphorically at least, serve to describe what happens in successful agitations. Borrowing the language of philosophical theology, he defines *identification* as "consubstantiality." In other words, ". . . in acting-together, men have common sensations, concepts, images, ideas, attitudes that make them consubstantial."[8]

If this is a correct concept, one would expect agitations to demonstrate a high degree of identification between speaker and audience. And indeed this is often true. Black men are better agitators for civil

[8]Kenneth Burke, *The Rhetoric of Motives*, New York, 1950, p. 21.

rights than white men; poor men talk about poverty more convincingly than the well-to-do; voteless men speak of extending the franchise with more force than do those who vote. The process of identification has already been largely accomplished before the speech begins. This does not mean that only members of an aggrieved group can attain identification with the group: a speech or a series of speeches on an issue of deep concern to the listeners may make the Negro audience color blind, or separate the prosperous man from the image of his affluence. The problem is more difficult, but not insurmountable. Thus a substantial number of agitators have risen directly from the masses they agitate; others have had to acquire identification through the causes they support.

In the British agitations of the 1830's and 1840's, the goal of all the agitators was ostensibly to improve the lot of ordinary workingmen. The Anti-Corn Law League speakers thought that this end could be achieved by economic measures: repeal the Corn Laws and lower the price of bread. Because this phase of the agitation did not propose to do anything about wages or rents, it appealed to middle class liberals, religious leaders, and manufacturers. The working classes were only marginally identified with the movement, and indeed the realities of politics did not demand that they should be. For workingmen had no votes and consequently no power to repeal the laws. Richard Cobden and John Bright, the leaders who organized the movement, were themselves enlightened and sincere men of substance and were excellent speakers, but they could not identify with workingmen, nor the workers with them. Their success was achieved by identification with stable and orderly elements of the population who saw in the repeal of the Corn Laws a way of bettering the lot of workingmen, who in turn would make fewer unacceptable demands upon society. The shift in the balance of political power which brought about repeal was from the agricultural interests to the industrial and commercial interests, but not to the working classes.

The Chartists, on the other hand, were men of more radical views. They were divided among themselves, in much the same way that the Civil Rights leaders of the 1960's were divided, between physical force and moral force advocates. But all were convinced that permanent and worthwhile improvements in the lot of workingmen could only be achieved by a revolutionary shift in the base of political power from the few to the many. Until free and frequent elections were granted and universal suffrage attained, reforms would be only palliative, and would serve to blunt the force of agitations aimed at permanent change. Chartist speakers were often drawn from the working classes themselves, so that identification was easily achieved. Among the better educated leaders were Richard Oastler, a displaced estate manager, Joseph Rayner Stephens, an unfrocked Wesleyan minister, and Feargus O'Connor, an unstable, power-seeking Irishman whose usefulness to the movement was enhanced by his ownership of the newspaper, *Northern Star*. These latter men were not of the working class, but their status as displaced members of more fortunate groups helped them to identify with their audiences.

The Message

The message of the speeches by the two groups showed a similar divergence. Cobden and Bright ran a tightly organized movement in which the wide divergence of belief on other issues was not allowed to obscure the central theme, repeal of the Corn Laws. Anyone who embraced repeal was welcome and received League support. Moreover, the Corn Law orators attained identification on the broadest possible level. Henry Jephson summarizes their appeals:

> This Corn Law had an innumerable train of the most evil consequences. "We plead," said a speaker at one of the Anti-Corn Law meetings, "against laws that have been enacted to debar mankind here, where God has been most bountiful, from participating in that which He has never withheld where He has been least bountiful. Men are starving, yet diamonds are let in duty free; corn is taxed, but turtle is let in free; corn is taxed, but pictures are free; industry is taxed, but that which the rich alone want is free; that, without which the poor cannot exist, and which God, through the bounty of our mother earth has given for all—*that* is prohibited by the lawmaking machinations of a sordid few whose rent-rolls to them are more sacred than the primeval charter of man's sovereignty over the globe, and God's ordination that the labourer is worth of his hire!"
>
> It was, as Cobden said, "A law which took from the poorest of the poor to add to the richest of the rich." The sole class which benefited by it was the class of landowners; it enriched them at the cost of the community. Every other class or interest suffered more or less. The farmers long hugged the delusion that they benefited by it, but even they were to discover their mistake at last. The agricultural labourers even did not profit by it, for the high price of corn brought them no higher wages, whilst they had to pay more for the first necessary of life. But it was upon the manufacturing and operative classes that the worst consequences of the law fell. It was a law which "destroyed our commerce, ruined our merchants, pauperised the population." By enhancing the price of bread, it led to the actual starvation of thousands, and to the misery and semi-starvation of millions and it was the direct and indirect cause of a very great portion of the crime, violence, and agitation which occurred in England during the first half of the present [nineteenth] century.
>
> "The Corn Law is, in fact," said Bright, in one of his speeches, "a law of the most ingeniously malignant character. The most demoniacal ingenuity could not have invented a scheme more calculated to bring millions of the working classes of this country to a state of pauperism, suffering, discontent, and insubordination than the Corn Law."[9]

[9]Jephson, *op cit.*, pp. 226–27.

Cobden and Bright, and the other Corn Law agitators as well, sought identification with a broad spectrum of the population. They tried to isolate the great landholders as a selfish group exercising political power out of keeping with their numbers or their economic strength in the community. They attempted to awaken an awareness of political power in middle class groups, many of whom could qualify for voting with a little effort. They played upon both sympathy for and fear of the workers. They sought to improve the economic lot of the workers without giving them the political power they sought. In the end the widespread suffering brought on by the failure of the Irish potato crop underlined the strength of their arguments and gave them the victory, but the success of the agitation was already in sight prior to this.

The problem of the Chartist agitators was somewhat different. They had little financial backing, lacked a disciplined organization, and were divided both as to ends and means. Although all were agreed that universal suffrage, the secret ballot, and frequent elections were necessary, there were many other causes embraced by the Chartists. Some sought an end to the new poor law; some were in favor of destroying factories; some sought better wages or cheaper bread. Some favored only peaceful demonstration; some sought to seize power by force.

Moreover they had few allies in the more fortunate classes. The violent speeches which characterized many of their meetings, magnified by lurid newspaper accounts and authenticated by occasional mob action, inspired fear rather than sympathy in those who had the political power. As a result their demands were scorned, and violent leaders used the inaction of the ruling authorities as evidence that only revolution could achieve results. Moderate men with social conscience were driven away from the movement and attracted instead to the more acceptable goals of the Anti-Corn Law League. To the Chartist speeches only the dispossessed and disfranchised could listen. The parallel with the Civil Rights Movement of the 1960's seems obvious.

So it was that the speeches of leading Chartists limited their appeals to the working classes. Their identification was with those "who, from earliest morn to latest night, are toiling in misery, yet starving while they toil; who, possessing all the anxieties of fond parents, cannot satisfy their children with bread; who, susceptible of every domestic affection, perceive their hearths desolate, and their little ones neglected, while the wives of their bosoms are exhausting every toiling faculty in the field or workshop, to add to the scanty portion which merely serves to protect their lives of careworn wretchedness."[10] Lurid descriptions of suffering, and impossible demands were reinforced by threats of violent action. The Reverend Joseph Rayner Stephens attacked the workhouses as "dungeons" where wife and husband, father and son were "sundered." "He

[10]William Lovett and J. Collins, *Chartism*. This is a book written in jail by two Chartists in 1840. (Cited by Jephson, *op. cit.*, pp. 159–60.)

was a revolutionist by fire—he was a revolutionist by blood, to the knife, to the death. . . . It would be law for every man to have his firelock, his cutlass, his sword, his pair of pistols or his pike, and for every woman to have her pair of scissors, and for every child to have its paper of pins, and its box of needles *[here the orator's voice was drowned in the cheers of the meeting]*, and let the men, with a torch in one hand and a dagger in the other, put to death any and all who attempted to sever man and wife."[11]

Similar speeches, directed more specifically to the principles set forth in the Charter, were made by Thomas Atwood, Richard Oastler, Feargus O'Connor, and others. Many of the leaders were prosecuted and imprisoned. Though the basic goals of the movement were attained in the reform acts of 1867 and 1884, the passage of nearly half a century before the culmination indicates that Chartism as such was unsuccessful. Yet there is reason to doubt that the repeal of the Corn Laws and a series of acts leading to better working conditions in factories would have come so quickly had it not been for the implicit threat of Chartism.

Typical Agitations

The twin movements of the Anti-Corn Law League and Chartism may serve as a model within which other agitations may be interpreted. An agitational movement is always based upon a grievance sufficiently strong to cause large numbers of people to demand action. It may be primarily rhetorical or primarily activist. If it is the latter it may be violent or nonviolent. It may be directed to those who are aggrieved and seek to organize them into a force powerful enough to demand action; or it may be directed to a broad spectrum of the community, seeking to win change by appeals to conscience as well as to self-interest. It may be tightly organized and directed toward a narrow goal with the intention of disbanding when the goal is achieved, or it may attempt to force a radical change in the social order resulting in a major shift of power to the advantage of the agitating group. It may be intelligently led and its spokesmen may talk sense; it may be merely an articulate statement of deeply felt grievances without insight into causes and without an attainable program. In spite of common origin and concern it may be impossible, as Roy Wilkins of the National Association for the Advancement of Colored People has suggested, "to have genuine cooperation, on an equal responsibility basis, with groups that do not have the same commitments, and which may very well be pursuing certain goals which have nothing to do with ... [the basic problem] at all."[12]

A brief glance at other British and American agitations may serve to clarify and support these concepts. In the late years of the fourteenth

---

[11]R. G. Gammage, *History of the Chartist Movement*, London, 1854, p. 65.
[12]*Los Angeles Times*, July 8, 1966, p. 3.

century the feudal system had ceased to have advantages for the serfs and yeoman farmers bound by feudal ties to the great lords. The decimations of the plague had produced an acute labor shortage both on the great estates and in the towns, and peasants were unable to profit by the demand for their labor. The great landholders, at most, suffered a little inconvenience; they continued to live in luxury while the peasants found their standard of living lowered. They needed articulate spokesmen, capable of consolidating their diffuse protests and identifying them with one another and with strong leaders. One such spokesman was an itinerant priest, John Ball. As a clergyman he might have been identified with the exploiting class, but he chose to be an agitating street preacher. For his protests against serfdom he was imprisoned by the Archbishop of Canterbury, but as soon as he was released he renewed his agitation against the aristocrats. The chronicler Froissart summarized the "crazy priest's" message in telling the story of the Peasants' Revolt of 1381:

> He was accustomed every Sunday after mass, as the people were coming out of the church, to preach to them in the market place and assemble a crowd around him; to whom he would say,—"My good friends, things cannot go well in England, nor ever will, until every thing shall be in common; when there shall neither be vassal nor lord, and all distinctions levelled; when the lords shall be no more masters than ourselves. How ill have they used us! and for what reason do they hold us in bondage? Are we not all descended from the same parents, Adam and Eve? And what can they show or what reasons give, why they should be more masters than ourselves? . . . They are clothed in velvets and rich stuffs, ornamented with ermine and other furs, while we are forced to wear poor cloth. They have wines, spices, and fine bread, when we have only rye and the refuse of the straw; and if we drink, it must be water. They have handsome seats and manors, when we must brave the wind and rain in our labours in the field; but it is from our labour they have wherewith to support their pomp. We are called slaves, and if we do not perform our services we are beaten."[13]

Partly as a result of such speeches the peasants of the southeastern counties revolted and marched on London under the temporal leadership of Wat Tyler. John Ball accompanied them as spiritual leader, and throughout their march he continued to preach his leveller doctrine. In the inevitable collapse of the Peasants' Revolt, Tyler and Ball were killed, and their ill-defined objectives were not attained. Yet, although the great lords remained rich and powerful, the lot of the peasants was somewhat improved by the gradual abolition of serfdom in the years that followed. Ball's methods in his agitation closely resembled those of the Chartist physical force faction, but he carried the logic of his words to their ultimate revolutionary conclusion, while the Chartists for the most part limited their weapons to loaded words.

[13]Sir John Froissart, *Chronicles of England, France, Spain, and the Adjoining Countries*, Vol. I, trans. Thomas Johnes, London, 1839, pp. 652–53.

In the nineteenth-century United States, the interconnected movements of abolitionism and secessionism seem at first glance to be different from other agitations. Neither movement addressed itself to an oppressed group. The abolitionists were denied access to the slaves and addressed their appeals to the altruism of audiences not directly affected by slavery. Illiterate black men could not read "Helper's Book"[14] and John Brown's raid caused hardly a ripple in the slave community of Virginia. Similarly the slaveholders who reacted so violently to Helper and John Brown and participated as speakers and audiences in the secessionist agitation were the dominant rather than the oppressed group in their society. They sought to rally Southerners to preserve their privileged position rather than to gain a new status.

Nevertheless, in other respects, both movements followed the pattern of agitation. Although the abolitionists and their audiences were not themselves affected, the grievance was real enough, and its statement was as "persistent and uncompromising" as that of any agitation in human history. Indeed William Lloyd Garrison's creed as set forth in the first issue of his abolitionist newspaper *The Liberator*, January 1, 1831, is almost a model for agitators: "I will be as harsh as Truth and as uncompromising as Justice. I am in earnest. I will not equivocate; I will not retreat a single inch; and I will be heard." The agitation was primarily rhetorical, but it had its activists: John Brown in Kansas and Virginia; the underground railroad in many places along the border and in the north; and even Henry Ward Beecher soliciting money from his pulpit to buy Sharp's rifles for free settlers in Kansas—Beecher's Bibles, they were called. As the Chartists did for the Anti-Corn Law League, the abolitionists won support for more moderate antislavery groups such as the Republican party, who seemed to the majority of Northerners to offer hope for the eventual extinction of slavery without the unacceptable disunionism of abolitionist leaders.

In many respects the secession agitation may be regarded as a counteragitation to abolitionism. Although it began simultaneously with Calhoun's doctrine of nullification as a protest against the tariff, it also had from the beginning a motive to protect the "peculiar institution" of the South. So long as Calhoun lived, his profession of Unionism kept the secessionists in check, but after his death the group led by Robert Barnwell Rhett, William L. Yancey, and others stepped up the tempo of their agitation. Such unionists as Alexander Stephens were overwhelmed by the flood of secessionist oratory which declared that the South must either elect a sympathetic President in 1860 or secede from the "Black Republican" dominated North. As Rhett put it in 1859, "If our rights are victorious in the next presidential election, we may con-

14Hinton R. Helper, *The Impending Crisis of the South*, New York, 1857. "Helper's Book" sought to prove that slavery had degraded and impoverished southern whites. The book was banned in the South as an insurrectionary document.

sider it as a kind of augury of a more auspicious future. If they are overthrown, let this election be the last contest between the North and South; and the long weary night of our dishonor and humiliation be dispersed at last, by the glorious day-spring of a Southern Confederacy."[15] Seventeen months later, on the eve of the South Carolina secession convention and only a few days after the election of Lincoln, Rhett delivered a speech of victory to the South Carolina Legislature, recapitulating all the points of the agitation since he had first declared in 1828, "To talk more must be a dastard's refuge," and urged "open resistance to the laws of the Union." To Rhett and his audience it appeared that his agitation had reached a successful culmination. All his energies were poured into bitter invective against the North. The *New York Weekly Tribune* on November 24, 1860, presented the full text of the speech on a page devoted completely to "The Secession Movement." A portion from the middle of the speech (about one seventh) will give the tone and general content. After reviewing the history of Northern "aggression" from the time of John Adams, he argued:

And now they have consummated their scheme of tyranny, by electing a Black Republican President to rule you. So long have you submitted, that they have lost all respect for you. They despise and contemn you. They think you a low, degraded, mean-spirited set of semi-barbarians, with very little more courage than your own negroes; and they have the audacity, the insolence, the unparalleled, the audacious insolence, to suppose that we of the South—we South Carolinians—would submit to a Black Republican President and a mulatto! (*cries of "Never! never!"*) Well my friends, what are we going to do? Or, rather, what have we done? Why, we have dissolved this Union with our oppressors. (*great applause*) We have said to the North, we are done with you. (*continued applause*) I read somewhere, the other day, that South Carolina was like a spoilt and fretful child, and needed spanking. (*laughter*) Do you hear that, fellow-citizens? Some Yankee says that South Carolina needs spanking, and is a spoilt child!

Fellow-citizens, I can tell them that we are the Sampson, that will take hold of the pillars of the temple of their idolatry, and pull it down upon them, and crush them beneath its fragments. (*applause*) Could I raise my voice, until its tones reached the majesty of thunder, I would cry in notes of thunder, until it rolled over every village and city and hamlet of the North: "this Union is dissolved!" Had I the power, I would go and write on the walls of their banqueting halls—"this Union is dissolved!" I would go to the fanatic, the manufacturer, to the plunderer who has fattened upon us like the vulture upon garbage and I would tell him in trumpet tones—"this Union is dissolved!" I would go to the politician, the cunning trickster who has deceived them, and not in the tones of thunder, but would whisper in his ear in the still small voice of conscience—"this Union is dissolved!" (*This passage of impassioned eloquence was received with silent and solemn admiration*

[15]H. Hardy Perritt, "Robert Barnwell Rhett's Speech, July 4, 1859," in *Antislavery and Disunion, 1858–1861*, ed. J. Jeffrey Auer, New York, 1963, p. 102.

*by the audience. Mr. Rhett presented the appearance of a tribune of
the people vindicating their liberties and predicting the ruin of their foes.)*

Rhett devoted the rest of the speech to ridiculing the probable efforts
of the North to cajole or force the seceding states to return, and pre-
dicted the emergence of a great empire extending to the Pacific "and
down through Mexico to the other side of the great gulf, and over the
isles of the sea."

There is an air of unreality about this diatribe in the light of the blood
and suffering of the Civil War and the total destruction of Rhett's dream.
But however dismal the ultimate outcome, at the time of delivery it
seemed to Rhett and his audience to be the triumphant culmination of
the secession agitation. The speech poured out the frustration of a class
which had seen its hold on power taken away, and now imagined that
the forces opposed to it had been defeated. All the stereotypes of evil
were seen in the oppressor; all the stereotypes of good were exemplified
in the "oppressed" Southern gentry. No compromise was possible or
desired. Rhett succeeded in identifying himself with the Southern culture
in which as Calhoun once put it, "Slavery is a positive good." In the
name of Justice and Liberty, Rhett and his fellow secessionists per-
petuated injustice and slavery for a few short and terrible years.

Agitation and Demagoguery

It is easy to dismiss the agitator by condemning him as a demagogue,
particularly when he poses a threat to our safety, our comfort, or our
cherished beliefs. It is simpler to pin such a label on Joseph Rayner
Stephens, John Ball, Robert Barnwell Rhett, or Malcolm X than it is
to evaluate and analyze the nature of their speaking. The terms demagogue and demagoguery have simple negative connotations which can
be applied easily to any of these, to Hitler, or to an effective speaker
of the opposing political party.

Because of its loose usage it is difficult to define demagoguery. To
the Greeks who invented the word, a demagogue was simply a leader
of the people. Although the present negative connotation was of later
origin, it is so firmly fixed that no purpose would be served by returning
to the earlier meaning. But the Greek usage does suggest a reason for
much of the confusion which surrounds the term. From ancient Greece
to the present time the tools of the demagogue have been precisely the
same as those used by any effective speaker, but the demagogue uses
them without considering the public interest.

Let us then say, as a working definition, that demagoguery is the
*process by which skillful speakers and writers try to influence public
opinion by using the traditional tools of rhetoric with complete indifference to truth. In addition, although demagoguery does not necessarily*

seek ends contrary to the public interest, its primary motivation is personal gain. This definition does not posit an absolute truth. Instead, it indicates that the demagogue is not interested in stating or interpreting facts objectively. The demagogue may be indifferent to objective data because he is too ignorant to discover them, because his prejudices prevent him from distinguishing between his and the public's interest, or because he maliciously distorts facts to gain his own ends.

Although even reputable speakers may occasionally fall into demagoguery, the habitual demagogue makes twisting the truth a way of life. He does not, however, need to invent new techniques; he merely distorts rhetorical devices taught by rhetoricians, practiced by orators, and praised by rhetorical critics from ancient Greece until now. He substitutes oversimplification for simplicity and directness, bogus evidence for genuine facts, pseudoreasoning for honest argument, emotionalism for factually based emotional appeal, and loaded language for colorful language. An agitator familiar with the sufferings and hardships of the poor may make a highly persuasive and moving argument without departing from facts at all. A demagogue may use the same facts merely as a point of departure to whip a mob into acts of senseless violence. An agitator may make a good case against unnecessary police force used to apprehend a traffic violator in a minority community. A demagogue may do as well in his denunciation of police who subdue an armed robber caught in the act.

It is easy to assume an identity between the agitator and the demagogue because the agitator so frequently directs his appeals to groups having a different set of values from our own. Hence his reasoning seems false and his facts twisted. Until we know what the facts are, however, it is better to suspend judgment, to seek out and evaluate the nature of the grievance, and to try to devise a reasonable solution to the problem on a broader base than that the agitator offers. As Henry George put it just after the publication of *Progress and Poverty*: "When, under institutions that proclaim equality, masses of men, whose ambitions and taste are aroused only to be crucified, find it a hard, bitter, degrading struggle even to live, is it to be expected that the sight of other men rolling in their millions will not excite discontent?" It was inevitable, he thought, that demagogues would appeal to discontent for the sake of votes, for political equality and social inequality could not exist side by side. The answer was for "thoughtful men" to consider the problems which were so evident, "trace them to their source, and popularize the remedy. It will not do to leave them to the ignorant poor and the ignorant rich."[16] The "thoughtful men" described by George might still be agitators, but they would be acting neither from ignorance nor self-interest and would therefore be free from demagoguery.

[16]Henry George, "The Kearney Agitation in California," *Popular Science Monthly,* XVII (August, 1880), 433–53.

Suggested Reading

For an agitator's evaluation of his own career, see Joseph R. Buchanan, *The Story of a Labor Agitator*, New York, 1903. An excellent historical study of an agitational movement may be found in John D. Hicks, *The Populist Revolt*, Minneapolis, 1931. Reinhard Luthin, *American Demagogues*, Boston, 1954, is an interesting study of a number of popular leaders. See also Forrest Davis, *Huey Long, A Candid Biography*, New York, 1935.

For agitational movements in nineteenth-century England, see Bonamy Dobrée, *English Revolts*, London, 1937; A. V. Dicey, *Law and Public Opinion in England during the 19th Century*, London, 1962; Mark Hovell, *The Chartist Movement*, London, 1925. For case studies in abolition and secession agitations, see J. Jeffrey Auer, ed., *Antislavery and Disunion, 1858–1861*, New York, 1963.

chapter 3

the role of the critic

Most of the speeches presented in this book are historical rather than contemporary. The issues which prompted them either no longer trouble the public, or they have so changed in form that they may be viewed dispassionately. Today we are more concerned with preserving the railroads as a part of our transportation system than with keeping railroad magnates from exploiting labor or maintaining arrogant political power. Most people regard anarchists as disorderly and unpleasant, but few fear them as instruments of senseless terrorism. Much of the platform of Eugene Debs's Socialists has been adopted by more conservative political groups. We can therefore observe the rhetoric of these movements without being caught up in the excitement of the day. We can assume the role of critic and evaluator. By reading and analyzing the rhetoric of agitation, we can determine for ourselves what agitators were actually saying about the society of their times. What charges did they bring against it? What evidence did they submit to support those charges, if any? Was the evidence complete and valid or partial and doctored? Were solutions offered? If so, did they make sense or did they have only a superficial relationship to the problems posed? What effect did the agitation have on public opinion? Was the change sought actually brought about? Did the agitation influence more moderate men to seek a solution as William Lloyd Garrison's agitation influenced Lincoln and Seward?

In answering these and similar questions, the critic is first a *social observer and reporter* and second a *judge of social utility*. In both of these roles he can be highly objective in a historical context. After further study, similarities among different agitators may emerge which can be phrased as generalizations about agitation. In doing this the critic becomes a *formulator of theory*. Finally the critic may be a *moralist* or a *judge of taste*. In this role he is seldom completely objective and indeed he cannot be. Students at Berkeley in 1965 offered far less support to the Filthy Speech Movement than to the Free Speech Movement. For personal reasons they discriminated between what seemed important and what seemed petty and in bad taste. The crude language of many nineteenth-century agitators will seem accurate, offensive, or amusing depending on the values of the contemporary reader. Thus it is difficult, even in the historical framework, to maintain objectivity in matters of taste and morals. For this reason the most useful criticism we may make of agitation will grow out of the first three roles. By maintaining objectivity in the historical framework we can describe events, evaluate results, and project theory that may give us a better understanding of contemporary agitation as well.

More specifically, how may these things be done? If you will look ahead at the speeches which comprise the major portion of this book, you will see that they are divided into four groups, The Rhetoric of Violence, The Rhetoric of Socialism and Social Reform, The Rhetoric of Civil Rights, and The Rhetoric of Anti-Communism. The first two groups contain no speeches later than 1920. Probably none of the issues discussed seems particularly important to present day readers, and certainly the speakers have long since ceased to disturb the sleep of even the most conservative. The third and fourth groups, however, contain some speeches by more contemporary figures, and some of the issues they deal with are highly relevant to our own time and may even seem incendiary or dangerously reactionary to some.

What we need to do, therefore, is to treat all the speeches as historical documents, even those that disturb our peace of mind. The introductions to the sections describe the social settings out of which the speeches grew, so that you can try to put yourself in the position of a listener sympathetic to the speaker. What grievance motivates the speech? Does the speaker develop the grievance in some detail or does he merely assert it? If he develops it, does he state new ideas or merely recall to the minds of the listeners information or beliefs they already possess? From your point of view as a favorable listener, would it be a better speech if he developed the grievance differently?

Now change your approach to the speech. Suppose you are a police reporter assigned to listen to the speech in order to discover if the speaker is trying to create a riot or induce the members of the audience to engage in seditious activity. Does the grievance appear in any different light from this point of view?

Finally, approach the speech as an interested, but uncommitted, observer. What effect does this approach have on your comprehension of the grievance? Does the speaker convince you that his case has validity? If not, what must he do to persuade you to accept his case?

From the grievance, turn to the solution. For speeches given many years ago, you have a special vantage point. It may be that the speaker's ideas have actually been tried in the intervening years since the speech was given. If so, find out how well they worked. Or perhaps the grievance has disappeared without any action, or by action quite different from that proposed. What conclusions can you draw about his speaking on the basis of these facts? If you cannot apply either of these tests, apply the same test you would for a contemporary speech. Is there a logical relationship between the grievance and the remedy? Would the adoption of the remedy really remove the causes which produced the condition? Does the speaker make such a relationship apparent, or does he merely assert it? As in the case of the grievance, you may want to consider these questions from the three points of view described earlier.

Having put yourself in the position of a member of the audience, you may want to change your point of view again. Does the speech deal with a specific problem, capable of solution within the existing order? Does the speech demand revolutionary changes in the existing order? Is the speech part of a counteragitation designed to perpetuate existing conditions? What would be the effect of adopting the program the speaker advocates? On the aggrieved group? On segments of society who profit by the conditions the speaker decries? On persons not directly affected by the grievance, nor profiting by it?

To which of these groups does the speaker address his speech? Is it constructed to reach a broad or a narrow segment of society? Insofar as he tries to reach groups other than the aggrieved one, how does he try to motivate them? By reason? By fear? By benevolence? By a combination of these or other motives? Does the speech seem likely to persuade large numbers of people to accept his solution? Does it seem likely to stimulate men of good will to study the problem in search of better solutions? Your answers to these questions will be partly dictated by the structure of the speech. If the development is clear, and the generalizations stated well and supported by facts, it is probable that the speaker is aiming beyond his immediate audience of aggrieved persons. If the speech consists largely of unsupported assertions vaguely tied to a solution, you may assume either that he is not trying to go beyond the aggrieved group, or that he lacks the rhetorical skill to do so.

In addition to the content, purpose, and structure of the speech, observe the language. Here too you will note considerable differences, and many of the questions in the paragraphs above will apply. As to the actual choice of language, however, our queries may be more specific. Consider, for example, the labels which a speaker might apply to his opponents, who, in his view are taking more than their share of profit from the economic system. Does he call them "our capitalist opponents," or "greedy profiteers," or "oppressors," or "thieves," or "captains of industry"? The choice of his terms may well set the whole tone of the speech. If the text of a speech reported by the *San Francisco Call* (Sept. 3, 1879), can be accepted as accurate, one of Dennis Kearney's speeches contained 37 name-calling phrases in succession to describe the character of his political opponents. But accurate or not, the report was close enough to the truth to be accepted in San Francisco. There is little question that such language is the dominant factor in the speeches of many agitators.

It is one thing, however, to use strong language in isolation and another to use it in the concluding section of a speech which contains supporting material which may justify it, or at least temper our condemnation of the speaker.

Observe also the rhetorical skill with which the language is structured. Is language used in antithesis to set good against evil, poverty against riches, innocence against police brutality, and so on? In what way does the use of such contrasts sharpen the idea being advanced? Are long and short sentences used jointly to enhance the cumulative effect of an idea? Are metaphors used? If so, are they trite and conventional, or original and stimulating? Do they make you think or react emotionally to the image?

When you have read a number of speeches, you will be ready to make some generalizations about the content, form, and language characteristic of speeches of agitation. This is not to say that all are alike, any more than all men are alike. Aside from the fact that they were seeking to change the social conditions of their day, there is hardly any similarity in personality between Henry George and Dennis Kearney, or between Daniel DeLeon and Eugene Debs. Yet there are some similarities in their speeches which are characteristic of a rhetoric of protest. If we can discover these common traits, perhaps we can better understand the agitators of our own time.

Suggested Reading

Traditional concepts of rhetorical criticism are set forth in Lester Thonssen and A. Craig Baird, *Speech Criticism*, New York, 1948. Recent short books on critical theory and method include Anthony Hillbruner, *Critical Dimensions*, New York, 1966; and Robert Cathcart, *Post Communication Criticism and Evaluation*, New York, 1966. For less orthodox, but provocative views of criticism, see Edwin Black, *Rhetorical Criticism*, New York, 1965; and Marie Hochmuth Nichols, *Rhetoric and Criticism*, Baton Rouge, 1963.

chapter 4

the rhetoric of violence

Almost any agitation which brings together large masses of discontented people is potentially violent. At least part of the impact of any agitation is the willingness of the establishment to make concessions in order to avoid violent confrontation or the extension of existing violent action. This is true even of dedicated nonviolent agitation such as that advocated by Martin Luther King. Authorities negotiate with such men to avoid confronting other more radical and less disciplined groups to whom the discontented will turn if nonviolent means produce no results.

But many agitators do not shy from violence as a part of their rhetoric. This may take the form of purposeless incitement to riot—"Burn, baby, burn"; or it may be offered as a threat to enforce demands made on political or economic authority, as in the midst of a bitterly contested strike; or it may be part of a revolutionary plan. Fortunately, active incitement to riot is an act of desperation or bravado which is relatively infrequent, and speeches given on such occasions are not normally preserved for study.[1] Outside of riotous action, the rhetoric of revolution sees violence as inevitable, and urges its listeners to arm and organize; but the time and place for the ultimate act will be determined by violence initiated by the police or the militia. Privately, particularly among anarchists of the nineteenth century, the speaker might urge assassinations, bombings, and other terrorist acts ("propaganda of the deed") for the purpose of keeping his cause before the public and hastening the

[1]Many such speeches are impromptu, and reporters are not prepared to make detailed notes. Moreover the speeches are usually accompanied by actions that are far more interesting to readers than what the speakers may have said.

day when repressive acts by the authorities would bring about wide-spread open revolt.[2]

Similarly a nonrevolutionary agitator such as Dennis Kearney, who sought to take political power from those he called "thieves" and "bummers," threatened hanging, burning, and shooting of his strongest opponents, particularly those who might have defected from his movement. But, though his audiences might call for "hemp," his counsels of violence were always for the future rather than for immediate mob action.

A second characteristic of the rhetoric of violence is that it is vague about the end result of violent action. The speaker may or may not develop a logical case in protest against the evils of the existing situation; he will certainly stimulate strong emotional response by utilizing the suffering, the fear, and the envy of those who hear him speak. But it is seldom clear in the speech how violence is going to improve the situation. The idyllic condition of society after the violence has been completed is usually developed only by assertion. It is believable only to those whose emotions are so involved in the protest that they believe any alternative self-evidently better than the present condition. In some cases the speaker seems to be carried away by his own eloquence; in others a naive idealism dominates; in a few cases malicious personal motives may be present.

The rhetoric of violence is basically destructive. It serves to bring social ills sharply into focus and to compel re-examination of frozen stereotypes. As Philosopher Pickett, a San Francisco eccentric, wrote of Kearneyism, "Let these ruffians yell, since such sounds the death knell of this plundercratic power...."[3] But violence offers little hope for the future, and constructive action did not emerge from the speeches or actions of Kearney, Most, or Parsons.

Dennis Kearney

The Chinese Must Go

In the late 1870's and early 1880's there was general labor unrest in many parts of the country. In San Francisco the period was marked by the rapid emergence

[2]For a good short study of the anarchist movement, see Barbara Tuchman, *The Proud Tower*, New York, 1966, Chapter 2.
[3]C. E. Pickett, *Philosopher Pickett's Anti-Plundercrat Pamphlet*, San Francisco, 1879.

of Dennis Kearney, founder and president of the Workingmen's Party of California.[4] Innocent of any understanding of economics, history, or politics, Kearney possessed one gift he used to make himself a national figure in a matter of weeks. "My Creator has given me a good pair of lungs and a tongue," he said of himself, "and Nature has furnished me with the power to use them."[5] Before he was thirty, through his intemperate speeches on the San Francisco sandlot, he had upset the equilibrium of California politics and acquired an international reputation as a dangerous incendiary orator.

Four basic contentions, uncluttered by either argument or evidence, appeared in his speeches: (1) "The Chinese must go," (2) grafting bankers and thieving railroad magnates must give up their spoil, (3) corrupt politicians should be "hung" to the nearest lamp post, and (4) unjust laws should be burned and new ones written to replace them. Kearney appealed to common knowledge and established prejudice, such as the prevailing anti-Chinese sentiment, magnifying real and fancied wrongs by describing them in the most lurid and intemperate language at his command. Epithets like "skunk," "thief," and "leprous, rat-eating Chinese slave" were common, as were threats of hanging, shooting, and burning. On his first trip to New York, the *Tribune* noted that, "His talk is of murder. He wants bondholders and other rich people hanged. He would like to make sausages of the Bonanza kings. . . . [His language] is of interest as disclosing the contents of a mind in which murderous images spawn and breed like serpents in a cave."[6] In a more sympathetic vein, Philosopher Pickett thought that the agitator "has some genius in coining words and phrases, with which to more properly depict the villains. Let him invent some new ones."[7]

Kearney neither wrote nor published his speeches, and surviving texts suffer both from the lack of knowledge and preparation of the speaker and from the imperfect reporting of his speeches in the newspapers. The text of the speech reproduced here cannot be regarded as either complete or accurate. At the time, the *San Francisco Chronicle* was engaged in bitter competition with the *Call* and *Alta California* for supremacy as the leading paper of San Francisco. In this battle, Kearney was "good copy." His stand against the Chinese was popular with all classes, although moderate men deplored the violence of his attack. There was enough truth in his charges of economic and political corruption to make them worth reporting, particularly when the charges supported the journal's editorial line.

[4]For a more detailed analysis of Kearney's rhetoric, see Charles W. Lomas. "Dennis Kearney: Case Study in Demagoguery," *Quarterly Journal of Speech,* XLI (October, 1955), 234–42.

[5]*San Francisco Call,* May 29, 1880.

[6]*New York Tribune,* August 5, 1878.

[7]Pickett, *op. cit.*

Though it was widely believed that the *Chronicle*, and later the *Call*, improved on Kearney's speeches in the printing, there is little evidence of such doctoring in the speech reported here. The text appears rather to consist of selected passages from a longer speech. It has no conclusion, and no points are developed in any detail. It seems probable, therefore, that the *Chronicle* chose those vivid phrases which suited its purpose. The distortion is one of selection rather than creation. The tone of the speech agrees with the unanimous reports of those who heard him speak—abusive, coarse, and violent.

The confusion which characterized Kearney's movement is well illustrated by passages from this speech. The Alameda election to which he refers was successful. The Workingmen elected their chosen candidate, W. R. Bones. But when he had taken his seat at Sacramento and turned against the party, Kearney responded with verbal violence only, in spite of many threats like those in this speech. Within this speech there are also mutually contradictory ideas. In one sentence he threatens violent revolution; in another he proposes cooperation with the authorities. Although some of this confusion may be in the reporting, it seems too consistent with extant texts of Kearney's other speeches to be disregarded.

The references in the speech to Judge Lake, Supervisor "Gag" Gibbs, and other political figures refer to unsuccessful efforts in San Francisco and Sacramento to prosecute Kearney or to pass legislation to limit or prevent his open air speeches. The text is from the *San Francisco Chronicle*, January 16, 1878, reporting a meeting of the Workingmen's Party.

I presume you know why we meet and what we mean. Our password is: The Chinese must go, and no humbug about it, Judge Lake or any other man to the contrary. Lake thought he was the only man in the city who knew how to persecute the Workingmen, and he was fired out of the City Criminal Court. He is the d——dest fool I ever saw, and ridiculed one of the Judges of the Supreme Court and said he was an illiterate ass.

I expect the villains who composed the last Grand Jury did not want to come into the City Criminal Court—the daylight thieves, the midnight assassins, the Mongolian lepers, for honest men to look at. But they must come, if it is only for me to look at them, and I will have their pictures taken.

Lake left the room in disgust today, and that was the first blood for the Workingmen. There are not enough villains in this State to crush us. I was told that a man wanted to blow up the city just for an experiment, but as Judge Lake lived close by him concluded he would not. I do not see much trouble now about driving out the d——d Chinese.

Gag Gibbs will have a seething, boiling hell to live in here in San Francisco.

The first time you find a man in the ranks who is not true to the core take him by the nape of the neck and chuck him into the street and then take the bloody shrimps by the throat and tell them you will put big stones around their necks and throw them into the bay.

We are going to give the others h––l, both inside and outside of the Courts. We are getting desperate now, and by the eternal God, if we have to take the Jimmy O'Brien reformers from the ranks, their friends won't know where to look for them. We have 1,000 secret men in our ranks, and I don't care how soon the reporters know it.

A man with a patent machine offered to take the lives of twenty men for $5. There are men in this city who are studying how to destroy us. What does it matter if they hang me, 10,000 men will rise up to avenge me. There is no law in this country to prevent men from revolutionizing. What does it mean? It means to depose the authorities and make our own laws to suit the people. We want a new party or a new country. We are going to win this fight anyhow, and there is no law which can prevent us. I favor trying the ballot first, but we may not be allowed an independent vote. We are going to try it in Alameda. It is the first time in the history of the country where the people have made an independent nomination. The Democratic thieves and Republican robbers do not like it, and want to compromise, but we will have nothing to do with the dirty villains. This is the first blood for us.

McCoppin called us a mob because we demanded work. There are too many villains in the Legislature who have no souls, but gizzards, and an honest man has got no chance to get a measure through up there.

The Supervisors may get up all the resolutions they like, but we won't stop the agitation until the last Mongolian leper leaves California. Resolutions are of no account. If they buy up the halls and stop our meetings, we will meet in secret and plot and concoct schemes that will destroy the villains; and we will put a man at the door with a musket in his hand and a bayonet on the end of it, and will admit none but friends.

When we have 40,000 men we will have another procession, but for a different purpose from the last one. We are going to use force now to carry out our plans. Is that your wish? (*all hands up*)

Let the Vigilantes, if they dare, go outside the law. How many of you have muskets? (*twenty or thirty hands up*) That's good. Form yourselves into a military organization, and when the next steamer comes here are you ready to march down to the wharf and stop the leprous Chinamen from landing? (*cries of "yes, yes"*) I will make all the necessary preparations and buy up all the second-hand gunshops [*sic*] we can get. We will call upon the Mayor and General Government to help us in our hour of peril, and prevent the Pacific Mail Steamship Company, the ocean pirates, from landing them.

Johann Most

The Beast of Property

The high priest of the cult of violence among late nineteenth-century agitators was Johann Most, a disciple of the anarchist, Michael Bakunin, rather than of Karl Marx. Exiled from both Germany and England, Most arrived in New York in 1882, bringing with him Bakunin's "conspiratorial form of organization, the cult of violence, the loathing of all authority, the quixotic vision of liberty and equality through destruction and chaos."[8]

In the 1880's Marxism was only one of many forms of socialism, and anticapitalist thought was split into many sections, none of them particularly influential with American workers. In the far west, Kearney's ignorant racism had captured the imagination of the masses at the expense of both reform and revolutionary movements. In New York and Chicago left-wing groups were weak and divided. But in all the great cities, masses of foreign-born laborers were concentrated in poverty pockets which belied the promise of the new world to which they had come to escape the oppression of the old.

It was to these groups rather than to the American-born that Johann Most addressed himself. He spoke English hesitantly and with a heavy accent. Indeed, his early speeches in the United States were almost entirely in German, a language in which he was unusually eloquent. A Detroit reporter, hearing Most speak in German (which the reporter could not understand), noted that the orator's delivery was of a "nature to prompt any patriot to deeds of heroic surgery." He was often interrupted by sudden bursts of applause, "which showed that the rough orator came to his points in no roundabout way but flung them naked to the floor and talked on in the midst of the applause."[9] Young Emma Goldman was at first repelled by Most's grotesquely twisted face, the result of clumsy surgery in his childhood. But as he warmed to his theme, "his disfigurement disappeared, his lack of physical distinction was for-

[8]Theodore Draper, *The Roots of American Communism*, New York, 1957, p. 14.
[9]*Detroit Evening News*, November 15, 1894. Clipping in Labadie Collection, University of Michigan Library.

gotten. He seemed transformed into some primitive power, radiating
hatred and love, strength and inspiration. The rapid current of his
speech, the music of his voice, and his sparkling wit, all combined
to produce an effect almost overwhelming."[10]

For a time Most became the leader of a growing anarchist group.
He learned to speak English more fluently, and he recruited young
English-speaking anarchists to carry his message. But the violent
revolution he proposed was unacceptable to most workers in an age
more tuned to Horatio Alger than to a philosophy of despair. His
diatribes against religion were directed to a society in which
evangelists often commanded more newspaper space than politicians.
He proposed a paradoxical society founded on extreme individualism
in which a bloody revolution would bring voluntary collective
action based on brotherly love.

The text of the speech reproduced here was originally composed
in German and was probably first delivered extemporaneously in
that language. Joseph Buchanan, editor of the Denver *Labor Enquirer*, stated that Most's Denver lecture in June, 1884, was the
first time Most ever delivered this lecture in English, and that the
Enquirer was the first to publish the English text.[11] The text is
nearly identical with a pamphlet version published by the New
Haven Group of the International Workingman's Association, un-
dated. Unlike Kearney's speeches, this text shows evidence of careful preparation both in content and style. There are a few German
constructions which mark it as a translation, but for the most part,
the language is fluent and hard hitting. Also unlike Kearney's
speeches, there is clear evidence that Most had a social goal, however utopian, beyond the mere acquisition of power.

"Among the beasts of prey man is certainly the worst." This expression, very commonly made nowadays, is only relatively true. Not man
as such, but man in connection with wealth is a beast of prey. The
richer a man, the greater his greed for more. We may call such monster
the "beast of property." It now rules the world, makes mankind miserable,
and gains in cruelty and voracity with the progress of our so-called
"civilization." This monster we will in the following characterize and
recommend to extermination.

Look about ye! In every so-called "civilized" country there are among
every 100 men about 95 more or less destitute and about 5 money-bags.

It is unnecessary to trace all the sneaking ways by which the latter
have gained their possessions. The fact that they own ALL, while the
others exist, or rather vegetate merely, admits of no doubt, that these
few have grown rich at the expense of the many.

Either by direct brute force, by cunning, or by fraud, this horde has
from time to time seized the soil with all its wealth. The laws of in-

[10]Emma Goldman, *Living My Life*, New York, 1934, pp. 6, 43.
[11]June 14, 1884.

heritance and entail, and the changing of hands, have lent a "venerable color to this robbery, and consequently mystified and erased the true character of such actions. For this reason the "beast of property" is not yet fully recognized, but is, on the contrary, worshipped with a holy awe.

And yet, all who do not belong to this class are its victims. Every off-spring of a non-possessor (poor man) finds every nook and corner of the earth occupied at his entrance into the world. There is nothing which is "lordless." Without labor nothing is produced; and in order to labor, there are required not only ability and will, but also room to work, tools, raw materials and means of sustenance. The poor man must, therefore, by force of necessity, apply to those who possess these things in plenty. And, behold! the rich give him permission to continue his existence. But in return for this he must divest himself of his skill and power. These qualities henceforth his pretended "saviors" use for themselves. They place him under the yoke of labor—they force him to the utmost of his mental and physical abilities to produce new treasures, which however he is not entitled to own. Should he desire to deliberate long before making so unequal a contract, his growling stomach will soon convince him that the poor man has no time for that, for there are millions in the same position as himself and he will risk that, while deliberating, hundreds of others will apply—his chance is gone and he again [will] be at the mercy of the winds.

It is the lash of hunger which compels the poor man to submit. In order to live he MUST SELL—"VOLUNTARILY" SELL—HIMSELF every day and hour to the "beast of property."

The bygone times, when the "ruling" classes, on their slave-hunting raids, threw their victims in chains and forced them to work, of which the rulers had all the benefit—the times when christian-germanic robbers stole entire countries, deprived the inhabitants of the soil, and pressed them to feudal service, were indeed terrible enough, but the climax of infamy has been reached by our present "law and order" system, for it has defrauded more than nine-tenths of mankind of their means of existence, reduced them to dependence upon an insignificant minority, and condemned them to self-sacrifice. At the same time it has disguised this relation with all sorts of jugglery that the thralls of today—the wage slaves—but partially recognize their serfdom and outlawed position, they rather incline to ascribe it to the caprices of fortune.

To perpetuate this state of affairs is the only aim of the "prominent" classes. Though not always united among themselves—one seeking to gain advantage over the other by tricks of trade, cunning in speculation and divers machinations of competition—yet in opposition to the proletariat they stand in one united hostile phalanx. Their political ideal is, therefore—in spite of all liberal phrases—a most powerful, centralized and brutal beadle government.

If the poor man, who is momentarily unable to sell himself to an exploiter of labor, or is already flayed to complete helplessness by the "beast of property," has recourse to begging—then the glutted bourgeois terms it vagrancy, and calls for police; he demands pillory and prison for the poor devil who refuses to starve between mountains of food.

Should the unemployed apply a little of the much vaunted self-help, that is, should he do in a small way, what the rich do daily with impunity on a grand scale, should he, in fact, steal, in order to live—the bourgeoisie will heap burning coals of "moral indignation" upon his head, and, with austere visage, hand him over relentlessly in charge of the state, that in its prisons he may be fleeced the more effectively, i.e., cheaper.

When the workers combine in order to obtain better wages, shorter hours of labor, or similar advantages, the money-bags immediately decry it as "conspiracy," which must be prevented.

When the workers organize politically, it is denounced as resistance to the "divine" order of things, which must be nullified by laws of exception or discrimination.

Should the people finally contemplate rebellion, an unceasing howl of rage raised by the "gold tigers" will be heard throughout the world— they pant for massacres and their thirst for blood is insatiable.

The life of the poor is valued as nothing by the rich. As the owner of vessels he places the lives of entire crews in jeopardy, when his object is to fraudulently obtain high insurance for half decayed hulks. Bad ventilation, deep excavation, defective supports, etc., etc., annually bring death to thousands of miners, but this system of operation saves expenses, therefore augments the gains, and gives the mine owners no occasion to be sorry. Neither does the factory-pasha care how many of "his" laborers are torn and rent apart by machinery, poisoned by chemicals, or slowly suffocated by dirt and dust. Profit is the main thing.

Women are cheaper than men: for this reason the capitalistic vampires with insatiate rapacity seek their blood. Besides, female labor procures them cheap mistresses.

Child flesh is the cheapest: what wonder then that the cannibals of modern society continually feast upon juvenile victims? What care they that the poor little ones are thereby bodily crippled and mentally ruined for life—that thousands of them, miserable and worn out at a tender age, sink into their graves? Stocks rise; that suffices.

As the bourgeoisie, by means of its capital, completely monopolizes all new inventions, every new machine, instead of shortening the hours of labor and enhancing the prosperity and happiness of ALL, causes, on the contrary, dismissal from employment for some, reduction of wages for others, and an increased and intensified state of misery for the entire proletariat.

When increase of production is accompanied by an augmented pauperization of the masses, consumption must simultaneously decrease, stagnation and crises must ensue. A superabundance of actual wealth in the hands of the few must create hunger, typhus, and other epidemics among the many. The injustice—yea the idiocy—of this state of affairs is evident. The money-bags of course merely shrug their shoulders. This they will continue to do until a rope well tied OVER their shoulders will end all further shrugging.

The worker is not only fleeced in manifold ways as producer, but also as consumer. Numberless parasites seek to despoil him of his paltry income.

After products have passed through various exchanges and storeage [sic], and their prices have been raised by jobbers and brokers' profits, by taxes and custom house duties, they finally reach the retailers, whose customers are almost exclusively the proletarians. The wholesalers "make" (that is, fraudulently obtain) perhaps 10 to 20 per cent profit by their transactions; the retailer is dissatisfied with less than 100 per cent. He makes use of all sorts of tricks for securing this result, especially the most shameless adulteration of food. In close relationship to these swindlers are the numberless poisoners and adulterators of beer, liquors, wine, etc., who render the streets in all our great cities and industrial centers unsafe with their nefarious traffic. Then there are the tenement-lords, who ceaselessly seek means to embitter the existence of the poor. The condition of the rooms become [sic] steadily worse, the rents higher, and the contracts more galling. The workers are crowded together more and more into rear houses, attics and cellar-holes, full of vermin, damp and musty. Prison cells are frequently far healthier than these pest-holes.

When the worker is out of employment, he is again at the mercy of a horde of speculators in hunger, who are ready to pounce on him in order to complete his ruin. Pawnbrokers and others of similar ilk advance small sums at high interest on the last possessions of the poor. Their contracts are usually so arranged that they can hardly be kept; the pawned objects [are] forfeited and the poor wretch takes another down-ward step. The cut-throats, however, amass fortunes in a short time. The beggar is looked upon as quite a well-paying figure by certain sharks. Every copper which he has gathered in his unenviable way arouses the covetousness of the keeper of dirty holes and vile dens. Even thieves are subject to this capitalistic spoliation. They are the slaves of crafty concealers and "fences," who receive their stolen goods for a song. Yes! even those unfortunate women, whom the present accursed system has driven to prostitution, are shamelessly plundered by keepers of brothels and houses of ill-fame.

This is the lot of the poor from the cradle to the grave. Whether he produces or consumes, whether he exists or merely vegetates, he is always surrounded of [sic] ravenous vampires who thirst for his last drop of blood. On the other hand, the rich man never stops his work of exploit-ing, though he may be utterly unable to assign a reason for his greed.

He that has $1,000,000 would have $10,000,000; he that has $100,000,000 would have $1,000,000,000.

The greed for wealth is closely associated with the greed for power. Wealth is not only a generator of more wealth, it is also a political power. Under the present capitalistic system venality is an all-pervading vice. It is as a rule a mere matter of price which will buy over those who may be of service either by speech or silence, by the pen or by the press, by acts of violence or any other means, to the "beast of property," which by its golden dictates is the absolute, almighty divinity.

In Europe and America there are several hundred thousand priests and ministers, specially provided for to poison the common sense of the masses.[12] Numberless missionaries wander from house to house spreading senseless tracts, or commit other "spiritual" mischief. In the schools strenuous attempts are made to nullify what little good the training in reading, writing, and ciphering may bring with it. Idiotic maltreatment of "history" excites that blatant prejudice which divides people, and prevents them from recognizing the fact, that their oppressors have long ago leagued together against them, and that all politics, past and present, has the only object in view, that of firmly establishing the power of the rulers, and thereby ensuing [sic] the exploitation of the poor by the rich.

The hawking trade in "loyalty and order intoxicants" is attended to by the inkslingers of the daily press, numerous literary perverters of history, by political heelers of the various predominating cliques, rings, combinations and organizations, by parliamentary windbags with seductive smiles, pledges on their lips and treason in their hearts, and hundreds of other politicians of all degrees and shades of villainy.

Whole squads of bushwhackers are specially employed in mystifying the social question. The professors of political economy for instance, play the part of lackeys to the bourgeoisie, extolling the golden calf as the true sun of life, and using falsehood and knavery so "scientifically," that they make the tanning of workingmen's hides appear as a benefaction to mankind. Some of those charlatans recommend social reform, or in other words, processes, based on the maxim of washing without wetting; not to mention their celebrated recipes for economizing and educating.

While thus bamboozling the masses the capitalistic knights of plunder continue to perfect their mechanism of power. New offices are created. High positions in these are filled in Europe by the progeny of the former highwaymen (now a "nobleman") in America by the most crafty office hunters and the most wily thieves, who combine with their original purpose of authoritatively gagging the proletariat, the very pleasant business of till-tapping and forgery on a grand scale. They command

[12]Most's second most celebrated lecture was entitled, "The Deistic Pestilence."

armies of soldiers, gendarmes, policemen, spies, judges, prison-keepers, toll-keepers, tax collectors, executors, etc., etc. The lower class of the beadledom are almost wholly recruited from the ranks of the non-possessors, and are only exceptionally [rarely] better paid. For all that they display great zeal as spies, eaves-droppers, and poke-noses, as claws, teeth, and suckers of the state, which institution is evidently nothing more nor less than the political organization of a horde of swindlers and spoliators, who without the tyrannizing machinery could not exist for one day before the just wrath and condemnation of the oppressed and plundered people.

In most of the old countries this system has naturally reached its point of culmination in the outer form. The entire disciplinary apparatus of the state concentrates in a monarchic power. Its representatives "by the grace of God" are, in accordance, the very quintessence of villainy. In them all vice and crime common to the ruling classes is developed to a monstrous degree. Their most agreeable occupation is a wholesale murder (war); when they rob, and they do it often, they always rob entire countries and hundreds, even thousands of millions. Incendiarism on a colossal scale serves to illuminate their atrocities. They adhere to the notion, that mankind exists for them to kick, cuff, and spit upon. At the best, they make it worth their while to select the most attractive women and girls from among their "subjects" to satiate their beastly lusts. The others have the right to "most obediently" die like dogs.

By direct blackmail these crowned murderers of Europe annually pocket $50,000,000. Militarism, their pet progeny, annually costs $1,000,-000,000, not taking in consideration the loss of life and labor. An equal sum is paid as interest on $20,000,000,000 of state-debts, which these scoundrels have incurred in a comparatively short time. Monarchism in Europe then cost annually $2,050,000,000 that is to say, more than 10,-000,000 of workers, the supporters of 50,000,000 of people, earn as wages in the same time.

In America the place of the monarchs is filled by the monopolists. Should monopolism in the alleged "free" United States of America develop at the rate it has in the last quarter of a century, there will remain free from monopolization only daylight and air. Five hundred million acres of land in the United States, about six times the area of Great Britain and Ireland, have been divided within a generation among the railroad companies and the great landlords of Europeo-aristocratic origin. Within a few decades Vanderbilt alone amassed $200,000,000; several dozen of his competitors in robbery bid fair to outdo him. San Francisco was settled hardly thirty years ago, to-day it harbors eighty-five millionaires! All the wealth of this great republic, although estab-lished but a century, its mines, its coalfields, its oilwells, etc., etc., has been "taken" from the people and are [sic] the property of a handful of daring adventurers and cunning schemers.

The "sovereignty of the people" falls prostrate into the dust before the influence of these money kings, railroad magnates, coal barons and factory lords. These fellows carry the whole United States in their pockets, and that which is vaunted as untrammeled legislation and free ballot is a farce, a delusion and a snare.

If this be the condition of the green wood, what may we not expect of the decayed timber? If this young American republic, with its nearly boundless territory and its almost inexhaustable [*sic*] natural resources has been so fatally corrupted and ruined in such a short time by the capitalistic system—why be surprised at the results of long continued abuses of similar nature in servile, rotten Europe?

Indeed it seems as though this young American republic had for the present but one historical mission, of demonstrating beyond controversy to the people on this side of the Atlantic as to those on the other by the presentation of bare, tangible facts what an outrageous monster the "beast of property" really is, and that neither the condition of the soil, nor the vastness of domain, nor the political forms of society can ever alter the viciousness of this beast of prey; but to the contrary, it proves, that the less a necessity naturally exists for individual greed and rapacity, the more dangerous to, and obtrusive upon society it becomes. It is not voracious to satisfy its wants—it devours for the sake of devouring only!

Let those who labor to live understand, that this monster cannot be tamed, nor be made harmless or useful to man; let them learn to know, that there is but one means of safety: unrelenting, pitiless, thorough, war of extermination! Gentle overtures are for naught; scorn and derision will be the result, if by petitions, elections, and like silly attempts the proletariat hopes to command the respect of its sworn enemies.

Some say, general education will bring about a change; but this advice is as a rule an idle phrase. Education of the people will only then be possible, when the obstructions thereto have been removed. And that will not take place until the entire present system has been destroyed.

But let it not be understood that nothing could or should be done by education. Far from it. Whoever has recognized the villainy of the present conditions, is in duty bound to raise his voice, in order to expose them, and thereby open the eyes of the people. Only avoid to reach this result by super-scientific reflections. Let us leave this to those well meaning scientists, who in this manner tear the mask of humanity from the "better class" and disclose the hideous countenance of the beast of prey. The language of and to the proletariat must be clear and forcible.

Whoever thus uses speech will be accused of inciting disturbance by the governing rabble; he will be bitterly hated and persecuted. This shows that the only possible and practical enlightenment must be of an inciting nature. Then let us incite!

Let us show the people how it is swindled out of its labor force by country and city capitalists; how it is euchered out of its meagre wages by the store, house, and other lords; how priests of pulpit, press, and party seek to destroy its intellect; how a brutal police is ever ready to maltreat and tyrannize it, and with a soldiery to spill its blood. Patience at last must forsake it! The people will rebel and crush its foes.

The revolution of the proletariat—the war of the poor against the rich, is the only way from oppression to deliverance!

But, some interpose, revolutions can not be made! Certainly not, but they can be prepared for by directing the people's attention to the fact that such events are iminent [sic], and calling upon them to be ready for all emergencies.

Capitalistic development, of which many theorists assert that it must proceed to the total extinction of the middle class, (small bourgeoisie), before the conditions favorable to a social revolution are at hand, has reached such a point of perfection, that its farther progress is almost impossible. Universal production (in civilized countries) can only be carried on, industrially as well as agriculturally, on a grand scale, when society is organized on a Communistic basis, and when (which will then be a truism) the reduction of the hours of labor keeps pace with the development of technical facilities, and augmented consumption with production.

This is easily comprehended. By wholesale production from 10 to 100 times more may be produced than the producers need in goods of equivalent value, and there lies the rub. Until lately, this entire surplus value has been but little noticed, because by far the greater portion of this so-called profit has been in turn capitalized, that is, used for new capitalistic enterprises, and because the industrially most advanced countries (the "beast of property" in those countries) export enormous quantities of merchandise. Now, however, the thing is beginning to weaken mightily. Industrialism has made great progress the world over, balancing exports and imports more and more, and for that reason new investments of capital become less profitable, and must, under such circumstances, soon prove entirely unremunerative. Universal crises must ensue and will expose these glaring incongruities.

Everything therefore is ripe for Communism; it is only necessary to remove its interested inveterate enemies, the capitalists and their abettors. During these crises the people will become sufficiently prepared for the struggle. Everything will then depend on the presence of a well trained revolutionary nucleus at all points, which is fit and able to crystalize around itself the masses of the people, driven to rebellion by misery and want of work, and which can then apply the mighty forces so formed to the destruction of all existing hostile institutions.

Therefore organize and enlarge everywhere the Socialistic revolutionary party before it be too late! The victory of the people over its tyrants and vampires will then be certain.

Instead of here developing a "programme," it is, under present conditions, of far greater importance to sketch what the proletariat must probably do immediately after the victorious battle to maintain its supremacy.

Most likely the following must be done: In every local community where the people have gained a victory, revolutionary committees must be constituted. These execute the decrees of the revolutionary army, which, reinforced by the armed workingmen, now rule like a new conqueror of the world.

The former (present) system will be abolished in the most rapid and thorough manner, if its supports—the "beasts of property" and horde of adherents—are annihilated. The case standing thus: If the people do not crush them, they will crush the people, drown the revolution in the blood of the best, and rivet the chains of slavery more firmly than ever. Kill or be killed is the alternative. Therefore massacres of the people's enemies must be instituted. All free communities enter into an offensive and defensive alliance during the continuance of the combat. The revolutionary communes must incite rebellion in the adjacent districts. The war can not terminate until the enemy (the "beast of property") has been pursued to its last lurking place, and totally destroyed.

In order to proceed thoroughly in the economic sense, all lands and so-called real estate, with everything upon it, as well as all movable capital will be declared the property of the respective communes. Until the thorough harmonious reorganization of society can be effected, the proclamation of the following principles and measures might render satisfaction.

Every pending debt is liquidated. Objects of personal uses which were pawned or mortgaged will be returned free. No rents will be paid. District committees on habitation, which will sit in permanence, allot shelter to those who are homeless or who have inadequate or unhealthy quarters; after the great purification there will be no want for desirable homes.

Until everyone can obtain suitable employment, the Commune must guarantee to all the necessities of life. Committees on supplies will regulate the distribution of confiscated goods. Should there be a lack of anything, which might be the case in respect to articles of food, these must be obtained by proper agents. Taking such things from neighboring great estates by armed columns of foragers would be a most expeditious way of furnishing them.

The preparation of provisions will be done effectively by communal associations of workmen, organized for that purpose.

The immediate organization of the workers according to the different branches of trade, and of placing at their disposal the factories, machines, raw materials, etc., etc., for co-operative production, will form the basis of the new society.

The Commune will—at least for the present—be supposed to mediate and regulate consumption. It, therefore, enters into contracts with the individual workers associations, makes periodical advances to them, which may consist in drafts upon the communal wares collected and stored, and thereby give the death stroke to the old monetary system.

Good schools, kindergartens, and other institutions for education must be founded without delay. The education of adults, which then will be possible, must not be neglected or postponed. Truth and knowledge must be taught in all churches, where no priestly cant will be tolerated. All printing presses must be put in operation to produce books, papers, and pamphlets of educational value by the million, to be distributed everywhere, particularly in regions not yet liberated from thralldom.

All law books, court and police records, registers of mortgages, deeds, bonds, and all so-called "valuable documents" must be burned. These indications only serve to show that the period of transition, which generally dismays those who otherwise energetically espouse a reorganization of society, because it appears difficult and arduous to them, need not be of such enervating nature.

And now let us take a look at the ideal of our aspirations.

Free society consists of autonomous, i.e., independent Communes. A network of federations, the result of freely made social contracts, and not of authoritative government or guardianship, surrounds them all. Common affairs are attended to in accordance with free deliberation and judgement by the interested Communes or associations. The people, without distinction of sex, meet frequently in parks or suitable halls, not indeed, to make laws or to bind their own hands, but in order to decide from case to case in all matters touching public affairs, or for appointing individuals to execute their resolves, and hear their reports.

The exterior appearance of these Communes will be entirely different from that of the present cities and villages. Narrow streets have vanished, tenement prisons are torn down, and spacious, well-fitted palaces, surrounded by gardens and parks, erected in their places, giving accommodation to larger or smaller associations brought together by identical interests, increasing comforts to a degree which no individual or family arrangement could reach.

In the country the people will be more concentrated. One agricultural Commune with city conveniences will take the place of several villages. The uniting farms hitherto separated, the general application and constant improvement of agricultural implements and chemical fertilizers, the growing perfection of the means of communication and transportation, etc., have simplified this process of concentration. The former contrast between city and country disappears, and the principle of equality gains one of its most important triumphs.

Private property exists no more. All wealth belongs to the Communes or the communal leagues. Everybody, whether able to work or not, can obtain from them such articles of necessity as he may desire. The sum total of necessities and comforts demanded, regulates the quantity of production.

The time of labor for the individual is limited to a few hours a day, because all those able to work, regardless of sex, take part in production, because useless, injurious, or similar work will not be done, and because technical, chemical, and other auxiliary means of production are highly developed and universally applied. By far the greater part of the day can be spent in the enjoyment of life.

The highest gratification will be found in freely chosen intellectual employment. Some spend their leisure time in the service of their fellow-men, and are busy for the common weal. Others can be found in the libraries, where they apply themselves to literary pursuits, or to gathering the material for educational lectures, or simply for private studies. Others again hasten to the lyceums, open to all, and there hear science. Academies of painting, sculpture, music, etc., offer chances of education for such as follow the fine arts.

Friends of childhood, especially those of the female sex, center about the places of education, where, under the direction of the real mentors of youth, they aid in the rearing and culture of the growing generation.

Teaching will be done only in well ventilated, light rooms, and during fair weather in the open air. And in order to secure the equal development of mind and body, merry play, gymnastics, and work will alternate with the close application of the mind.

Theaters and concert halls will offer free seats to all.

Forced or procured marriages are unknown; mankind has returned to the natural state and love rules unconstrained.

Vice and crime have disappeared with their original causes, private property and general misery.

Diseases to a great extent cease to appear because bad lodging, murderous workshops, impure food and drink, over-exertion, etc., etc., have become things unknown.[13]

Man at last can enjoy life. THE "BEAST OF PROPERTY" IS NO MORE!!!

Albert Parsons

The Board of Trade: Legalized Theft

In 1883 Johann Most succeeded in uniting many segments of the American radical movement in the anarchist International Working People's Association. Like their leader, most of the members of this Association were

---

[13]Most's description of his idyllic society was so persuasive that Emma Goldman was astonished to discover that it was not being attained in the Soviet Union in the early 1920's (*op. cit.*, pp. 726–927).

addicted to rhetorical violence. The strongest and most numerous chapter was in Chicago. Although most leaders and members of this group were German or Slavic by birth, the most eloquent of the group was Albert Parsons, editor of the English-language anarchist journal, *The Alarm*. Parsons was American-born, and had tried unsuccessfully for a political career before joining the anarchist movement. His career came to an abrupt end when he was hanged with three other anarchists of the Chicago group for alleged complicity in the Haymarket bombing of 1886. Since no evidence was produced that linked Parsons and the others to the actual bombing, most investigators believe that it was their incendiary speeches and writings that brought about their conviction.

There is no question that Parsons was guilty of rhetorical violence. *The Alarm* was filled with violent invective. The police were "bloodhounds of law and order" (January 9, 1885); the rich were "devils bred in hell and dogs with hearts of stone" (September 24, 1885); the industrial system was "legalized robbery and murder" (December 26, 1885). Parsons published translations from Most's pamphlet, *Revolutionäre Kriegswissenschaft*, a manual of guerrilla warfare containing directions for making nitroglycerine, dynamite, bombs, and poison. As early as 1878, Allan Pinkerton, of the detective agency, had singled Parsons out as "a young man . . . of flippant tongue, . . . capable of making a speech that will tingle the blood of that class of characterless rascals that are always standing ready to grasp society by the throat; and while he can excite his auditors, of this class, to the very verge of riot, has that devilish ingenuity in the use of words which has permitted himself to escape deserving punishment."[14]

There is some reason to suppose that Parsons did not really want violence, in spite of the incendiarism of his speeches. At the Haymarket trial he excused his use of intemperate language: "Well, possibly I have said some foolish things. Who has not? As a public speaker, probably I have uttered some wild and possibly incoherent assertions. Who, as a public speaker, has not done so?" He was outraged, he said, by seeing "little children suffering, men and women starving," while others were "rolling in luxury and wealth and opulence, out of the unpaid-for labor of the laborers." Meanwhile the militia were drilling in the streets, preparing to "butcher their fellow-men when they demand the right to work and partake of the fruits of their labor! Seeing these things . . . , may I not say some things then that I would not in cooler moments?"[15]

The speech presented here was given at an anarchist rally in front of the newly completed Board of Trade building in Chicago on April 28, 1885. The text is from *The Alarm*, May 2, 1885. Parsons probably spoke extemporaneously and then wrote out the text for

[14]Allan Pinkerton, *Strikers, Communists, Tramps and Detectives*, New York, 1878, pp. 388–89.
[15]Lucy Parsons, *Life of Albert Parsons*, Chicago, 1903, pp. 147–48.

publication. It cannot be regarded as a completely accurate text. However, since Parsons was a literate and practiced speaker, and since he was constantly writing and speaking on similar themes, the text undoubtedly reflects the topics he used, and similar if not identical language. Since *The Alarm* was read mainly by the same people who attended the rally, there was no reason to make extensive changes.

At five o'clock this morning over one hundred thousand men, women and children, wage workers in the city of Chicago, arose from their lowly beds and hastily partaking of their frugal morning meal, could be seen in thousands swarming their way to the factories, workshops, and other places of labor where they gave from 10 to 12 or 14 or 16 hours of hard work for a sum barely enough to keep themselves from actual want. Twenty thousand able-bodied men tramp the streets of this city, vainly searching for employment, with compulsory idleness, enforced poverty, and the misery resulting therefrom. Tonight the propertied class—the robbers of labor's product—were engaged in dedicating a temple to the God of Mammon; a temple which was to be devoted exclusively to the plunder and destruction of the people.

We have assembled as anarchists and communists to enter our solemn protest against the methods and practices of the existing society, which is founded upon the exploitation of man by his fellow man. We are here to declare in tones that may be heard within the banquet halls of this board of thieves, who, like Belschazzer, may read the handwriting on the walls of their temple, "weighed in the balance and found wanting." (*applause*) What is the Board of Trade? What is it but an institution devoted exclusively to the work of making the food of the people both dear and scarce. It is an establishment to the chicanery of legalized theft, and the people are its victims. It is the business of the Board of Trade to "run corners" and force up or down the market; compelling the farmer who produces to sell at a price which does not remunerate him for his labor, and then compels the working class of the industrial centers, who are the principal consumers of the country, to buy at enhanced prices. Their sword is two-edged; it cuts down the consumer and the producer, and levies a tribute from both which goes to make up the splendor and magnificence that this banquet represents.

The people of the whole northwest pour their wealth into this gambling hell, where these social vampires and parasites have assembled tonight. There is not a stone of the building which has not been carved out of the flesh and blood of labor, and cemented by the sweat and tears of the women and children of toil. These are the [men?] whose practices send our little ones supperless to bed, and bring wretchedness and woe where peace and plenty should prevail. When the cornerstone of this Board of Trade was laid, amid great pomp and ceremony, last year, a devout, pious man named Bishop Cheney was there to bless and baptize it. (*laughter*) What a truthful follower that man must be of the tramp Nazarine, Jesus, that son of a carpenter, who had nowhere to lay his head, and who scourged the profit mongers of the Board of Trade from the temple of Jerusalem and denounced them as a gang of thieves and a den of vipers. (*cheers*) Another pious fraud to take part in the present ceremonies is that eminent divine the Rev. Clinton Locke. (*shouts and laughter*) Let us not be foolish. Let us not be deceived about these grave matters any longer. Have we the right to live? (*cries of "yes" and "no"*) Do we want to possess and enjoy our natural rights? (*cries of "yes"*) If we do then we must take the necessary steps to acquire and maintain them.

Is not our natural right to life, liberty, and happiness the equal to anyone else? But we have yet to acquire these inalienable rights. The present social system makes private property of the means of labor and the resources of life—capital—and thereby creates classes and inequalities; conferring upon the holders of property the power to live upon the labor product of the propertyless. Whoever owns our bread owns our ballots, for a man who must sell his labor or starve must sell his vote when the same alternative is presented. The inequalities of our social system, its classes, its privileges, its enforced poverty and misery, arises out of the institution of private property, and so long as this system prevails our wives and children will be driven to toil, while their fathers and brothers are thrown into enforced idleness and the men of the Board of Trade and all other profit mongers and legalized gamblers who live by fleecing the people will continue to accumulate millions at the expense of their helpless victims. This grand conspiracy against our liberty and lives is maintained and upheld by statute law and the constitution and enforced by the military arm of the state. If we would achieve our liberation from economic bondage and acquire our natural right to life and liberty, every man must lay by a part of his wages, buy a Colt's navy revolver (*cheers*), a Winchester Rifle (A VOICE: "*And 10 pounds of dynamite.*") and learn how to make and use dynamite. Then raise the flag of rebellion, the scarlet banner of liberty, fraternity, equality and strike down to the earth every tyrant that lives upon this globe. Tyrants have no right that we should respect. Until this is done you will continue to be robbed, to be plundered, to be at the mercy of the privileged few. Therefore, agitate for the purpose of organization, organize for the purpose of rebellion, for wage slaves have nothing to lose but their chains; they have a world of freedom and happiness to win.

Suggested Reading

Chester M. Destler, *American Radicalism, 1865–1901*, New York, 1963. This book was originally published as a Connecticut College Monograph, and is a discerning analysis of a number of significant radical activities in the period it covers. Destler has made extensive use of materials in the anarchist Labadie Collection at the University of Michigan as well as collections in the Wisconsin State Historical Society Library and the New York Public Library. An important book both for this and the next chapter is J. R. Commons et al., *History of Labour in the United States*, New York, 1946. Volume II makes clear the nature of the division between socialist and anarchist beliefs and organization. The best treatment of the Haymarket riot is to be found in Henry David, *History of the Haymarket Affair*, New York, 1958.

chapter 5

the rhetoric of socialism
and social reform

Native-born American socialism has seldom followed orthodox patterns. Marxism is too doctrinaire to be applied in the pragmatic climate of American politics, and American-born workers have consistently been more interested in getting a larger share of the profit of American industry than in destroying the system. As for anarchism, more Americans were attracted to the individualism of Thoreau or the undisciplined freedom of the frontier than to the idyllic society pictured by Johann Most. Most American Socialist movements, therefore, had an ill-defined philosophical base, and tended to emphasize immediate rather than long-range goals. In method they were evolutionary rather than revolutionary. Some were romantic and utopian, like the Nationalist movement based on Edward Bellamy's novel, *Looking Backward*; some were loose alliances of the discontented, like the Populist Party, and their goals were vague enough to embrace a variety of conflicting interests; some were grouped around an attractive personality, such as Henry George or Eugene Debs, and tried to develop mass support which each of several lesser leaders hoped to be able to control. The only doctrinaire Socialist group with long continuity (prior to the formation of the Communist Party), was Daniel DeLeon's Socialist Labor Party. DeLeon sacrificed a mass movement for the sake of party discipline and succeeded in developing a party which has maintained its identity from about 1890 to the present as a revolutionary group with virtually no influence beyond its tiny membership.

None of the socialist movements has attracted a sufficient body of votes from organized labor to become a major political threat, but many of the ideas developed by Henry George and Eugene Debs have been adopted by more potent political groups. As Joseph Buchanan, a nine-teenth-century labor organizer, put it, "The average workingman will not leave his old party so long as there is one plank in its platform he supports, and will not join a new party so long as there is one plank in its platform he does not support."[1]

Regardless of their divergent backgrounds, all socialists and most social reformers were sure of one thing: there must be a better economic system than that which produced great wealth for some and extreme poverty for others in a country of unbounded resources and productive capacity. In the charges they made against the existing order, there was remarkable unanimity. In the view of socialists and neosocialists the existing economic system returned to the producers only a small portion of that which they produced. The rest was going into the hands of nonproducers. Henry George thought it was going to the owners of the land. Most socialists thought it was going to the owners of the tools. In any case the gross discrepancy between the income of the workers and that of the owners allowed socialist speakers to claim that distributing the differential among the workers would bring a high standard of living to all. When their arithmetic was questioned, they fell back on a secondary argument that capitalists deliberately restricted production in order to keep working men in wage slavery, or more rationally, perhaps, that the system itself made workers and employers alike the victims of cycles of prosperity and depression.

As to the remedy, however, socialists could not agree whether socialism was an economic or a political movement, whether capitalism should be destroyed or gradually transformed, whether the political arm of the movement should seek to elect public officials or merely to educate the workers. There was also great divergence in the nature of the society to be attained. Georgists thought that economic equality could be reached by taxing the profit in land speculation and using the proceeds for public services. Anarchists thought a cooperative society would emerge spontaneously from the ashes of violent revolution; Daniel DeLeon's Socialist Labor Party intended to impose a highly structured and thoroughly planned socialist state. Victor Berger believed that socialism could be attained through elections in a democratic society. Militant leaders of the Industrial Workers of the World, originally supported by almost all socialist factions,[2] thought that workers could seize control of industry by organizing labor on industrial rather than craft lines.

[1]Joseph R. Buchanan, *Story of a Labor Agitator*, New York, 1903, p. xi.

[2]Although both Debs and DeLeon submerged their differences to participate in the organizing convention of the IWW in 1905, neither remained with the organization long enough to have much influence on its activities. It soon fell into the hands of anarchosyndicalists who committed it to a course of violence, whereas other socialist leaders, although not completely ruling out violent revolution, preferred to seek a political solution.

Eugene Debs, perhaps the best speaker and certainly the best loved of all socialist leaders of the early twentieth century, represented in his own person the shifting uncertainty of socialist aims and methods. In a span of ten years Debs was successively leader of a militant labor union, a Bryan Democrat, a utopian, the presidential candidate of the Socialist Party, and a founder of the IWW. It is little wonder that there was confusion among the rank and file.

Because of this confusion, socialist and reform speeches were most effective in their attacks on the existing order. To document the need for a change, they were filled with lively examples and analogies, and they made effective use of factual data, including statistics. Different speakers were likely to use the same data; the same enemies were castigated; the same basic arguments were advanced. The language was colorful and showed a high degree of rapport between speaker and audience.

As to solutions, the arguments were less compelling. Because they proposed new and untested remedies, they were sometimes too vague to be understandable, or at the other extreme too dogmatic to be appealing. Moreover, hostility and rivalry among the leaders caused their arguments to cancel each other out, while personal attacks on each other undermined the influence of all the socialist speakers with the rank and file. The greatest influence of the socialist speakers may well have been the documentation of economic ills and the stimulation of new ideas for reform in the progressive wings of the Republican and Democratic Parties.

Henry George

Acceptance Speech—1886

One of the most original thinkers among American agitators was Henry George, founder of a school of economic theory which came to be known as the Single Tax. In George's view as set forth in 1880 in *Progress and Poverty*, land was the gift of God to all men and free access to it was a natural right. But grasping individuals had seized the land and held it for speculative purposes, profiting from values derived from the increased density of the population. The owners then charged exorbitant rents or sold the land at inflated prices, although they may have contributed nothing of social value through their ownership of the land. George's solution was to take this "unearned increment" for public use by the taxation of land values, exclusive of improvements. The revenue so derived would pay all the expenses of government and allow greatly expanded services.

The simplicity of George's scheme attracted a large personal following, and in 1886 an alliance of labor unions, socialists, and reformers invited him to become their candidate for mayor of New York City. As a condition of accepting their nomination he asked and received pledges of support on petitions signed by more than 30,000 voters. In a campaign of less than a month George spoke more than a hundred times; five speeches were a typical evening's work, and on one evening he spoke to eleven separate audiences, chiefly out of doors.

On the occasion of his acceptance speech in Cooper Union, the unfriendly *New York Tribune* reported that the crowds were jammed "clear to the walls, . . . packed as sheep might be in a mammoth freight car."[3] Outside, another five hundred waited impatiently for him to address them at the end of the meeting.

Although earlier in his career George had been somewhat pedantic and ineffective with audiences,[4] the acceptance speech is audience-centered and lively. He makes excellent use of examples, and his statistics on crowded conditions in New York could hardly have been presented more impressively. As the text of the speech shows, the audience responded warmly throughout his address.

The entrenched power of Tammany Hall was too much for George to overcome in a few short weeks of even the most strenuous campaign, though he polled 68,000 votes to some 90,000 for Abram Hewitt, a respectable candidate put up by Tammany to stave off the threat of a labor victory. A young and untried Republican named Theodore Roosevelt polled 60,000 votes. Some observers believe that George won the election at the polls but lost it to Tammany at the counting tables.

The text given here is basically that in Louis Post and Fred Leubuscher, *An Account of the George-Hewitt Campaign*, New York, 1886. Their version is nearly identical with that printed on October 6, 1886, by the *New York World*, except for the elimination of the *World's* reports of audience reactions. In the text given here, audience reactions have been restored by collating the *World* text with those of the *New York Tribune*, the *New York Star*, and a partial text in the *New York Times*, all dated October 6. The reporting in all these sources appears to be accurate; minor differences may be attributed to the drowning of the speaker's voice by audience reactions, or to occasional lapses in a reporter's ability to keep up with the speaker. In addition to restoration of audience responses and a few minor changes, three more extensive revisions were made in the Post and Leubuscher text, and are explained in notes as they occur.

[3]*New York Daily Tribune*, October 6, 1886.
[4]For a discussion of this point, see Charles W. Lomas, "Kearney and George: The Demagogue and the Prophet," *Speech Monographs*, XXVIII (March, 1961), 50–59.

The step I am about to take has not been entered upon lightly. When my nomination for Mayor of New York was first talked of I regarded it as a nomination which was not to be thought about. I did not desire to be Mayor of New York. (*Applause and cries of, "But you shall be."*) I have had in my time political ambition, but years ago I gave it up. I saw what practical politics meant; I saw that under the conditions as they were a man who would make a political career must cringe and fawn and intrigue and flatter, and I resolved that I would not so degrade my manhood. (*Great applause and cries of "Bully for you."*) Another career opened to me; the path that I had laid before—that my eyes were fixed upon—was rather that of a pioneer—that of the men who go in advance of politics (*applause*), the men who break the road that after they have gone will be trod by millions. It seemed to me that there lay duty and that there lay my career, and since this nomination has been talked about my friends here and through the country and beyond the seas have sent me letter after letter, asking me not to lower, as they are pleased to term it, the position I occupied by running for a municipal office. But I believe, and have long believed, that working men ought to go into politics. (*applause and cheers*) I believe, and I have long believed, that through politics was the way, and the only way, by which anything real and permanent could be secured for labor. In that path, however, I did not expect to tread. That, I thought, would devolve upon others, but when the secretary of this nominating convention came to me and said, "You are the only man upon whom we can unite, and I want you to write me a letter either accepting or refusing to accept, and giving your reasons," that put a different face on the matter. I had made up my mind to refuse, but when he came in that way I could not refuse. (*applause*) But I made my conditions. I asked for a guarantee of good faith of the men who put me forward; I asked for some tangible evidence that my fellow-citizens of New York really wanted me to act. That evidence you have given me. All I asked, and more.

(*Then turning to the chairman and grasping his hand, Mr. George continued impressively:*) John McMackin, Chairman of the Convention of Organized Labor, I accept your nomination, and in grasping your hand I grasp in spirit the hand of every man in this movement. From now henceforward let us stand together.

Working-men of New York—organized laborers of New York, I accept your nomination. (*enthusiastic cheering*) For weal or for woe, for failure or for success, henceforward I am your candidate. (VOICE: "*And the next Mayor, too.*") I am proud of it from the bottom of my heart. I thank you for the compliment you have paid me. Never in my time has any American citizen received from his fellow-citizens such a compliment as has been consummated to-night; never shall any act of mine bring discredit upon that compliment. (A VOICE: "That we are sure of.")

(*Then dropping the chairman's hand, and coming to the front of the platform again, Mr. George said, with much solemnity:*) Working-men of New York, I am your candidate; now it devolves upon you to elect me. (CHORUS OF VOICES: *"We will."*) In your name I solicit the suffrages of all citizens, rich or poor, white or black, native or foreign-born; if any organization of citizens sees fit to indorse your nomination, well and good; but as you have asked me for no pledges, so you may rely on me; I will make no pledge to any man or body of men. As you have nominated me unsolicited, I will solicit the indorsement of no other party. Whoever accepts me must accept me as the candidate of organized labor standing alone. And now it devolves upon you to elect me. You can; but look in the face what is against us. This, in my opinion, will be one of the fiercest contests that ever took place in this or any other American city. If money can beat me, I shall be beaten. Every influence that can be arrayed against me will be used. There will be falsehood and slanders, everything that money and energy and political knowledge and experience can command. Don't imagine that those who have their hands in the pockets of this city through their control of the municipal departments will give up easily (*laughter*); don't imagine that the politicians who have made a business of politics for years and have grown fat upon it will allow the working-men to smash their machines without trying their utmost to prevent it. But I do believe, as your chairman has said, that we shall win in spite of all. And I believe it because I see, in this gathering en-thusiasm—a power that is stronger than money (*prolonged applause*), more potent than trained politicians; something that will meet and throw them aside like chaff before a gale. (*renewed applause*)

Standing now as your candidate for the Mayoralty of New York City, it is meet and fitting that I should say something with regard to the office to which you propose to elect me. It is an important office; it is a powerful position, but any man who obtains it will be fettered by a bad system. Our system of government here is very bad. What we should have is one similar to that of the United States—one executive, responsible to the people, and the heads of the various departments appointed by him removable at his pleasure and responsible to him. Then you will have somebody to call to account. Under our present system you have dual commissions, commissions of three, or four, or five persons, and the consequence is you can fix no responsibility anywhere. These men have to provide for their friends, and therefore there are all sorts of trading and dickering. Nevertheless the Mayor of New York has large powers, he has absolute power in appointing commissioners, though he has no power, as he ought to have, to remove them, with the exception of two very important commissioners—the Commissioners of Accounts; these he may appoint and remove at pleasure. Their business is to go through the departments and see that everything is all correct. But the Mayor has a greater power, the power of visitation and inquisition, finding out how things are going; and he has another great power, that of appealing to public opinion. If elected, as I believe I shall be elected, Mayor, I will do my utmost to discharge its duties faithfully and well—I will do my utmost to give you an honest and a clean government. (*applause*) I will do my utmost to bring about such changes in legislation as will remedy defects which have been proved, and I will enforce the laws.

I want this to be distinctly understood—that when I take the oath of office as Mayor of New York I will be Mayor of the whole city. (*prolonged cheering, ending with three rounds and a tiger from some men in the rear*) I will preserve order at all risks; I will enforce the law against friends as fully as against enemies. (*applause*) But there are some things that, if I am Mayor of New York, I shall stop if I can prevent them. There will be no more policemen acting as censors of what shall be said at public meetings. (*This last word seemed to be anticipated and was drowned in a tempest of applause.*) I will support to the utmost of my power and my influence the peace officers of the city, but if it is in my power to put a stop to it I will put a stop to the practice which seems to be common among many of the hoodlums of the force, of turning themselves into judge, jury, and executioner, and clubbing anybody whom they think ought to be clubbed. Without fear and without favor I will try to do my duty. I will listen as readily to the complaint of the richest man in this city as I will to the complaint of the poorest. (A VOICE: "*The rich have nothing to complain of.*") Some of them are under the impression that if I am elected they may have. No: you are right about it. The rich in this city have very little to complain of. Corrupt government always is and always must be the government of the men who have money. Under our republican forms, while we profess to believe in the equality of all men, the rich have virtually ruled the administration of the law. It reminds me of an old fable I used to read in a French book. There was a terrible pestilence among the animals once upon a time. The lion made proclamation and called all the beasts together. They were suffering for their sins, he said, and ought to investigate who it was that provoked the wrath of Heaven, and then offer him up as a sacrifice. And so all the animals met. They elected the fox as chairman. (*laughter*) The lion said he was a great sinner; that he had eaten many flocks of sheep, and even once eaten a shepherd. (*laughter*) The fox said to the lion that the sheep ought to be complimented to be eaten by his majesty, and as for the shepherd, it served him right, "for evidently," went on the fox, "he had been throwing stones at your majesty." And then the wolf and the hyena and the tiger and so on confessed their several sins, until it came to the fox, who said he had eaten a great many chickens, but they crowed so in the morning that they disturbed him very much. Lastly came the donkey, who said that as he was carrying a load of hay to the market for his master he turned around and took a mouthful. "Wicked monster," cried the fox. "But I was hungry," continued the ass. "He had forgotten to give me my breakfast." "That makes no difference," cried the fox, and it was unanimously decided that it was the sin of the ass that brought the pestilence (*laughter*), and all the animals fell on him and tore him to pieces by way of sacrifice. It is so with many rich criminals and it is so on the other side of the question. The Theiss boycotters are still in prison. Is there not something in the State of New York that recalls that battle of the animals? (*A voice near one of the doors here shouted out, "Mr. George, there are three or four ex-convicts who have been sent here as heelers for Tammany Hall."*) I should not be at all surprised at that.

The politicians whom you have disturbed by your nomination, and a good many of the respectable journals, think very poorly of this movement, because they term it, "class movement." They dislike to see class movements in our politics; they would rather you would go on in the old way voting for Tammany Hall, or the County Democracy, or the Republicans. Class movement! What class is it? The working class! Do you ever ask yourselves how it is that the working-men came to constitute a class? In the beginning all men had to work. Is it not the dictate of Scripture: "Thou shalt earn thy bread by the sweat of thy brow"? Nature gives to man nothing. Without work nothing can be produced. Work is the producer of all wealth. How, then, is it that there came to be distinctively a working class? How is it that that working class is everywhere the poorer class? It is that some men devise schemes by which they can live without working, by throwing the burden of their work upon their fellows. An English writer has divided all men into three classes— working-men, beggar-men, and thieves (*loud cheers*)— and this is correct. There are only three ways of getting the product of labor—by working for it, by having it given to you, and by stealing it. (*laughter*) If this is a class movement, then it is a movement of the working class against the beggar-men and the thieves. (*applause*) A class movement! No. (*cheers*) It is what Gladstone said of that great movement on the other side of the water—it is a movement of the masses against robbery by the classes, and is it not time that there should be in this city of New York some such movement as this? The political condition of this city—the metropolis of the western world—is to-day a hissing and a reproach through all the monarchies of Europe. Go over there on the other side and venture to say one word against their aristocratic institutions and see how quickly you will be met with the retort that there is no place where there is such open-faced corruption as in this city of New York. Speak to an Englishman about his rulers and see how quickly he will answer you to your disadvantage. (*A voice: "To hell with them!"*) Oh, no! Not to hell with any country. The man who is in this labor movement truly and heartily, the man who feels its spirit and its impulse, becomes a citizen of the world (*loud cheers*), a worker for the emancipation of the race. All over the world the working classes are brothers. (*cheers*) The quicker and sooner they recognize that, the quicker the day of redemption will come. I sat on the platform last night when Mr. Justin McCarthy delivered his masterly address, and I was very pleased to notice the charity to all men that was manifest throughout it. Ireland is not struggling for its rights alone, but for the rights of the English people as well. The Land League movement has brought out the burning declaration of the land for the people, and is doing its work on both sides of the sea.[5]

But to come back to our own government and time. This government of New York City—our whole political system—is rotten to the core. It needs no investigation to discover it. An assemblyman ordinarily "puts up" more than he can honestly expect to get back in salary. The ordinary expenditure of a candidate for Congress, I am told, is about $10,000, and he can make the expenses of his campaign go as high as $80,000. Even our judges pay some $20,000 for the privilege of running. It is well understood that a candidate for Mayor must be prepared to spend $75,000, and it is said that, in a recent campaign, the candidate spent something like $200,000. Look how money flows everywhere. This morning we read of Alderman Divver barbecuing an ox and letting beer run like water—and this distance from election, too! Is this vast amount of money thrown out for simple salaries? The money that is habitually spent in campaigning in this city is put in as a business investment (*applause*) —money out to get money in. Corruption!

Just consider, for a moment, the contemptuous manner in which this movement of our working class is treated. And why? Just because they think we haven't the "sinews of war." Because, as Mr. "Fatty" Walsh says, "Those labor fellows ain't got no inspectors of election." And under the beautiful system of local politics here, one rogue is turned out and another let in. Does that improve things? Do you suppose that Mr. Rollin M. Squire was a sinner above all other office-holders in this city? (*cries of "no"*) Is not the present incumbent applying the same old official axe—chopping off Tammany heads and putting in County Democrats in the same good old fashion? Is it not well understood that without some such deal tickets cannot be got up nor candidates run? Look at the outcry that has gone up over this movement. The cry of alarm, "The Democracy must unite," is heard everywhere. How has the party of Jefferson and of Jackson fallen when its two local wings must be called upon to unite, and even the power of the National Administration

[5]The preceding seven sentences do not appear in the Post and Leubuscher or *World* texts, nor does the audience interruption which prompted the remarks. The language here is from the *Star*, supported by similar remarks in the abbreviated version in the *Times*. It seems probable that the *World* reporter missed the interplay with the audience because of crowd noise, and simply omitted the passage.

brought in to help that unity! And against what? Against the working man! Why don't they unite, then, when the obligation is so imperative? Because the difficulty lies in parcelling out the spoils—in giving out the offices and getting the proper kind of pledges. As to the principle of the thing, they care nothing for that. Isn't it time that fresh breath was infused into this corruption?

In this movement of ours there is hope of better things. In a city where it has long been held that a man must be rich, very rich, to hold its highest office, you have put up a poor man. (*cheers*) In a city where it is a standing rule that a candidate must disburse money, you propose to furnish your own money. And you have a candidate who is free from pledges. Can your Johnny O'Briens say that when their candidate is nominated? (*cries of "no, no!"*) If the much hoped for union of Tammany Hall and Irving Hall and the County Democracy does take place, can it be said of their candidate that he stands free of pledges as to how he will parcel out the jobs in his gift? Remember that until you can elect men who are free you cannot expect an unfettered administration.

This movement aims at political reform; but that is not all. That is not the entire significance of my candidacy. We aim, too, at social reform. (*applause*) As declared in the platform you heard here to-night we aim at equal rights for all men. Chattel slavery is dead, but what we do tonight is to unfurl again the standard of the equal rights of man, to take up again the sentiment of the Declaration of Independence. (*applause*) Upon us devolves the duty of overthrowing that more insidious form of slavery which results in industrial slavery. This movement is a revolt of the masses not simply against political corruption, but against social injustice. (*applause*) And is it not time, and is this not the place?[6] (*cries of "yes," and applause*) Look over our vast city, and what do we see? On one side a very few men richer by far than it is good for men to be, and on the other side a great mass of men and women struggling and worrying and wearying to get a most pitiful living. In this big metropolis in this year of grace, 1886, we have a vast surging class of so-called free and independent citizens, with none of whom the wild, Red Indian, in anything like his native state, could afford to exchange. We have hordes of citizens living in want and in vice born of want, existing under conditions that would appall a heathen. Is this by the will of our Divine Creator? (A VOICE: *"No."*) It is the fault of men (*applause*), and as men and citizens on us devolves the duty of removing this wrong; (*applause*) and in that platform that the convention has adopted and on which I stand, the first true step in that direction is taken. Why should there be such abject poverty and destitu-

---

[6]The preceding four sentences are from the *Tribune* report, supported by similar language in the *Star*. The *World* text has the same idea, but it is considerably shorter. Again crowd noise may have been a factor.

tion in this city on the one side and such wealth on the other? There is one great fact that stares in the face anyone who chooses to look at it. That fact is that the vast majority of men and women and children in New York have no legal right to live here at all. Most of us—99 per cent at least—must pay the other one per cent by the week or month or quarter for the privilege of staying here and working here.

See how we are crowded in New York. London has a population of 15,000 to the square mile. Canton, in crowded China, has 35,000 inhabitants within the same area. New York has 54,000 to the square mile, and leaving out the uninhabited portion it has a population of 85,000 to the square mile. In the Sixth Ward there is a population of 149,000 to the square mile; in the Tenth Ward, 276,000; in the Thirteenth, 224,000, including roads, yards, and all open places. Why, there is one block in this city that contains 2,500 living beings and every room in it a workshop. There is in one ward a tenement covering one quarter of an acre, which contains an average of 1,350 people. At that rate a square mile would contain 3,456,000.[7] Nowhere else in the civilized world are men and women and children packed together so closely. As for children, they die almost as soon as they enter the world. In the district known as the Mulberry Bend, according to Commissioner Wingate's report, there is an infant death-rate of 65 per cent, and in the tenement district he says that a large percentage of the children die before they are five years of age.

Now, is there any reason for such overcrowding? There is plenty of room on this island. There are miles and miles and miles of land all around this nucleus. Why cannot we take that and build houses upon it for our accommodation? Simply because it is held by dogs in the manger who will not use it themselves, nor allow anybody else to use it, unless they pay an enormous price for it—because what the Creator intended for the habitation of the people whom He called into being is held at an enormous rent or an enormous price. Did you ever think, men of New York, what you pay for the privilege of living in this country? I do not ask what you pay for bricks and mortar and wood, but for rent; and the rent is mainly the rent of the land. Bricks and mortar and wood are of no greater value here than they are in Long Island or in Iowa. When what is called real estate advances it is the land that is getting more valuable; it is not the houses. All this enormous value that the growth of population adds to the land of this city is taken by the few individuals and goes for the benefit of the idle rich, who look down upon those who earn their living by their labor.

But what do we propose to do about it? We propose, in the first place, as our platform indicates, to make the buildings cheaper by taking

[7]The preceding sentence is found in the *Tribune* and *Star* accounts but not in others.

the tax off buildings. We propose to put that tax on land exclusive of improvements, so that a man who is holding land vacant will have to pay as much for it as if he was using it, just upon the same principle that a man who goes to a hotel and hires a room and takes the key and goes away would have to pay as much for it as if he occupied the room and slept in it. In that way we propose to drive out the dog in the manger who is holding from you what he will not use himself. We propose in that way to remove this barrier and open the land to the use of labor in putting up buildings for the accommodation of the people of the city. (*applause*) I am called a Socialist. I am really an individualist. I believe that every individual man ought to have an individual wife, and is entitled to an individual home. (*applause*) I think it is monstrous, such a state of society as exists in this city. Why, the children, thousands and thousands, have no place to play. It is a crime for them to play ball in the only place in which they can play ball. It is an offence for them to fly their kites. The children of the rich can go up to Central Park, or out into the country in the summer time; but the children of the poor, for them there is no playground in the city but the streets; it is some charity excursion which takes them out for a day, only to return them again to the same sweltering condition. There is no good reason whatever why every citizen of New York should not have his own separate house and home; and the aim of this movement is to secure it. We hold that the land belongs to the entire people. We hold that the value of the land of this city, by reason of the presence of this great population, belongs to us to apply to the welfare of the people. Everyone should be entitled to share in it. It should be for the use of the whole people, and for the beautifying and adornment of the city, for providing public accommodations, playgrounds, schools, and facilities for education and recreation. Why, here is this building in which we are assembled, the Cooper Institute; its superintendent told me only a little while ago they accommodated only about one tenth of the young people who are flocking here to get an education to enable them to make a livelihood. Instead of relying upon the beneficence of individuals, we, the people of New York, ought to furnish the institutions ourselves. We ought to have in this city of New York twenty such institutions as this. What the platform aims at is the taking for the use of the people all that value and benefit which result from social growth. We believe that the railroads of this city ought to be taken properly and legally by the people and run for the benefit of the people of New York. (*applause*) Why should it not be so? Any individual putting up a big building, such as the Norse building, the Cyrus Field building, the Western Union building, puts in an elevator. But he does not put in that elevator a man with a bell-punch strung around his neck to collect fares. He gains the advantage in the increased value of his building. So we could take their railroads and run them. We could take those railroads and run them free, let everybody ride who would, and we could pay for it out of the increased value of the people's property in consequence. These are but steps, but the aim of this movement, and this is its significance, is the assertion of the equal rights of man—the assertion of his equal and inalienable right to life and to all the elements that the Creator has furnished for the maintenance of that life.

Here is the heart of the labor question, and until we address ourselves to that the labor question never can be solved. These little children who die in our tenement districts, have they no business here? Do they not come into life with equal rights from the Creator? In the early days of New Zealand, when the English colonists bought land from the natives, they encountered a great difficulty. After they had bought and paid for a piece of land, the women would come with babes in their arms and would say: "We want something for these babes." The reply was: "We paid you for your land!" Then they who had parted with the land answered: "Yes, yes, yes, but you did not pay these babes. They were not born then."

I expect, my friends, to meet you many times during this campaign, and expect to make my voice heard in all parts of this city. I am ready to meet any questions that may be addressed to me, and to do whatever in me lies for the success of our ticket. (*applause*) I am your candidate for Mayor of New York. (*vociferous cheers, followed by three cheers and a rattling tiger*) It is something that a little while ago I never dreamt of. Years ago I came to this city from the West, unknown, knowing nobody, and I saw and recognized for the first time the shocking contrast between monstrous wealth and debasing want. And here I made a vow, from which I have never faltered, to seek out and remedy, if I could, the cause that condemned little children to lead such a life as you know them to lead in the squalid districts. It is because of that that I stand before you tonight, presenting myself for the chief office of your city—espousing the cause, not only of your rights but of those who are weaker than you. Think of it! Little ones dying by thousands in this city; a veritable slaughter of the innocents before their time has come. Is it not our duty as citizens to address ourselves to the adjustment of social wrongs that force out of the world those who are called into it almost before they are here—that social wrong that forces girls upon the streets and our boys into the grogshops and then into penitentiaries? We are beginning a movement for the abolition of industrial slavery, and what we do on this side of the water will send its impulse across the land and over the sea, and give courage to all men to think and act. Let us, therefore, stand together. Let us do everything that is possible for men to do from now until the second of next month, that success may crown our efforts, and that to us in this city may belong the honor of having led the van in this great movement. (*great enthusiasm and cheering*)

Daniel DeLeon

What Means This Strike?

The most brilliant, strong-minded, and intolerant of all American Socialist leaders at the turn of the century was Daniel DeLeon, for many years editor of *The People*, official publication of the Socialist Labor Party. DeLeon joined the party at the age of 35, after he had been introduced to Socialism by party members active with him in Henry George's campaign for mayor of New York in 1886. More than any other American socialist, DeLeon had a clear grasp of the implications of the writings of Marx and Engels, and in his later years he developed a logical method of implementing these theories when the party should obtain power.

But, like many strong-minded men, DeLeon quarreled with most of the prior leaders of the Socialist Labor party, with the officials of the American Federation of Labor, with the Socialist Party of Eugene Debs and Victor Berger, and with social and political reformers of all colors. Rejecting all but his own brand of Marxist orthodoxy, he effectively forestalled the development of a mass radical party embracing a larger spectrum of political opinion.

Yet in spite of his violent attacks upon other left-wing leaders, he was highly effective with labor audiences whenever he had a chance to address them. His rapport with his listeners is apparent in the stenographic report of DeLeon's speech in the City Hall of New Bedford, Massachusetts, February 11, 1898. Sometimes the language is scholarly, and it would seem that a workingman's attention might lag. Then a passage in direct address will follow, or a striking application of principle to the particular situation the New Bedford workers were experiencing at the moment, or a slashing attack on "thieving capitalists" or "labor fakirs." At times he builds his audience to a high pitch of excitement, evoking applause on nearly every sentence.[8]

Some of DeLeon's attacks were oversimplifications even in 1898; many others have been outdated by changes in the position of organized labor and the attitudes of management. The value of

[8]Arnold Petersen, National Secretary of the Socialist Labor Party, in a partisan evaluation, contrasts DeLeon favorably with "second rank" orators like Daniel Webster, and "such vulgar practitioners of vocal acrobatics as Robert Ingersoll and William Jennings Bryan." Arnold Petersen, *Daniel DeLeon: Orator*, New York, 1942, p. 14.

the speech to a contemporary student of agitation is in the methods
he used to arouse his audience and in the content and style of his
speech.

The text reproduced here is from a pamphlet printed by the
New York Labor News, publishers of the Socialist Labor Party
literature. It was first printed shortly after the speech was delivered, and has been reissued many times since.

Working men and working women of New Bedford; ye striking textile
workers; and all of you others, who, though not now on strike, have
been on strike before this, and will be on strike some other time —:

It has been the habit in this country and in England that, when a
strike is on, "stars" in the Labor Movement are invited to appear on
the scene, and entertain the strikers; entertain them and keep them in
good spirits with rosy promises and prophesies, funny anecdotes, bom-
bastic recitations in prose and poetry; stuff them full of rhetoric and
wind—very much in the style that some Generals do, who, by means of
bad whiskey, seek to keep up the courage of the soldiers whom they are
otherwise unable to beguile. Such has been the habit in the past; to a
great extent it continues to be the habit in the present; it was so during
the late miners' strike; it has been so to some extent here in New Bedford; and it is so everywhere, to the extent that ignorance of the Social
Question predominates. To the extent, however, that Socialism gets a
footing among the working class such false and puerile tactics are thrown
aside. The Socialist workingmen of New Bedford, on whose invitation
I am here; all those of us who are members of that class-conscious revolutionary international organization of the working class, that throughout
the world stands out to-day as the leading and most promiseful feature
of the age;—all such would consider it a crime on the part of the men,
whom our organization sends forth to preach the Gospel of Labor, if
they were to spend their platform time in "tickling" the workers. Our
organization sends us out to teach the workers, to enlighten them on
the great issue before them, and the great historic drama in which most
of them are still unconscious actors. Some of you, accustomed to a
different diet, may find my speech dry; if there be any such here, let
him leave; he has not yet graduated from that primary school reared by
experience in which the question of wages is forced upon the workers
as a serious question, and they are taught that it demands serious thought
to grapple with, and solve it. If, however, you have graduated from
that primary department, and have come here with the requisite earnest-
ness, then you will not leave this hall without having, so to speak, caught
firm hold of the cable of the Labor Movement; then the last strike of
this sort has been seen in New Bedford; then, the strikes that may follow
will be as different from this as vigorous manhood is from toddling in-
fancy; then you will have entered upon that safe and sure path along

which, not, as heretofore, eternal disaster will mark your tracks, but New Bedford, Massachusetts, and the nation herself will successively fall into your hands, with freedom as the crowning fruit of your efforts. (*applause*)

Three years ago I was in your midst during another strike. The superficial observer who looks back to your attitude during that strike, who looks back to your attitude during the strikes that preceded that one, who now turns his eyes to your attitude in the present strike, and who discovers substantially no difference between your attitude now and then might say, "Why, it is a waste of time to speak to such men; they learn nothing from experience; they will eternally fight the same hopeless battle; the battle to establish 'safe relations' with the capitalist class, with the same hopeless weapon: the 'pure and simple' organization of labor!" But the Socialist does not take that view. There is one thing about your conduct that enlists for and entitles you to the warm sympathy of the Socialist, and that is that, despite your persistent errors in fundamental principles, in aims and methods, despite the illusions that you are chasing after, despite the increasing poverty and cumulating failures that press upon you, despite all that you preserve manhood enough not to submit to oppression, but rise in the rebellion that is implied in a strike. The attitude of workingmen engaged in a bona fide strike is an inspiring one. It is an earnest [belief] that slavery will not prevail. The slave alone who will not rise against his master, who will meekly bend his back to the lash and turn his cheek to him who plucks his beard—that slave alone is hopeless. But the slave, who, as you of New Bedford, persists, despite failures and poverty, in rebelling, there is always hope for. This is the reason I have considered it worth my while to leave my home and interrupt my work in New York, and come here, and spend a few days with you. I bank my hopes wholly and build entirely upon this sentiment of rebellion within you.

What you now stand in need of, aye, more than of bread, is the knowledge of a few elemental principles of political economy and of sociology. Be not frightened at the words. It is only the capitalist professors who try to make them so difficult of understanding that the very mentioning of them is expected to throw the workingman into a palpitation of the heart. The subjects are easy of understanding.

The first point that a workingman should be clear upon is this: What is the source of the wages he receives; what is the source of the profits his employer lives on? The following dialogue is not uncommon:

Workingman—"Do I understand you rightly, that you Socialists want to abolish the capitalist class?"

Socialist—"That is what we are after."

Workingman—"You are!? Then I don't want any of you. Why, even now my wages are small; even now I can barely get along. If you abolish the capitalist I'll have nothing; there will be nobody to support me."

Who knows how many workingmen in this hall are typified by the workingman in this dialogue!

When, on pay-day, you reach out your horny, "unwashed" hand it is empty. When you take it back again, your wages are on it. Hence the belief that the capitalist is the source of your living, that he is your bread-giver, your supporter. Now that is an error, an optic illusion.

If, early in the morning you go on top of some house and look east-ward, it will seem to you that the sun moves and that you are standing still. Indeed, that was at one time the general and accepted belief. But it was an error, based upon an optic illusion. So long as that error pre-vailed the sciences could hardly make any progress. Humanity virtually stood stock still. Not until the illusion was discovered and the error over-thrown, not until it was ascertained that things were just the other way, that the sun stood still, and that it was our planet that moved at a break-neck rate of speed, was any real progress possible. So likewise with this illusion about the source of wages. You can not budge, you can not move one step forward unless you discover that, in this respect also, the fact is just the reverse of the appearance: that, not the capitalist, but the workingman, is the source of the worker's living; that it is not the capitalist who supports the workingman, but the workingman who sup-ports the capitalist (*loud applause*); that it is not the capitalist who gives bread to the workingman, but the workingman who gives himself a dry crust, and sumptuously stocks the table of the capitalist. (*long and loud applause*) This is a cardinal point in political economy; and this is the point I wish first of all to establish in your minds. Now, to the proof.

Say that I own $100,000. Don't ask me where I got it. If you do, I would have to answer you in the language of all capitalists that "Such a question is un-American." You must not look into the source of this my "original accumulation": It is un-American to pry into such secrets. (*laughter*) Presently I shall take you into my confidence. For the present I shall draw down the blinds, and keep out your un-American curiosity. I have $100,000, and am a capitalist. Now, I may not know much; no capitalist does; but I know a few things, and among them is a little plain arithmetic. I take a pencil and put down on a sheet of paper "$100,000." Having determined that I shall need at least $5,000 a year to live with comfort, I divide the $100,000 by $5,000; the quotient is 20. My hair then begins to stand on end. The 20 tells me that, if I pull $5,000 an-nually out of $100,000, these are exhausted during that term. At the be-ginning of the 21st year I shall have nothing left. "Heaven and earth, I would then have to go to work if I wanted to live!" No capitalist relishes that thought. He will tell you, and pay his politicians, professors and political parsons, to tell you, that "labor is honorable." He is perfectly willing to let you have that undivided honor, and will do all he can that you may not be deprived of any part of it; but, as to himself, he has for work a constitutional aversion; the capitalist runs away from work like the man bitten by a mad dog runs away from water. I want to live without work on my $100,000 and yet keep my capital untouched. If you ask any farmer, he will tell you that if he invests in a Durham cow she will yield him a supply of 16 quarts a day, but, after some years, the supply goes down; she will run dry; and then a new cow must be got. But I, the capitalist, aim at making my capital a sort of $100,000 cow, which I shall annually be able to milk $5,000 out of, without her ever running dry. I want, in short, to perform the proverbially impossible feat of eating my cake, and yet having it. The capitalist system performs that feat for me. How?

I go to a broker. I say, Mr. Broker, I have $100,000; I want you to invest that for me. I don't tell him that I have a special liking for New Bedford mills' stock; I don't tell him I have a special fancy for railroad stock; I leave the choosing with him. The only direction I give him is to get the stock in such a corporation as will pay the highest dividend. Mr. Broker has a list of all these corporations, your New Bedford corporations among them, to the extent that they may be listed; he makes the choice, say of one of your mills right here in this town. I hire a vault in a safe deposit company and I put my stock into it. I lock it up, put the key in my pocket, and I go and have a good time. If it is too cold in the north I go down to Florida; if it is too hot there I go to the Adirondack mountains; occasionally I take a spin across the Atlantic and run the gauntlet of all the gambling dens in Europe; I spend my time with fast horses and faster women; I never put my foot inside the factory that I hold stock of; I don't even come to the town in which it is located, and yet, lo and behold, a miracle takes place!

Those of you versed in Bible lore surely have read or heard about the miracle that God performed when the Jews were in the desert and about to die of hunger. The Lord opened the skies and let manna come. But the Jews had to get up early in the morning, before the sun rose; if they overslept themselves the sun would melt the manna, and they would have nothing to eat. They had to get up early, and go out, and stoop down and pick up the manna and put it in baskets and take it to their tents and eat it. With the appearance of the manna on earth the miracle ended.[9] But the miracles that happen in this capitalist system of production are so wonderful that those recorded in the Bible don't hold a candle to them. The Jews had to do some work, but I, stockholding capitalist, need do no work at all. I can turn night into day, and day into night. I can lie flat on my back all day and all night; and every three months my manna comes down to me in the shape of dividends. Where does it come from? What does the dividend represent?

In the factory of which my broker bought stock, workmen, thousands of them, were at work; they have woven cloth that has been put upon the market to the value of $7,000; out of the $7,000 that the cloth

[9]For the Biblical story, see the sixteenth chapter of Exodus.

is worth my wage workers receive $2,000 in wages, and I receive the $5,000 as profits or dividends. Did I, who never put my foot inside of the mill; did I, who never put my foot inside of New Bedford; did I, who don't know how a loom looks; did I, who contributed nothing whatever toward the weaving of that cloth; did I do any work whatever toward producing those $5,000 that came to me? No man, with brains in his head instead of sawdust, can deny that those $7,000 are exclusively the product of the wage workers in that mill. That out of the wealth thus produced by them alone, they get $2,000 in wages, and I, who did nothing at all, I get the $5,000. The wages these workers receive represent wealth that they have themselves produced; the profits that the capitalist pockets represent wealth that the wage workers produced, and that the capitalist, does what?—let us call things by their names—that the capitalist steals from them.

You may ask, But is that the rule, is not that illustration an exception? —Yes, it is the rule; the exception is the other thing. The leading industries of the United States are to-day stock concerns, and thither will all others worth mentioning move. An increasing volume of capital in money is held in stocks and shares. The individual capitalist holds stock in a score of concerns in different trades, located in different towns, too many and too varied for him even to attempt to run. By virtue of his stock, he draws his income from them; which is the same as saying that he lives on what the workingmen produce but are robbed of. Nor is the case at all essentially different with the concerns that have not yet developed into stock corporations.

Again, you may ask, The conclusion that what such stockholders live on is stolen wealth because they evidently perform no manner of work is irrefutable, but are all stockholders equally idle and superfluous; are there not some who do perform some work: are there not "Directors"?— There are "Directors," but these gentlemen bear a title much like those "Generals" and "Majors" and "Colonels" who now go about, and whose generalship, majorship and colonelship consisted in securing substitutes during the war. (applause) These "Directors" are simply the largest stock-holders, which is the same as to say that they are the largest sponges; their directorship consists only in directing conspiracies against rival "Directors," in bribing Legislatures, Executives and Judiciaries, in picking out and hiring men out of your midst to serve as bell-wethers, that will lead you, like cattle, to the capitalist shambles, and tickle you into contentment and hopefulness while you are being fleeced. The court decisions removing responsibility from the "Directors" are numerous and increasing; each such decision establishes, from the capitalist Government's own mouth, the idleness and superfluousness of the capitalist class. These "Directors," and the capitalist class in general, may perform some "work," they do perform some "work," but that "work" is not of a sort that directly or indirectly aids production;—no more than the intense mental strain and activity of the "work" done by the pickpocket is directly or indirectly productive. (*applause*)

Finally, you may ask, No doubt the stockholder does no work, and hence lives on the wealth we produce; no doubt these "Directors" have a title that only emphasizes their idleness by a swindle, and, consequently, neither they are other than sponges on the working class; but did not your own illustration start with the supposition that the capitalist in question had $100,000; is not his original capital entitled to some returns? —This question opens an important one; and now I shall, as I promised you, take you into my confidence; I shall raise the curtain which I pulled down before the question, Where did I get it? I shall now let you pry into my secret.

Whence does this original capital, or "original accumulation," come? Does it grow on the capitalist like hair on his face, or nails on his fingers and toes? Does he secrete it as he secretes sweat from his body? Let me take one illustration of many.

Before our present Governor, the Governor of New York was Levi Parsons Morton. The gentleman must be known to all of you. Besides having been Governor of the Empire State, he was once Vice-President of the Nation, and also at one time our Minister to France. Mr. Morton is a leading "gentleman"; he wears the best of broadcloth; his shirt-bosom is of spotless white; his nails are trimmed by manicurists; he uses the elitest language; he has front pews in a number of churches; he is a pattern of morality, law and order; and he is a multi-millionaire capitalist. How did he get his start millionaire-ward? Mr. Morton being a Republican, I shall refer you to a Republican journal, the *New York Tribune*, for the answer of this interesting question. The *Tribune* of the day after Mr. Morton's nomination for Governor in 1894 gave his biography. There we are informed that Mr. Morton was born in New Hampshire of poor parents; he was industrious, he was clever, he was pushing, and he settled, a poor young man, in New York city, where in 1860, mark the date, he started a clothing establishment; then, in rapid succession, we are informed that he failed, and—STARTED A BANK! (*loud laughter and applause*) A man may start almost any kind of a shop without a cent. If the landlord gave him credit for the rent, and the brewer, the shoe manufacturer, the cigar manufacturer, etc., etc., give him credit for the truck, he may start a saloon, a shoe shop, a cigar shop, etc., etc., without any cash, do business and pay off his debt with the proceeds of his sales. But there is ONE shop that he cannot start in that way. That shop is the banking shop. For that he must have cash on hand. He can no more shave notes without money than he can shave whiskers without razors. Now, then, the man who just previously stood up before a notary public and swore "So help him, God," he had no money to pay his creditors, immediately after, without having in the meantime married an heiress, has money enough to start a bank on! Where did he get it? (*applause*)

Read the biographies of any of our founders of capitalist concerns by the torch-light of this biography, and you will find them all to be essentially the same, or suggestively silent upon the doings of our man during the period that he gathers his "original accumulation." You will find that "original capital" to be the child of fraudulent failures and fires, of high-handed crime of some sort or other, or of the sneaking crime of appropriating trust funds, etc. With such "original capital,"—gotten by dint of such "cleverness," "push" and "industry,"—as a weapon, the "original" capitalist proceeds to fleece the working class that has been less "industrious," "pushing" and "clever" than he. If he consumes all his fleecings, his capital remains of its original size in his hands, unless some other gentleman of the road, gifted with greater "industry," "push" and "cleverness" than he, comes around and relieves him of it; if he consume not the whole of his fleecings, his capital moves upward, million-ward.

The case is proved: Labor alone produces all wealth. Wages are that part of Labor's own product that the workingman is allowed to keep; profits are the present and running stealings perpetrated by the capitalist upon the workingman from day to day, from week to week, from month to month, from year to year; capital is the accumulated past stealings of the capitalist—corner-stoned upon his "original accumulation." (*long applause*)

Who of you before me fails now to understand, or would still deny that, not the capitalist supports the workingman, but the workingman supports the capitalist; or still holds that the workingman could not exist without the capitalist? If any there be, let him raise his hand and speak up now——

None? Then I may consider this point settled; and shall move on.

The second point, on which it is absolutely necessary that you be clear, is the nature of your relation, as working people, to the capitalist in this capitalist system of production. This point is an inevitable consequence of the first.

You have seen that the wages you live on and the profits the capitalist riots in are the two parts into which is divided the wealth that you produce. The workingman wants a larger and larger share, so does the capitalist. A thing can not be divided into two shares so as to increase the share of each. If the workingman produces, say $4 worth of wealth a day, and the capitalist keeps 2, there are only 2 left for the workingman; if the capitalist keeps 3, there is only 1 left for the workingman; if the capitalist keeps 3½ there is only ½ left for the workingman. Inversely, if the workingman pushes up his share from ½ to 1, there are only 3 left to the capitalist; if the workingman secures 2, the capitalist will be reduced to 2; if the workingman push still onward and keep 3, the capitalist will have to put up with 1;—and if the workingman makes up his mind to enjoy all that he produces, and keep all the 4, THE CAPITALIST WILL HAVE TO GO TO WORK. (*long applause*) These plain figures upset the theory about the Workingman and the Capitalist being brothers. Capital, meaning the Capitalist Class, and Labor, have been portrayed by capitalist illustrated papers as Chang and Eng; this, I remember, was done notably by *Harper's Weekly*, the property of one of the precious "Seeley Diners" (*laughter*);—you remember that "dinner." (*laughter*) The Siamese Twins were held together by a piece of flesh. Wherever Chang went Eng was sure to go; if Chang was happy, Eng's pulse throbbed harder; if Chang caught cold, Eng sneezed in chorus with him; when Chang died, Eng followed suit within five minutes. Do we find that to be the relation of the workingman and the capitalist? Do you find that the fatter the capitalist, the fatter also grow the workingmen? Is not your experience rather that the wealthier the capitalist, the poorer are the workingmen? That the more magnificent and prouder the residences of the capitalist, the dingier and humbler become those of the workingmen? That the happier the life of the capitalist's wife, the greater the opportunities of his children for enjoyment and education, the heavier becomes the cross borne by the workingmen's wives, while their children are crowded more and more from the schools and deprived of the pleasures of childhood? Is that your experience, or is it not? (VOICES ALL OVER THE HALL: *"It is!"* and applause.)

The pregnant point that underlies these pregnant facts is that between the Working Class and the Capitalist Class, there is an irrepressible conflict, a class struggle for life. No glib tongued politician can vault over it, no capitalist professor or official statistician can argue it away; no capitalist parson can veil it; no labor fakir can straddle it; no "reform" architect can bridge it over. It crops up in all manner of ways, like in this strike, in ways that disconcert all the plans and all the schemes of those who would deny or ignore it. It is a struggle that will not down, and must be ended only by either the total subjugation of the Working Class, or the abolition of the Capitalist Class. (*loud applause*)

Thus you perceive that the theory on which your "pure and simple" trade organizations are grounded, and on which you went into this strike, is false. There being no "common interests," but only HOSTILE INTERESTS, between the Capitalist Class and the Working Class, the battle you are waging to establish "safe relations" between the two is a hopeless one.

Put to the touchstone of these undeniable principles the theory upon which your "pure and simple"[10] trade organizations are built, and you

[10]Throughout this speech, as in the pages of *The People*, of which he was editor, DeLeon attacks the American Federation of Labor, Samuel Gompers, and other labor leaders who preferred to use the unions merely as means to obtain a larger share of the profits of industry, rather than to seek to change the system. As Ira Kipnis points out, DeLeon and his associates "were devoting most of their energies to expelling heretics, suspending and reorganizing numerous sections, and destroying socialist newspapers." *The American Socialist Movement, 1897–1912*, New York, 1952, p. 26.

will find it to be false; examined by the light of these undeniable principles the road that your false theory makes you travel and the failures that have marked your career must strike you as its inevitable result. How are we to organize and proceed? you may ask. Before answering the question let me take up another branch of the subject. Its presentation will sweep aside another series of illusions that beset the mind of the working class, and will, with what has been said, give us a sufficient sweep over the ground to lead us to the right answer.

Let us take a condensed page of the country's history. For the sake of plainness, and forced to it by the exigency of condensation, I shall assume small figures. Place yourselves back a sufficient number of years with but ten competing weaving concerns in the community. How the individual ten owners came by the "original accumulations" that enabled them to start as capitalists you now know. (*laughter*) Say that each of the ten capitalists employs ten men; that each man receives $2 a day, and that the product of each of the ten sets of men in each of the ten establishments is worth $40 a day. You know now also that it is out of these $40 worth of wealth, produced by the men, that each of the ten competing capitalists takes the $20 that he pays the ten men in wages, and that out of that same $40 worth of wealth he takes the $20 that he pockets as profits. Each of these ten capitalists makes, accordingly, $120 a week.

This amount of profits, one should think, should satisfy our ten capitalists. It is a goodly sum to pocket without work. Indeed, it may satisfy some, say most of them. But if for any of many reasons it does not satisfy any one of them, the whole string of them is set in commotion. "Individuality" is a deity at whose shrine the capitalist worships, or affects to worship. In point of fact, capitalism robs of individuality, not only the working class, but capitalists themselves. The action of any one of the lot compels action by all; like a row of bricks, the dropping of one makes all the others drop successively. Let us take No. 1. He is not satisfied with $120 a week. Of the many reasons he may have for that, let's take this: He has a little daughter; eventually, she will be of marriageable age; whom is he planning to marry her to? Before the public, particularly before the workers, he will declaim on the "sovereignty" of our citizens, and declare the country is stocked with nothing but "peers." In his heart, though, he feels otherwise. He looks even upon his fellow capitalists as plebeians; he aspires at a Prince, a Duke, or at least a Count for a son-in-law; and in visions truly reflecting the vulgarity of his mind, he beholds himself the grandfather of Prince, Duke, or Count grandbrats. To realize this dream he must have money; Princes, etc., are expensive luxuries. His present income, $120 a week, will not buy the luxury. He must have some more. To his employees he will recommend reliance on heaven; he himself knows that if he wants more money it will not come from heaven, but must come from the sweat of his employees' brows. As all the wealth produced in his shop is $40 a day, he knows that, if he increases his share of $20 to $30, there will be only $10 left for wages. He tries this. He announces a wage reduction of 50 per cent. His men spontaneously draw themselves together and refuse to work; they go on strike. What is the situation?

In those days it needed skill, acquired by long training, to do the work; there may have been corner-loafers out of work, but not weavers; possibly at some great distance there may have been weavers actually obtainable, but in those days there was neither telegraph nor railroad to communicate with them; finally, the nine competitors of No. 1, having no strike on hand, continued to produce, and thus threatened to crowd No. 1 out of the market. Thus circumstanced, No. 1 caves in. He withdraws his order of wage reduction. "Come in," he says to his striking workmen, "let's make up; Labor and Capital are brothers; the most loving of brothers sometimes fall out; we have had such a falling out; it was a slip; you have organized yourselves in a union with a $2 a day wage scale; I shall never fight the union; I love it, come back to work." And the men did.

Thus ended the first strike. The victory won by the men made many of them feel bold. At their first next meeting they argued: "The employer wanted to reduce our wages and got left; why may not we take the hint and reduce his profits by demanding higher wages; we licked him in his attempt to lower our wages, why should we not lick him in an attempt to resist our demand for more pay?" But the labor movement is democratic. No one man can run things. At that union meeting the motion to demand higher pay is made by one member, another must second it; amendments and amendments to the amendments are put with the requisite seconders; debate follows; points of order are raised, ruled on, appealed from and settled;—in the meantime it grows late, the men must be at work early the next morning, the hour to adjourn arrives, and the whole matter is left pending. Thus much for the men.

Now for the employer. He locks himself up in his closet. With clenched fists and scowl on brow, he gnashes his teeth at the victory of his "brother" Labor, its union and its union regulations. And he ponders. More money he must have and is determined to have. This resolution is arrived at with the swiftness and directness which capitalists are able to. Differently from his men, he is not many, but one. He makes the motion, seconds it himself, puts it, and carries it unanimously. More profits he SHALL HAVE. But how? Aid comes to him through the mail. The letter-carrier brings him a circular from a machine shop. Such circulars are frequent even to-day. It reads like this: "Mr. No. 1, you are employing ten men; I have in my machine shop a beautiful machine with which you can produce, with 5 men, twice as much as now with 10; this machine does not chew tobacco; it does not smoke (some of these circulars are cruel and add:) this machine has no wife who gets sick and keeps it home to attend to her; it has no children who die, and whom to bury it must stay away from work; it never goes on strike; it works and grumbles not; come and see it."

Right here let me lock a switch at which not a few people are apt to switch off and be banked. Some may think "Well, at least that machine capitalist is entitled to his profits; he surely is an inventor." A grave error. Look into the history of our inventors, and you will see that those who really profited by their genius are so few that you can count them on the fingers of your hands, and have fingers to spare. The capitalists either take advantage of the inventor's stress and buy his invention for a song; the inventor believes he can make his haul with his next invention; but before that is perfected, he is as poor as before, and the same advantage is again taken of him; until finally the brown of his brains being exhausted, he sinks into a pauper's grave, leaving the fruit of his genius for private capitalists to grow rich on; or the capitalist simply steals the invention and gets his courts to decide against the inventor. From Eli Whitney down, that is the treatment the inventor, as a rule, receives from the capitalist class.

Such a case, illustrative of the whole situation, happened recently. The Bonsack Machine Co. discovered that its employees made numerous inventions, and it decided to appropriate them wholesale. To this end, it locked out its men, and demanded of all applicants for work that they sign a contract whereby, in "consideration of employment" they assign to the company all their rights in whatever invention they may make during the term of their employment. One of these employees, who had signed such a contract, informed the Company one day that he thought he could invent a machine by which cigarettes could be held closed by crimping at the ends, instead of pasting. This was a valuable idea; and he was told to go ahead. For six months he worked at this invention and perfected it; and, having during all that time, received not a cent in wages or otherwise from the company, he patented his invention himself. The company immediately brought suit against him in the Federal Courts, claiming that the invention was its property; and—THE FEDERAL COURT DECIDED IN FAVOR OF THE COMPANY, THUS ROBBING THE INVENTOR OF HIS TIME, HIS MONEY, OF THE FRUIT OF HIS GENIUS, AND OF HIS UNQUESTIONABLE RIGHTS!! (*cries of "shame" in the hall*) "Shame"? Say not "Shame"! He who himself applies the torch to his own house has no cause to cry "Shame!" when the flames consume it. Say rather "Natural!" and smiting your own breasts say "Ours the fault!" Having elected into power the Democratic, Republican, Free Trade, Protection, Silver, or Gold platforms of the capitalist class, the working class has none but itself to blame, if the official lackeys of that class turn against the working class the public powers put into their hands. (*loud applause*)—The capitalist owner of the machine shop that sends the circular did not make the invention.

To return to No. 1. He goes and sees the machine; finds it to be as represented; buys it; puts it up in his shop; picks out of his 10 men the 5 least active in the late strike; sets them to work at $2 a day as before; and full of bows and smirks, addresses the other 5 thus: "I am sorry I have no places for you; I believe in union principles and am paying the union scale to the 5 men I need; I don't need you now; good bye. I hope I'll see you again." And he means this last as you will presently perceive.

What is the situation now? No. 1 pays, as before, $2 a day, but to only 5 men; these, with the aid of the machine, now produce twice as much as the 10 did before; their product is now $80 worth of wealth; as only $10 of this goes in wages, the capitalist has a profit of $70 a day, or 250 per cent more. He is moving fast towards his Prince, Duke, or Count son-in-law. (*laughter and applause*)

Now watch the men whom his machine displaced; their career throws quite some light on the whole question. Are they not "American citizens?" Is not this a "Republic with a Constitution?" Is anything else wanted to get a living? Watch them! They go to No. 2 for a job; before they quite reach the place, the doors open and 5 of that concern are likewise thrown out upon the street.—What happened there? The "individuality" of No. 2 yielded to the pressure of capitalist development. The purchase of the machine by No. 1 enabled him to produce so much more plentifully and cheaply; if No. 2 did not do likewise, he would be crowded out of the market by No. 1; No. 2, accordingly, also invested in a machine, with the result that 5 of his men are also thrown out.

These 10 unemployed proceed to No. 3, hoping for better luck there. But what sight is that that meets their astonished eyes? Not 5 men, as walked out of Nos. 1 and 2, but all No. 3's 10 have landed on the street; and, what is more surprising yet to them, No. 3 himself is on the street, now reduced to the condition of a workingman along with his former employees.—What is it that happened there? In this instance the "individuality" of No. 3 was crushed by capitalist development. The same reason that drove No. 2 to procure the machine, rendered the machine indispensable to No. 3. But having, differently from his competitors Nos. 1 and 2, spent all his stealings from the workingmen instead of saving up some, he is now unable to make the purchase; is, consequently, unable to produce as cheaply as they; is, consequently, driven into bankruptcy, and lands in the class of the proletariat, whose ranks are thus increased.

The now 21 unemployed proceed in their hunt for work, and make the round of the other mills. The previous experiences are repeated. Not only are there no jobs to be had, but everywhere workers are thrown out, if the employer got the machine; and if he did not, workers with their former employers, now ruined, join the army of the unemployed.

What happened in that industry happened in all others. Thus the ranks of the capitalist class are thinned out, and the class is made more powerful, while the ranks of the working class are swelled, and the class is made weaker. This is the process that explains how, on the one hand, your New Bedford mills become the property of ever fewer men: how, according to the census, their aggregate capital runs up to over $14,000,-000; how, despite "bad times," their profits run up to upwards of $1,300,-000; how, on the other hand, your position becomes steadily more precarious.

No. 1's men return to where they started from. Scabbing they will not. Uninformed upon the mechanism of capitalism, they know not what struck them; and they expect "better times,"—just as so many equally uninformed workingmen are expecting to-day; in the meantime, thinking thereby to hasten the advent of the good times, No. 1's men turn out the Republican party and turn in the Democratic, turn out the Democratic and turn in the Republican,—just as our misled workingmen are now doing (*applause*) not understanding that, whether they put in or out Republicans, Democrats, Protectionists or Free Traders, Gold-bugs or Silverbugs, they are every time putting in the capitalist platform, upholding the social principle that throws them out of work or reduces their wages. (*long applause*)

But endurance has its limits. The Superintendent of the Pennsylvania Railroad for the Indiana Division, speaking, of course, from the capitalist standpoint, recently said: "Many solutions are being offered for the labor question; but there is just one and no more. It is this: Lay a silver dollar on the shelf, and at the end of a year you have a silver dollar left; lay a workingman on the shelf, and at the end of a month you have a skeleton left. (*loud applause*) This," said he, "is the solution of the labor problem." In short, starve out the workers. No. 1's men finally reach that point. Finally that happens that few if any can resist. A man may stand starvation and resist the sight of starving wife and children; but if he has not wherewith to buy medicine to save the life of a sick wife or child, all control is lost over him. On the heels of starvation, sickness follows, and No. 1's men throw to the wind all union principles; they are now ready to do anything to save their dear ones. Cap in hand, they appear before No. 1, the starch taken clean out of them during the period they "lay on the shelf." They ask for work; they themselves offer to work for $1 a day. And No. 1, the brother of labor, who but recently expressed devotion to the union, what of him? His eyes sparkle at "seeing again" the men he had thrown out; at their offer to work for less than the men now employed, his chest expands, and, grabbing them by the hand in a delirium of patriotic ecstacy, he says: "Welcome, my noble American citizens (*applause*); I am proud to see you ready to work and earn an honest penny for your dear wives and darling children (*applause*); I am delighted to notice that you are not, like so many others, too lazy to work (*applause*); let the American eagle screech in honor of your emancipation from the slavery of a rascally union (*long applause*); let the American eagle wag his tail an extra wag in honor of your freedom from a dictatorial walking delegate (*long applause*); you are my long lost brothers (*laughter and long applause*); go in, my $1-a-day brothers!" and he throws his former $2-a-day brothers heels over head upon the sidewalk. (*long and prolonged applause*)

When the late $2-a-day men have recovered from their surprise, they determine on war. But what sort of war? Watch them closely, and you may detect many a feature of your own in that mirror. "Have we not struck," argue they, "and beaten this employer once before? If we strike again, we shall again beat him." But the conditions have wholly changed.

In the first place, there were no unemployed skilled workers during that first strike; now there are; plenty of them, dumped upon the country, not out of the steerage of vessels from Europe, but by the native-born machine;

In the second place, that very machine has to such an extent eliminated skill that, while formerly only the unemployed in a certain trade could endanger the jobs of those at work in that trade, now the unemployed of all trades (virtually the whole army of the unemployed) bear down upon the employed in each; we know of quondam shoemakers taking the jobs of hatters; quondam hatters taking the jobs of weavers; quondam weavers taking the jobs of cigarmakers; quondam cigarmakers taking the jobs of "machinists"; quondam farm hands taking the jobs of factory hands, etc., etc., so easy has it become to learn what is now needed to be known of a trade;

In the third place, telegraph and railroads have made all of the unemployed easily accessible to the employer;

Finally, different from former days, the competitors have to a great extent consolidated; here in New Bedford, for instance, the false appearance of competition between the mill owners is punctured by the fact that to a great extent seemingly "independent" mills are owned by one family, as is the case with the Pierce family.

Not, as at the first strike, with their flanks protected, but now wholly exposed through the existence of a vast army of hungry unemployed; not, as before, facing a divided enemy, but now faced by a consolidated mass of capitalist concerns; how different is now the situation of the strikers! The changed conditions brought about changed results; instead of VICTORY, there was DEFEAT (*applause*); and we have had a long series of them. Either hunger drove the men back to work; or the unemployed took their places; or, if the capitalist was in a hurry, he fetched in the help of the strong arm of the government, now HIS GOVERNMENT.

We now have a sufficient survey of the field to enable us to answer the question, How shall we organize so as not to fight the same old hopeless battle?

Proceeding from the knowledge that labor alone produces all wealth; that less and less of this wealth comes to the working class, and more and more of it is plundered by the idle class or capitalist; that this is the result of the working class being stripped of the tool (machine), without which it cannot earn a living; and finally, that the machine or tool has reached such a state of development that it can no longer be operated by the individual but needs the collective effort of many;—proceeding from this knowledge, it is clear that the aim of all intelligent class-conscious workingmen must be the overthrow of the system of private ownership in the tools of production because that system keeps them in wage slavery.

Proceeding from the further knowledge of the use made of the Government by the capitalist class, and of the necessity that class is under to own the Government, so as to enable it to uphold and prop up the capitalist system;—proceeding from that knowledge, it is clear that the aim of all intelligent, class-conscious workingmen must be to bring the Government under the control of their own class by joining and electing the American wing of the International Socialist party—the Socialist Labor Party of America, and thus establishing the Socialist Co-operative Republic. (applause)

But in the meantime, while moving toward that ideal, though necessary, goal, what to do? The thing cannot be accomplished in a day, nor does election come around every 24 hours. Is there nothing that we can do for ourselves between election and election?

Yes; plenty.

When crowded, in argument, to the wall by us New Trade Unionists, by us of the Socialist Trade and Labor Alliance, your present, or old and "pure and simple" organizations, yield the point of ultimate aims; they grant the ultimate necessity of establishing Socialism; but they claim "the times are not yet ripe" for that; and, not yet being ripe, they lay emphasis upon the claim that the "pure and simple" union does the workers some good NOW by getting something NOW from the employers and from the capitalist parties. We are not "practical" they tell us; they are. Let us test this theory on the spot. Here in New Bedford there is not yet a single New Trade Unionist organization in existence. The "pure and simple" trade union has had the field all to itself. All of you, whose wages are NOW higher than they were five years ago, kindly raise a hand.(No hand is raised.) All of you whose wages are now lower than five years ago, please raise a hand. (The hands of the large audience go up.) The proof of the pudding lies in the eating. Not only does "pure and simpledom" shut off your hope of emancipation by affecting to think such a state of things is unreachable now, but in the meantime and RIGHT NOW, the "good" it does to you, the "something" it secures for you "from the employers and from the politicians" is lower wages. (prolonged applause) That is what their "practicalness" amounts to in point of fact. Presently I shall show you that they prove "practical" only to the labor fakirs who run them, and whom they put up with. No, no; years ago, before capitalism had reached its present development, a trade organization of labor could and did afford protection to the workers, even if, as the "pure and simple" union, it was wholly in the dark on the issue. THAT TIME IS NO MORE.

The New Trade Unionist knows that no one or two, or even half a dozen elections will place in the hands of the working class the Government of the land; and New Trades Unionism, not only wishes to do something now for the workers, but it knows that the thing can be done, and how to do it.

"Pure and Simple" or British trade unionism has done a double mischief to the workers: Besides leaving them in their present pitiable plight, it has caused many to fly off the handle and lose all trust in the power of trade organization. The best of these, those who have not become pessimistic and have not been wholly demoralized, see nothing to be done but voting right on election day—casting their vote straight for the S. L. P. This is a serious error. By thus giving over all participation in the industrial movement, they wholly disconnect themselves from the class struggle that is going on every day; and by putting off their whole activity to a single day in the year—election day, they become floaters in the air. I know several such. Without exception they are dreamy and flighty and unbalanced in their methods.

The utter impotence of "pure and simple" unionism today is born of causes that may be divided under two main heads.

One is the contempt in which the capitalist and ruling class holds the working people. In 1886, when instinct was, unconsciously to myself, leading me to look into the social problem, when as yet it was to me a confused and blurred interrogation mark, I associated wholly with capitalists. Expressions of contempt for the workers were common. One day I asked a set of them why they treated their men so hard, and had so poor an opinion of them. "They are ignorant, stupid, and corrupt," was the answer, almost in chorus.

"What makes you think so?" I asked. "Have you met them all?"

"No," was the reply, "we have not met them all individually, but we have had to deal with their leaders, and they are ignorant, stupid, and corrupt. Surely these leaders must be the best among them, or they would not choose them."

Now, let me illustrate. I understand that two days ago, in this city, Mr. Gompers went off at a tangent and shot off his mouth about me. What he said was too ridiculous for me to answer. You will have noticed that he simply gave what he wishes you to consider as his opinion; he furnished you no facts from which he drew it, so that you could judge for yourselves. He expected you to take him on faith. I shall not insult you by treating you likewise. Here are the facts on which my conclusion is based:

In the State of New York we have a labor law forbidding the working of railroad men more than ten hours. The railroad companies disregarded the law; in Buffalo, the switchmen struck in 1892 to enforce the law;

thereupon the Democratic Governor, Mr. Flower, who had himself signed the law, sent the whole militia of the State into Buffalo to help the railroad capitalists break the law, incidentally to commit assault and battery with intent to kill, as they actually did, upon the workingmen. Among our State Senators is one Jacob Cantor. This gentleman hastened to applaud Gov. Flower's brutal violation of his oath of office to uphold the constitution and the laws; Cantor applauded the act as a patriotic one in the defense of "Law and Order." At a subsequent campaign, this Cantor being a candidate for re-election, the New York *Daily News*, a capitalist paper of Cantor's political complexion, published an autograph letter addressed to him and intended to be an indorsement of him by Labor. This letter contained this passage among others: "If any one says you are not a friend of Labor, he says what is not true." By whom was this letter written and by whom signed?—by Mr. Samuel Gompers, "President of the American Federation of Labor." (*hisses*)

Whom are you hissing, Gompers or me? (MANY VOICES: *"Gompers!"* *followed by prolonged applause.*)

Do you imagine that the consideration for that letter was merely the "love and affection" of Senator Cantor? (*laughter*)

Again: The Republican party, likewise the Democratic, is a party of the capitalist class; every man who is posted knows that; the conduct of its Presidents, Governors, Judges, Congresses, and Legislatures can leave no doubt upon the subject. Likewise the free coinage of silver, or Populist party, was, while it lived, well known to be a party of capital; the conduct of its runners, the silver mine barons, who skin and then shoot down their miners, leaves no doubt upon that subject. But the two were deadly opposed: one wanted Gold, the other Silver. Notwithstanding these facts, a "labor leader" in New York city appeared at a recent campaign standing, not upon the Republican capitalist party platform only, not upon the Free-Silver capitalist party platform only, but—ON BOTH; he performed the acrobatic feat of being simultaneously for Gold and against Silver, for Silver against Gold. Who was that "labor leader"?— Mr. Samuel Gompers, "President of the American Federation of Labor."

Again: In Washington there is a son of a certain labor leader with a Government job. He is truly "nonpartisan." Democrats may go and Republicans may come, Republicans may go and Democrats may come, but he goeth not; the Democratic and the Republican capitalists may fight like cats and dogs, but on one thing they fraternize like cooing doves, to wit, to keep that son of a labor leader in office. Who is the father of that son?—Mr. Samuel Gompers, "President of the A. F. of L."

Again: You have here a "labor leader," named Ross (*applause in several parts of the hall*)—Unhappy men! Unhappy men! As well might you applaud the name of your executioner. When I was here about three years ago I met him. He was all aglow with the project of a bill that he was going to see through your Legislature, of which he was and is now a member. It was the anti-fines bill; that, thought he, was going to put an end to an infamous practice of the mill owners. I argued with him that it does not matter what the law is; the all important thing was, which is the class charged with enforcing it. So long as the capitalist class held the Government, all such labor laws as he was straining for, were a snare and a delusion. What I said seemed to be Greek to him. He went ahead and the bill passed. And what happened? You continued to be fined after, as before; and when one of you sought to enforce the law, was he not arrested and imprisoned? (VOICES: *"That's so."*) And when another brought the lawbreaking mill owner, who continued to fine him, into court, did not the capitalist court decide in favor of the capitalist (VOICES: *"That's so."*), and thus virtually annulled the law? And where was Mr. Ross all this time? In the Massachusetts Legislature. Do you imagine that his ignorance of what a capitalist Government means, and of what its "labor laws" amount to, did not throw its shadow upon and color you in the capitalist's estimation? Do you, furthermore, imagine that his sitting there in that Legislature, a member of the majority party at that, and never once demanding the prompt impeachment of the Court that rendered null that very law that he had worked to pass,— do you imagine that while he plays such a complaisant role he is a credit to the working class?

No need of further illustrations. The ignorance, stupidity and corruption of the "pure and simple" labor leaders is such that the capitalist class despises you. The first prerequisite for success in a struggle is the respect of the enemy. (*applause*)

The other main cause of the present impotence of "pure and simple" unionism is that, through its ignoring the existing class distinctions, and its ignoring the close connection there is between wages and politics, it splits up at the ballot box among the parties of capital, and thus unites in upholding the system of capitalist exploitation. Look at the recent miners' strike; the men were shot down and the strike was lost; this happened in the very midst of a political campaign; and these miners, who could at any election capture the Government, or at least, by polling a big vote against capitalism announce their advance towards freedom, are seen to turn right around and vote back into power the very class that had just trampled upon them. What prospect is there in sight of such conduct, of the capitalists becoming gentler? or of the union gaining for the men anything NOW except more wage reductions, enforced by bullets? None! The prospect of the miners and other workers doing the same thing over again, a prospect that is made all the surer if they allow themselves to be further led by the labor fakirs whom the capitalists keep in pay, renders sure that capitalist outrages will be repeated and further capitalist encroachments will follow. Otherwise were it if the union, identifying politics and wages, voted against capitalism; if it struck at the ballot box against the wage system with the same solidarity that it demands for the strike in the shop. Protected once a year by the guns of an increasing class-conscious party of labor, the union could be a valuable fortification behind which to conduct the daily class struggle in the shops. The increasing Socialist Labor Party vote alone would not quite give that temporary protection in the shop that such an increasing vote would afford if in the shop also the workers were intelligently organized, and honestly, because intelligently, led. Without organization in the shop, the capitalist could outrage at least individuals. Shop organization alone, unbacked by that political force that threatens the capitalist class with extinction, the working class being the overwhelming majority, leaves the workers wholly unprotected. But the shop organization that combines in its warfare the annually recurring class-conscious ballot, can stem capitalist encroachment from day to day. The trade organization IS impotent if built and conducted upon the impotent lines of ignorance and corruption. The trade organization IS NOT impotent if built and conducted upon the lines of knowledge and honesty; if it understands the issue and steps into the arena fully equipped, not with the shield of the trade union only, but also with the sword of the Socialist ballot.

The essential principles of sound organization are, accordingly, these:

1st—A trade organization must be clear upon the fact that, not until it has overthrown the capitalist system of private ownership in the machinery of production, and made this the joint property of the people, thereby compelling every one to work if he wants to live, is it at all possible for the workers to be safe. (applause)

2nd—A labor organization must be perfectly clear upon the fact that it cannot reach safety until it has wrenched the Government from the clutches of the capitalist class; and that it cannot do that unless it votes, not for MEN but for PRINCIPLES, unless it votes into power its own class platform and programme: THE ABOLITION OF THE WAGES SYSTEM OF SLAVERY.

3rd—A labor organization must be perfectly clear upon the fact that politics are not, like religion, a private concern, any more than the wages and the hours of a workingman are his private concern. For the same reason that his wages and hours are the concern of his class, so is his politics. (applause) Politics is not separable from wages. For the same reason that the organization of labor dictates wages, hours, etc., in the interest of the working class, for that same reason must it dictate politics also; and for the same reason that it execrates the scab in the shop it must execrate the scab at the hustings. (applause)

Long did the Socialist Labor Party and New Trade Unionists seek to deliver this important message to the broad masses of the American proletariat, the rank and file of our working class. But we could not reach, we could not get at them. Between us and them there stood a solid wall of ignorant, stupid, and corrupt labor fakirs. Like men groping in a dark room for an exit, we moved along the wall, bumping our heads, feeling ever onwards for a door; we made the circuit and no passage was found. The wall was solid. This discovery once made, there was no way other than to batter a breach through that wall. With the battering ram of the Socialist Trade & Labor Alliance we effected a passage; the wall now crumbles; at last we stand face to face with the rank and file of the American proletariat (*long and continued applause*); and we ARE DELIVERING OUR MESSAGE (*renewed applause*)—as you may judge from the howl that goes up from that fakirs' wall that we have broken through.

I shall not consider my time well spent with you if I see no fruit of my labors; if I leave not behind me in New Bedford Local Alliances of your trades organized in the Socialist Trade & Labor Alliance. That will be my best contribution toward your strike, as they will serve as centers of enlightenment to strengthen you in your conflict, to the extent that it may now be possible.

In conclusion, my best advice to you for immediate action, is to step out boldly upon the streets, as soon as you can; organize a monster parade of the strikers and of all the other working people in the town; and let the parade be headed by a banner bearing the announcement to your employers:

> We will fight you in this strike to the bitter end; your money bag may beat us now; but whether it does or not, that is not the end, it is only the beginning of the song; in November we will meet again at Philippi, and the strike shall not end until, with the falchion of the Socialist Labor Party ballot, we shall have laid you low for all time! (*loud applause*)

This is the message that it has been my agreeable privilege to deliver to you in the name of the Socialist Labor Party and of the New Trade Unionists or Alliance men of the land. (*prolonged applause*)

William D. Haywood

Industrial Unionism

"Big Bill" Haywood was representative of the type of labor leadership which emerged from the peculiar conditions of the American West in the late nineteenth century. Western pioneer miners were an independent breed, and they did not take readily to the regimentation of corporate management of the mines. Accustomed to settling personal differences with violence, their unions, formed to defend themselves against corporate exploitation, were always ready to turn to dynamite and gunfire in labor disputes. Similarly, with or without union provocation, mine owners resorted to Pinkerton police and state militia to settle labor conflicts.

In 1905 the Western Federation of Miners, successful in several bloody conflicts with employers, sent Haywood to Chicago to participate in the formation of a nation-wide industrial union which was to be known as the Industrial Workers of the World (IWW). Most of the participants were members of one of the socialist factions. At first, however, they suppressed their differences, conceiving of the IWW as the economic arm of socialism, while the Socialist Party and the Socialist Labor Party were the political arms. Daniel DeLeon and Eugene Debs were both present and spoke to the convention. The American Federation of Labor, with most of its constituent members, refused to participate, and the "labor fakirs" were roundly condemned by most of the speakers.

Within a year, however, it became evident that the dominant leadership of the IWW was opposed to political action. Debs withdrew to devote himself wholly to the Socialist Party. In 1908 DeLeon also withdrew when it became evident that the Socialist Labor Party was unable to control the actions of the IWW. The major remaining leaders of the organization were anarchosyndicalist and revolutionary, and more and more inclined to violent action. Haywood remained, growing progressively more radical along with the remnant of the IWW.[11]

At the 1905 convention, however, Haywood's speeches, like those of other leaders, stressed unity and cooperation among all elements of the labor movement. Even the AFL unions would be welcome when they should see the light. There was only a hint of possible violence, but his goal was clear: "... the ultimate aim of this organization is to get control of the supervision of industry."

The speech presented here was given by Haywood at the closing session of the IWW convention of June 27–July 8, 1905. The text is taken from the official proceedings of the convention as stenographically reported. Audience reactions indicate that his earthy language and vivid examples were enthusiastically received. The speech is hortatory, rather than argumentative, its intent being to send delegates away determined to put the ideas of the convention into practice.

Fellow Workers:—The first thing that it is necessary for me to say to you this evening is to correct the introduction of our little chairlady. I am not the president of the Western Federation of Miners, but am holding the position of secretary-treasurer at the present time. The president of the Western Federation of Miners is as close to me, however, as any

[11]Haywood remained a leader in the Socialist Party until his expulsion from the national executive committee in 1912. *Ibid.*, p. 417.

man can be, and I very much regret that you will not this evening have the opportunity of listening to the president; a man who has suffered as much for the cause of labor as any man in this country was ever called upon to suffer.

The theme for this evening is "Industrial Unionism." For nearly two weeks there have been assembled in this hall over two hundred men and women gathered in your city for the purpose of organizing, not a rival to the American Federation of Labor, not a rival to any other organization—but to organize a labor movement for the working class. Those of us who have studied conditions in this country recognize the fact that up to the launching of this organization there was not a labor organization in this country that represented the working class. (*applause*) This industrial union is an organization that stands with the gates wide open to take in every man and woman, and, if necessary, child, that is working for wages with either brain or muscle. (*applause*) This organization is broad enough in its scope to take in the men who work in the sewer, or our journalistic friends here on the platform who think that they are professional men. (*applause*) There are a great many professional men who don't know the difference between a professional man and a laborer. For instance—begging the pardon of the journalists—there are some scrub reporters that are working on a police assignment who imagine they are professional men working for a salary. They get about $15 a week, and are lucky at that. There are a great many skilled artisans that are getting $3.50 and $4 a day, who recognize their position as workingmen, and their remuneration, their compensation, as wages. (*applause*) I simply want to demonstrate that a $3 a day hod-carrier is just as good as a $15 a week reporter, and it does not make a bit of difference whether he is a Negro or a white man. (*applause*) (A VOICE: "*As long as he is a union man.*") It does not make any difference whether he is an American or a foreigner. (*applause*) Although I am an American, it is no fault of mine. I am still of the opinion that an American is just as good as a foreigner as long as he behaves himself, and no longer. (*laughter*)

The organization that has been launched in your city recognizes neither race, creed, color, sex, or previous condition of servitude. (*laughter*) We came out of the west to meet the textile worker of the east. We men of the west are getting more wages per day than those men are getting. We recognize the fact that unless we bring them up to our condition they of necessity will drag us down to theirs. (*applause*) We propose that this industrial movement shall provide, for every man and woman that works, a decent livelihood. Is that something worth working for? Now, understand me—or rather, do not misunderstand me. I do not mean that this organization is going to improve the condition of purely the skilled workers, the bricklayer, the carpenter, or the type-setter; but I mean that we are going down in the gutter to get at the mass of the workers and bring them up to a decent plane of living. (*applause*) I do not care the snap of my finger whether or not the skilled workers join this industrial movement at the present time. When we get the unorganized and the unskilled laborer into this organization the skilled worker will of necessity come here for his own protection. (*applause*) As strange as it may seem to you, the skilled worker to-day is exploiting the laborer beneath him, the unskilled man, just as much as the capitalist is. (*applause*) To make myself better understood, the skilled laborer has organized for himself a union, recognizing that in unity there is strength. He has thrown a high wall around that union which prohibits men from joining the organization. He exacts that a man to become a member of the labor union must of necessity serve an apprenticeship to develop his skill. What for? For the benefit of the union? No, but for the benefit of his employer, who is a member of the Citizens' Alliance (*applause*), and who is trying to crush out of existence that same union that has endeavored to develop skilled mechanics for the benefit of the capitalist class. (*applause*) What I want to demonstrate to you is that the skilled mechanic, by means of the pure and simple trades union, is exploiting the unskilled laborer. I think that will be easy for me to do. The unskilled laborer has not been able to get into the skilled laborer's union because that union exacts that a man must needs have served a term of years as an apprentice. Again, there are unions in this country that exact an initiation fee, some of them as high as $500. There is the glass blowers', to be specific, how long would it take a man working for a dollar or a dollar and a quarter a day and providing for a family, to save up enough money to pay his initiation fee into that union? Why, he might just as well figure on a trip to "Paree." To demonstrate the point that I wanted to get at, it is this: That the unskilled laborer's wages have been continually going down, that the prices of commodities have been continually going up, and that the skilled mechanic through his union has been able to hold his wages at a price and upon a scale that has insured to him even at these high prices a reasonable decent living; but the laborer at the bottom, who is working for a dollar or a dollar and a quarter a day, has been ground into a state of destitution. (*applause*)

Now, ladies and gentlemen, this condition does not exist as generally throughout the west as it does here and farther east, and especially is this true in the camps where the Western Federation of Miners is thoroughly organized, because in those camps we have established a minimum wage of $3 a day for every man or boy that is employed around the mines. Now we have no objections to a man getting as much more as he can, but we exact that he shall get at least those decent wages that will justify him in maintaining a family and doing it respectably, and we are coming here to Chicago and we are going further east to see if it is not possible to bring the common laborer up to a plane something like we enjoy in the mining camps of the west. (*applause*) And that can only be brought about by organization. Not an organization with a $500 initiation fee; not an organization that demands that you shall serve a three years' apprenticeship to any trade for the benefit of a member of the Citizens' Alliance, but an organization that has the doors wide open so that any man that is working at any calling can come in and join hands with us. (*applause*) Though we are enjoying very good conditions, we recognize, as I stated before, that our conditions can only be maintained by upholding the conditions or endeavoring to uplift the fellow who is at the bottom.

Now, don't get discouraged, folks, you of the working class, because here in Chicago you have lost some strikes. Remember that you never could have lost those strikes if you had been organized industrially as the workers in Russia are organized (*applause*)—organized into an organization that takes in every man, woman, and child working in an industry. For instance, in the packing plants, the butchers' organization was one of the best organizations in this country, reputed to be 50,000 strong. They were well disciplined, which is shown from the fact that when they were called on strike they quit to a man. That is, the butchers quit, but did the engineers quit, did the firemen quit, did the men who were running the ice plants quit? They were not in the union, not in that particular union. They had agreements with their employers which forbade them quitting. The result was that the butchers' union was practically totally disrupted, entirely wiped out. Now, presuming that every man around the packing houses, from the printer to the pig sticker, belonged to one union; that when they went out on strike the engineers, firemen, and men that ran the ice plants all quit; that millions of dollars of produce were in a state so that it would rapidly perish, don't you believe that those packing house companies would have capitulated? Don't you believe that if to-day the organized workers of your great city would not go on strike, but that they would stay home for three or four days, that the teamsters would win the strike that they are now engaged in? (*applause*) One union man is no better than another union man, and any union man that will stand back because a company has an agreement with him, and who will scab on his fellow union man, he may be a union man, but in my opinion he is a technical scab. (*applause*) On the Santa Fe Railroad some time ago the telegraphers went out on strike, and they presented their grievance to the company. The company says: "We cannot do anything for you." They appealed to the different brotherhoods of railroad men. Those various brotherhoods appointed their grievance committees to see the management. When they went to the management the management said to them: "Gentlemen, haven't we schedules with you?" The committee said "Yes." "Well," said the company, "you carry out your schedules with us and we will attend to the telegraphers." They attended to the telegraphers to the extent that there is not a union telegrapher on the Santa Fe system. Then the machinists went on strike on the same system, and they appealed to the brotherhoods, and the brotherhoods in the same manner appealed to the management. The management called their attention to their agreements, and told them to attend to their business and carry out the rates and rules of those schedules, and they would attend to the machinists; and the machinists to-day are the victims of the sacred contract of the union man with his employer. There never was a contract so sacred, drawn up between a union and an employer, but what the employer would break it if he felt it was to his interest to do so. (*applause*) So that in my opinion and in the opinion of the delegates that have assembled here, no union will have the right or be empowered to enter into a contract with any company or corporation unless that contract is in keeping with and to the welfare of the general labor movement. (*applause*)

Some of the labor leaders of this country have been quoted as saying that it is possible for the capitalist, the corporationist—or the employer, if you will—to get together with the workingmen and adjust the conditions that exist between them. Some of them have said that if we only sit down at a table and look each other in the eye and talk these matters over that there would never be another strike. Well, now, that proposition of looking each other in the eye suggests to me that out in Colorado and further west this is a sort of a poker player's game. (*laughter*) A man sitting behind a full hand of four aces looks the other fellow in the eye and tries to make him believe he has only got two deuces. (*laughter*) Now, the capitalist is always ready to sit down and look the other fellow in the eye, and he has always got the best of it. Why? Because he owns the tools that the other fellow works with. (*applause*) Without the tools the other man could not live, and when a man or a company or corporation has possession of the tools, the means of production, the economic power, the means of life, he has your life absolutely in his possession. (*applause*) Why, folks, rather than be one of the residents of the ghetto down here, a place that I was through last night, I would rather be a big buck nigger on a plantation in the south before the days when chattel slavery was wiped out.[12] Why? Because—size me up pretty well now—I would be worth about $3,000 to a plantation holder. It would be to his interest to provide me with good shelter, with suitable clothing, with proper food, with proper medical attendance, because I represent to him a monetary value of $3,000. Suppose I was to go to some plantation owner to-day—and we have not any slavery in this country. He would size me up and he would say: "You are worth just about $2 or $1.50 a day to work on this ranch. If you get sick you take care of yourself. If you die it is no loss to me. I care nothing about your family. Your little pickaninnies, there is no value to them. Your little red-headed

---

[12]Haywood's previous references to race in the speech make it clear that there are no racist connotations in his use of a word, the implications of which have changed greatly since 1905.

girl does not represent five cents of value to me." Is this system more cruel than that of slavery days? A hundred thousand times more. (*applause*) The wage system is worse than chattel slavery.

Now, are there any of you who feel that your interests and the capitalist's interests are identical? Don't you know that there is not an employing capitalist or corporation manufactory in this country that if it were possible would not operate his or its entire plant or factory by machines and dispose of every human being employed? (*applause*) The corporation does not hire you. The employer never looks at your face; he never looks you in the eye. He cares nothing about your feelings. He does not care anything about your surroundings. He cares nothing about your twinges of anguish or your heartaches. He wants your hands and as much of your brain as is necessary to attach yourself to a machine. (*applause*) Remember, that to-day there are no skilled mechanics. Down in the packing house there are no butchers. There is a train of specialized men that do just their part, that is all. The machine is the apprentice of yesterday; the machine is the journeyman of to-day. The machine is rapidly taking your place, and it will have you entirely displaced pretty soon, and it is a question as between you and the capitalist as to who is going to own and control and manipulate and supervise that machine. (*applause*)

That is the purpose of this industrial union. Now, let no man make a mistake. While we are going to do everything that we can to improve and take advantage of every opportunity that is offered to us to improve the condition of the working class as we go along, the ultimate aim of this organization is to get control of the supervision of industry. (*applause*) We propose to say to the employing class what the hours of labor shall be and what the remuneration shall be. We are the people who do the work, and we have got tired of those who do nothing but shirk, reaping all of the benefits. That is the definition of industrial unionism; the absolute control and supervision of industry. And when the working class are sufficiently well organized to control the means of life, why then the system that the speaker before me told you about, the ownership of legislatures and senates and militias and police will be of little avail to them, because a condition such as exists in Chicago at the present time could not exist. The army or police that would raise a hand, a club or a gun against a workingman would have to leave this community or starve to death. (*applause*) And we are going further than that. We are going to say to the employer: You must take your place in the productive system of this country or you will starve. (*applause*)

Now, remember, that we fellows out west were once east; that if we don't know what we are going up against, our fathers probably did. My great-great-grandfather lived in Boston. My great-grandfather came as far west as Ohio. My grandfather lived in Iowa. My father carried the mail in Colorado before there was a railroad. I have been still farther west, until they told me that it was only a few miles to the rolling billows of the Pacific, and I concluded that the Haywood family had better turn back, that we had been driven to the frontiers until there were no more frontiers. So I have come back to Chicago, and am still on the frontier; that is, on the frontier of this industrial union movement, which I hope to see grow throughout this country until it takes in a great majority of the working people, and that those working people will rise in revolt against the capitalist system as the working class in Russia are doing to-day. (*great applause*)

Eugene Debs

The Socialist Party and the

Working Class

For more than twenty years Eugene Debs was the dominant figure in the Socialist Party of the United States. As its presidential candidate in five campaigns he spoke to thousands of people in Socialist rallies throughout the country, trying to organize a mass party capable of taking power and putting socialist ideas into practice. Although he wrote extensively for Socialist publications, his most effective communication was from the platform where his warm personality and forceful delivery won him a strong personal following.

As the candidate of the newly formed and somewhat disorganized Social Democratic Party in 1900, Debs polled nearly 97,-000 votes. Four years later his vote as the candidate of the Socialist Party, successor to SDP, was 408,000. There were many factors in this dramatic increase. In 1904 the Democratic Party lost the Populist vote by nominating a conservative instead of the popular idol, Bryan, and those thus dispossessed could take their choice between the flamboyant trust buster, Theodore Roosevelt, and the Socialist candidate, Debs. Those who chose Debs found a much improved spokesman compared with the candidate of four years earlier. His speaking style was more concrete and more colorful than in 1900. He was surer of his beliefs, confident that socialism would be achieved very soon, and he struck out at the old parties in language that reflected that confidence.

The speech given here is Debs's opening speech in the campaign of 1904, delivered at Indianapolis, September 1. The text is from

The International Socialist Review for September, 1904. There is no indication in the source as to whether the speech was taken from a manuscript or stenographically recorded, but the short paragraph structure suggests that it is a manuscript prepared for easy reading. A later edition, printed in *Writings and Speeches of Eugene V. Debs,* New York, 1948, contains a few modifications, although it is essentially the same. None of these changes except one or two which clarify the sense has been adopted in the version given here.

Mr. Chairman, Citizens and Comrades:

There has never been a free people, a civilized nation, a real republic on this earth. Human society always consisted of masters and slaves, and the slaves have always been and are today, the foundation stones of the social fabric.

Wage-labor is but a name; wage-slavery is a fact.

The twenty-five millions of wage-workers in the United States are twenty-five millions of twentieth-century slaves.

This is the plain meaning of what is known as the labor market, and the labor market follows the capitalist flag.

The most barbarous fact in all christendom is the labor market. The mere term sufficiently expresses the animalism of commercial civilization.

They who buy and they who sell in the labor market are alike dehumanized by the inhuman traffic in the brains and blood and bones of human beings.

The labor market is the foundation of so-called civilized society. Without these shambles, without this commerce in human life, this sacrifice of manhood and womanhood, this barter of babes, this sale of souls, the capitalist civilizations of all lands and all climes would crumble to ruin and perish from the earth.

Twenty-five millions of wage-slaves are bought and sold daily at prevailing prices in the American Labor Market.

This is the paramount issue in the present national campaign.

Let me say at the very threshold of this discussion that the workers have but the one issue in this campaign, the overthrow of the capitalist system and the emancipation of the working class from wage-slavery.

The capitalists may have the tariff, finance, imperialism, and other dust-covered and moth-eaten issues entirely to themselves.

The rattle of these relics no longer deceives workingmen whose heads are on their own shoulders.

They know by experience and observation that the gold standard, free silver, fiat money, protective tariff, free trade, imperialism, and anti-imperialism all mean capitalist rule and wage-slavery.

Their eyes are open and they can see; their brains are in operation and they can think.

The very moment a working man begins to do his own thinking he understands the paramount issue, parts company with the capitalist politician and falls in line with his own class on the political battlefield.

The political solidarity of the working class means the death of despotism, the birth of freedom, the sunrise of civilization.

Having said this much by way of introduction I will now enter upon the actualities of my theme: the class struggle.

We are entering tonight upon a momentous campaign. The struggle for political supremacy is not between political parties merely, as appears upon the surface, but at bottom it is a life and death struggle between two hostile economic classes, the one the capitalist and the other the working class.

The capitalist class is represented by the Republican, Democratic, Populist, and Prohibition parties, all of which stand for private ownership of the means of production and the triumph of any one of which will mean continued wage-slavery to the working class.

As the Populist and Prohibition sections of the capitalist party represent minority elements which propose to reform the capitalist system without disturbing wage-slavery, a vain and impossible task, they will be omitted from this discussion with all the credit due the rank and file for their good intentions.

The Republican and Democratic parties, or, to be more exact, the Republican-Democratic party, represents the capitalist class in the class struggle. They are the political wings of the capitalist system and such differences as arise between them relate to spoils and not to principles.

With either of these parties in power one thing is always certain and that is that the capitalist class are in the saddle and the working class under the saddle.

Under the administration of both these parties the means of production are private property, production is carried forward for capitalist profit purely, markets are glutted and industry paralyzed, workingmen become tramps and criminals while injunctions, soldiers, and riot guns are brought into action to preserve "law and order" in the chaotic carnival of capitalistic anarchy.

Deny it as may the cunning capitalists who are clear-sighted enough to perceive it, or ignore it as may the torpid workers who are too blind and unthinking to see it, the struggle in which we are engaged today is a class struggle, and as the toiling millions come to see and understand it and rally to the political standard of their class, they will drive all capitalist parties of whatever name into the same party, and the class struggle will then be so clearly revealed that the hosts of labor will find their true place in the conflict and strike the united and decisive blow that will destroy slavery and achieve their full and final emancipation.

In this struggle the workingmen and women and children are represented by the Socialist Party and it is my privilege to address you in the
name of that revolutionary and uncompromising party of the working
class.

What shall be the attitude of the workers of the United States in the
present campaign? What part shall they take in it? What party and what
principles shall they support by their ballots? And why?

These are questions the importance of which are not sufficiently recognized by workingmen or they would not be the prey of parasites and the
servile tools of scheming politicians who use them only at election time
to renew their masters' lease of power and perpetuate their own ignorance, poverty, and shame.

In answering these questions I propose to be as frank and candid as
plain-meaning words will allow, for I have but one object in this discussion and that object is not office, but the truth, and I shall state it as I
see it if I have to stand alone.

But I shall not stand alone, for the party that has my allegiance and
may have my life, the Socialist Party, the party of the working class, the
party of emancipation, is made up of men and women who know their
rights and scorn to compromise with their oppressors; who want no votes
that can be bought and no support under any false pretenses whatsoever.

The Socialist Party stands squarely upon its proletarian principles and
relies wholly upon the forces of industrial progress and the education of
the working class.

The Socialist Party buys no votes and promises no offices. Not a farthing
is spent for whiskey or cigars. Every penny in the campaign fund is the
voluntary offering of workers and their sympathizers and every penny is
used for education.

What other parties can say the same?

Ignorance alone stands in the way of socialist success. The capitalist
parties understand this and use their resources to prevent the workers
from seeing the light.

Intellectual darkness is essential to industrial slavery.

Capitalist parties stand for Slavery and Night.

The Socialist Party is the herald of Freedom and Light.

Capitalist parties cunningly contrive to divide the workers upon dead
issues.

The Socialist Party is uniting them upon the living issue:

Death to Wage Slavery!

When industrial slavery is as dead as the issues of the Siamese capitalist
parties the Socialist Party will have fulfilled its mission and enriched
history.

And now to our questions:

First, every workingman and woman owe it to themselves, their class and their country to take an active and intelligent interest in political affairs.

The ballot of united labor expresses the people's will and the people's will is the supreme law of a free nation.

The ballot means that labor is no longer dumb, that at last it has a voice, that it may be heard and if united must be heeded.

Centuries of struggle and sacrifice were required to wrest this symbol of freedom from the mailed clutch of tyranny and place it in the hand of labor as the shield and lance of attack and defense.

The abuse and not the use of it is responsible for its evil.

The divided vote of labor is the abuse of the ballot and the penalty is slavery and death.

The united vote of those who toil and have not will vanquish those who have and toil not and solve forever the problem of democracy.

Since the race was young there have been class struggles. In every state of society, ancient and modern, labor has been exploited, degraded, and in subjection.

Civilization has done little for labor except to modify the forms of its exploitation.

Labor has always been the mudsill of the social fabric—is so now and will be until the class struggle ends in class extinction and free society.

Society has always been and is now built upon exploitation—the exploitation of a class—the working class, whether slaves, serfs, or wage-laborers, and the exploited working class have always been, instinctively or consciously, in revolt against their oppressors.

Through all the centuries the enslaved toilers have moved slowly but surely toward their final freedom.

The call of the Socialist Party is to the exploited class, the workers in all useful trades and professions, all honest occupations, from the most menial service to the highest skill, to rally beneath their own standard and put an end to the last of the barbarous class struggles by conquering the capitalist government, taking possession of the means of production and making them common property of all, abolishing wage-slavery and establishing the co-operative commonwealth.

The first step in this direction is to sever all relations with capitalist parties. They are precisely alike and I challenge their most discriminating partisans to tell them apart in relation to labor.

The Republican and Democratic Parties are alike capitalist parties—differing only in being committed to different sets of capitalist interests—they have the same principles under varying colors, are equally corrupt and are one in their subservience to capital and their hostility to labor.

The ignorant workingman who supports either of these parties forges his own fetters and is the unconscious author of his own misery. He can and must be made to see and think and act with his fellows in supporting the party of his class and this work of education is the crowning virtue of the socialist movement.[13]

Let us briefly consider the Republican Party from the worker's standpoint. It is capitalist to the core. It has not and can not have the slightest interest in labor except to exploit it.

Why should a workingman support the Republican Party?

Why should a millionaire support the Socialist Party?

For precisely the same reason that all the millionaires are opposed to the Socialist Party, all the workers should be opposed to the Republican Party. It is a capitalist party, is loyal to capitalist interests, and entitled to the support of capitalist voters on election day.

All it has for workingmen is its "glorious past" and a "glad hand" when it wants their votes.

The Republican Party is now and has been for several years, in complete control of government.

What has it done for labor? What has it not done for capital?

Not one of the crying abuses of capital has been curbed under Republican rule.

Not one of the petitions of labor has been granted.

The eight-hour and anti-injunction bills, upon which organized labor is a unit, were again ruthlessly slain by the last Congress in obedience to the capitalist masters.

David M. Parry has greater influence at Washington than all the millions of organized workers.

Read the national platform of the Republican Party and see if there is in all its bombast a crumb of comfort for labor. The convention that adopted it was a capitalist convention and the only thought it had of labor was how to abstract its vote without waking it up.

In the only reference it made to labor it had to speak easy so as to avoid offense to the capitalists who own it and furnish the boodle to keep it in power.

The labor platforms of the Republican and Democratic Parties are interchangeable and nonredeemable. They both favor "justice to capital and justice to labor." This hoary old platitude is worse than meaningless. It is false and misleading and so intended. Justice to labor means that labor shall have what it produces. This leaves nothing for capital.

Justice to labor means the end of capital.

The old parties intend nothing of the kind. It is false pretense and false promise. It has served well in the past. Will it continue to catch the votes of unthinking and deluded workers?

---

[13]Although the following portion of this speech resembles one which might be given at any party convention, the tone which has been established at the beginning and to which the speaker returns at the end shows that the aim of the speech is more than to secure a partisan victory; rather it urges fundamental changes in the structure of society.

What workingmen had part in the Republican national convention or were honored by it?

The grand coliseum swarmed with trust magnates, corporation barons, money lords, stock gamblers, professional politicians, lawyers, lobbyists, and other plutocratic tools and mercenaries, but there was no room for the horny-handed and horny-headed sons of toil. They built it, but were not in it.

Compare that convention with the convention of the Socialist Party, composed almost wholly of working men and women and controlled wholly in the interest of their class.

But a party is still better known by its chosen representatives than by its platform declarations.

Who are the nominees of the Republican Party for the highest offices in the gift of the nation and what is their relation to the working class?

First of all, Theodore Roosevelt and Charles W. Fairbanks, candidates for President and Vice President, respectively, deny the class struggle and this almost infallibly fixes their status as friends of capital and enemies of labor. They insist that they can serve both; but the fact is obvious that only one can be served and that one at the expense of the other. Mr. Roosevelt's whole political career proves it.

The capitalists made no mistake in nominating Mr. Roosevelt. They know him well and he has served them well. They know that his instincts, associations, tastes, and desires are with them, that he is in fact one of them and that he has nothing in common with the working class.

The only evidence of the contrary is his membership in the Brotherhood of Locomotive Firemen which seems to have come to him coincident with his ambition to succeed himself in the presidential chair. He is a full fledged member of the union, has the grip, signs and pass word, but it is not reported that he is attending meetings, doing picket duty, supporting strikes and boycotts and performing such other duties as his union obligation imposes.

When Ex-President Grover Cleveland violated the constitution and outraged justice by seizing the state of Illinois by the throat and handcuffing her civil administration at the behest of the crime-sustained trusts and corporations, Theodore Roosevelt was among his most ardent admirers and enthusiastic supporters. He wrote in hearty commendation of the atrocious act, pronounced it most exalted patriotism and said he would have done the same thing himself had he been president.

And so he would and so he will!

How impressive to see the Rough Rider embrace the Smooth Statesman! Oyster Bay and Buzzard's Bay! "Two souls with but a single thought, two hearts that beat as one."

There is also the highest authority for the statement charging Mr. Roosevelt with declaring about the same time he was lauding Cleveland that if he was in command he would have such as Altgeld, Debs, and other traitors lined up against a dead wall and shot into corpses. The brutal remark was not for publication but found its way into print and Mr. Roosevelt, after he became a candidate, attempted to make denial, but the distinguished editor who heard him say it pinned him fast, and the slight doubt that remained was dispelled by the words themselves which sound like Roosevelt and bear the impress of his war-like visage.

Following the Pullman strike in 1894 there was an indignant and emphatic popular protest against "government by injunction," which has not yet by any means subsided.

Organized labor was, and is, a unit against this insidious form of judicial usurpation as a means of abrogating constitutional restraints of despotic power.

Mr. Roosevelt with his usual zeal to serve the ruling class and keep their protesting slaves in subjection, vaulted into the arena and launched his vitriolic tirade upon the mob that dared oppose the divine decree of a corporation judge.

"Men who object to what they style 'government by injunction,'" said he, "are, as regards the essential principles of government, in hearty sympathy with their remote skinclad ancestors, who lived in caves, fought one another with stone-headed axes and ate the mammoth and woolly rhinoceros. They are dangerous whenever there is the least danger of their making the principles of this ages-buried past living factors in our present life. They are not in sympathy with men of good minds and good civic morality."

In direct terms and plain words Mr. Roosevelt denounces all those who oppose "Government by Injunction" as cannibals, barbarians, and anarchists, and this violent and sweeping stigma embraces the whole organized movement of labor, every man, woman, and child that wears the badge of union labor in the United States.

It is not strange in the light of these facts that the national Congress, under President Roosevelt's administration, suppresses anti-injunction and eight-hour bills and all other measures favored by labor and resisted by capital.

No stronger or more convincing proof is required of Mr. Roosevelt's allegiance to capital and opposition to labor, nor of the class struggle and class rule which he so vehemently denies; and the workingman who in the face of these words and acts, can still support Mr. Roosevelt must feel himself flattered in being publicly proclaimed a barbarian, and sheer gratitude, doubtless, impels him to crown his benefactor with the highest honors of the land.

If the working class are barbarians, according to Mr. Roosevelt, this may account for his esteeming himself as having the very qualities necessary to make himself Chief of the Tribe.

But it must be noted that Mr. Roosevelt denounced organized labor as savages long before he was a candidate for president. After he became a candidate he joined the tribe and is today, himself, according to his own dictum, a barbarian and the enemy of civic morality.

The labor union to which President Roosevelt belongs and which he is solemnly obligated to support, is unanimously opposed to "Government by Injunction." President Roosevelt knew it when he joined it and he also knew that those who oppose injunction rule have the instincts of cannibals and are a menace to morality, but his proud nature succumbed to political ambition, and his ethical ideas vanished as he struck the trail that led to the tribe and, after a most dramatic scene and impressive ceremony, was decorated with the honorary badge of international barbarism.

How Theodore Roosevelt, the trade-unionist, can support the presidential candidate who denounced him as an immoral and dangerous barbarian he may decide at his leisure, and so may all other men in the United States who are branded with the same vulgar stigma, and their ballots will determine if they have the manhood to resent insult and rebuke its author, or if they have been fitly characterized and deserve the humiliation and contempt.

The appointment of Judge Taft to a cabinet position is corroborative evidence, if any be required, of President Roosevelt's fervent faith in Government by Injunction. Judge Taft first came into national notoriety when, some years ago, sitting with Judge Ricks, who was later tried for malfeasance, he issued the celebrated injunction during the Toledo, Ann Arbor, and North Michigan railroad strike that paralyzed the Brotherhoods of Locomotive Engineers and Firemen and won for him the gratitude and esteem of every corporation in the land. He was hauled to Toledo, the headquarters of the railroad, in a special car pulled by a special engine, on special time, and after hastily consulting the railroad magnates and receiving instructions, he let go the judicial lightning that shivered the unions to splinters and ended the strike in total defeat. Judge Taft is a special favorite with the trust barons and his elevation to the cabinet was ratified with joy at the court of St. Plute.[14]

Still again did President Roosevelt drive home his arch-enmity to labor and his implacable hostility to the trade-union movement when he made Paul Morton, the notorious union hater and union wrecker, his secretary of the navy. That appointment was an open insult to every trade unionist in the country and they who lack the self-respect to resent it at the polls may wear the badge, but they are lacking wholly in the spirit and principles of union labor.

Go ask the brotherhood men who were driven from the C. B. & Q. and the striking union machinists on the Santa Fe to give you the pedigree of Mr. Morton and you will learn that his hate for union men is coupled only by his love for the scabs who take their places.

[14]Plutocrat.

Such a man and such another as Sherman Bell the military ferret of the Colorado mine owners are the ideal patriots and personal chums of Mr. Roosevelt and by honoring these he dishonors himself and should be repudiated by the ballot of every working man in the nation.

Mr. Fairbanks, the Republican candidate for Vice President, is a corporation attorney of the first class and a plutocrat in good and regular standing. He is in every respect a fit and proper representative of his party and every millionaire in the land may safely support him.

In referring to the Democratic Party in this discussion we may save time by simply saying that since it was born again at the St. Louis convention it is near enough like its Republican ally to pass for a twin brother.[15]

The former party of the "common people" is no longer under the boycott of plutocracy since it has adopted the Wall street label and renounced its middle class heresies.

The radical and progressive element of the former Democracy have been evicted and must seek other quarters. They were an unmitigated nuisance in the conservative counsels of the old party. They were for the "common people" and the trusts have no use for such a party.

Where but to the Socialist Party can these progressive people turn? They are now without a party and the only genuine Democratic party in the field is the Socialist Party and every true Democrat should thank Wall street for driving him out of a party that is democratic in name only and into one that is democratic in fact.

The St. Louis convention was a trust jubilee. The Wall street reorganizers made short work of the free silver element. From first to last it was a capitalistic convocation. Labor was totally ignored. As an incident, two thousand choice chairs were reserved for the Business Men's League of St. Louis, an organization hostile to organized labor, but not a chair was tendered to those whose labor had built the convention hall, had clothed, transported, fed, and wined the delegates and whose votes are counted on as if they were so many dumb driven cattle, to pull the ticket through in November.

As another incident, when Lieutenant Richmond Hobson dramatically declared that President Cleveland had been the only president who had ever been patriotic enough to use the federal troops to crush union labor, the trust agents, lobbyists, tools, and claquers scrambled with delight and the convention shook with applause.

The platform is precisely the same as the Republican platform in relation to labor. It says nothing and means the same. A plank was proposed condemning the outrages in Colorado under Republican administration, but upon order from the Parryites it was promptly thrown aside.

[15]After two campaigns with Bryan as the standard-bearer and a platform borrowed from the Populists, the Democrats turned in 1904 to conservative Judge Alton B. Parker and a gold standard platform.

The editor of *American Industries,* organ of the Manufacturers' Association, commented at length in the issue of July 15th, on the triumph of capital and the defeat of labor at both Republican and Democratic national conventions. Among other things he said: "The two labor lobbies, partly similar in make-up, were, to put it bluntly, thrown out bodily in both places." And that is the simple fact and is known of all men who read the papers. The capitalist organs exult because labor, to use their own brutal expression, was kicked bodily out of both the Republican and Democratic national conventions.

What more than this is needed to open the eyes of workingmen to the fact that neither of these parties is their party and that they are as strangely out of place in them as Rockefeller and Vanderbilt would be in the Socialist Party?

And how many more times are they to be "kicked out bodily" before they stay out and join the party of their class in which labor is not only honored but is supreme, a party that is clean, that has conscience and convictions, a party that will one day sweep the old parties from the field like chaff and issue the Proclamation of Labor's Emancipation?

Judge Alton B. Parker corresponds precisely to the Democratic platform. It was made to order for him. His famous telegram in the expiring hour removed the last wrinkle and left it a perfect fit.

Thomas W. Lawson, the Boston millionaire, charges that Senator Patrick McCarren who brought out Judge Parker for the nomination is on the pay roll of the Standard Oil company as political master mechanic at twenty thousand dollars a year, and that Parker is the chosen tool of Standard Oil. Mr. Lawson offers Senator McCarren one hundred thousand dollars if he will disprove the charge.

William Jennings Bryan denounced Judge Parker as a tool of Wall street before he was nominated and declared that no self-respecting Democrat could vote for him, and after his nomination he charged that it had been dictated by the trusts and secured by "crooked and indefensible methods." Mr. Bryan also said that labor had been betrayed in the convention and need look for nothing from the Democratic Party. He made many other damaging charges against his party and its candidates, but when the supreme test came he was not equal to it, and instead of denouncing the betrayers of the "common people" and repudiating their made-to-order Wall street program, he compromised with the pirates that scuttled his ship and promised with his lips the support his heart refused and his conscience condemned.

The Democratic nominee for President was one of the Supreme judges of the State of New York who declared the eight-hour law unconstitutional and this is an index of his political character.

In his address accepting the nomination he makes but a single allusion to labor and in this he takes occasion to say that labor is charged with having recently used dynamite in destroying property and that the perpetrators should be subjected to "the most rigorous punishment known to the law." This cruel intimation amounts to conviction in advance of trial and indicates clearly the trend of his capitalistically trained judicial mind. He made no such reference to capital, nor to those ermined rascals who use judicial dynamite in blowing up the Constitution while labor is looted and starved by capitalistic freebooters who trample all law in the mire and leer and mock at their despoiled and helpless victims.

It is hardly necessary to make more than passing reference to Henry G. Davis, Democratic candidate for Vice President. He is a coal baron, railroad owned and, of course, an enemy to union labor. He has amassed a great fortune exploiting his wage-slaves and has always strenuously resisted every attempt to organize them for the betterment of their condition. Mr. Davis is a staunch believer in the virtue of the injunction as applied to union labor. As a young man he was in charge of a slave plantation, and his conviction is that wage-slaves should be kept free from the contaminating influence of the labor agitator and render cheerful obedience to their master.

Mr. Davis is as well qualified to serve his party as is Senator Fairbanks to serve the Republican Party, and wage-workers should have no trouble in making their choice between this precious pair of plutocrats, and certainly no intelligent workingman will hesitate an instant to discard them both and cast his vote for Ben Hanford, their working class competitor, who is as loyally devoted to labor as Fairbanks and Davis are to capital.

In what has been said of other parties I have tried to show why they should not be supported by the common people, least of all by workingmen, and I think I have shown clearly enough that such workers as do support them are guilty, consciously or unconsciously, of treason to their class. They are voting into power the enemies of labor and are morally responsible for the crimes thus perpetrated upon their fellow-workers and sooner or later they will have to suffer the consequences of their miserable acts.

The Socialist Party is not, and does not pretend to be, a capitalist party. It does not ask, nor does it expect the votes of the capitalist class. Such capitalists as do support it do so seeing the approaching doom of the capitalist system and with a full understanding that the Socialist Party is not a capitalist party, nor a middle class party, but a revolutionary working class party, whose historic mission is to conquer capitalism on the political battle-field, take control of government and through the public powers take possession of the means of wealth production, abolish wage-slavery, and emancipate all workers and all humanity.

The people are as capable of achieving their industrial freedom as they were to secure their political liberty and both are necessary to a free nation.

The capitalist system is no longer adapted to the needs of modern society. It is outgrown and fetters the forces of progress. Industrial and commercial competition are largely of the past. The handwriting blazes on the wall. Centralization and combination are the modern forces in industrial and commercial life. Competition is breaking down, and co-operation is supplanting it.

The hand tools of early times are used no more. Mammoth machines have taken their places. A few thousand capitalists own them and many millions of workingmen use them.

All the wealth the vast army of labor produces above its subsistence is taken by the machine owning capitalists, who also own the land and the mills, the factories, railroads, and mines, the forests and fields, and all other means of production of transportation.

Hence wealth and poverty, millionaires and beggars, castles and caves, luxury and squalor, painted parasites on the boulevard and painted poverty among the red lights.

Hence strikes, boycotts, riots, murder, suicide, insanity, prostitution on a fearful and increasing scale.

The capitalist parties can do nothing. They are a part, an iniquitous part of the foul and decaying system.

There is no remedy for the ravages of death.

Capitalism is dying and its extremities are already decomposing. The blotches upon the surface show that the blood no longer circulates. The time is near when the cadaver will have to be removed and the atmosphere purified.

In contrast with the Republican and Democratic conventions, where politicians were the puppets of plutocracy, the convention of the Socialist Party consisted of working men and women fresh from their labors, strong, clean, wholesome, self-reliant, ready to do and dare for the cause of labor, the cause of humanity.

Proud indeed am I to have been chosen by such a body of men and women to bear aloft the proletarian standard in this campaign, and heartily do I endorse the clear and cogent platform of the party which appeals with increasing force and eloquence to the whole working class of the country.

To my associate upon the national ticket I give my hand with all my heart. Ben Hanford typifies the working class and fitly represents the historic mission and revolutionary character of the Socialist Party.

These are stirring days for living men. The day of crisis is drawing near and socialists are exerting all their power to prepare the people for it.

The old order of society can survive but little longer. Socialism is next in order. The swelling minority sounds warning of the impending change. Soon that minority will be the majority and then will come the co-operative commonwealth.

Every workingman should rally to the standard of his class and hasten the full-orbed day of freedom.

Every progressive Democrat must find his way in our direction and if he will but free himself from prejudice and study the principles of socialism he will soon be a sturdy supporter of our party.

Every sympathizer with labor, every friend of justice, every lover of humanity should support the Socialist Party as the only party that is organized to abolish industrial slavery, the prolific source of the giant evils that afflict the people.

Who with a heart in his breast can look upon Colorado without keenly feeling the cruelties and crimes of capitalism! Repression will not help her. Brutality will only brutalize her. Private ownership and wage-slavery are the curse of Colorado. Only socialism will save Colorado and the nation.

The overthrow of capitalism is the object of the Socialist Party. It will not fuse with any other party and it would rather die than compromise.

The Socialist Party comprehends the magnitude of its task and has the patience of preliminary defeat and the faith of ultimate victory.

The working class must be emancipated by the working class.

Woman must be given her true place in society by the working class.

Child labor must be abolished by the working class.

Society must be reconstructed by the working class.

The working class must be employed by the working class.

The fruits of labor must be enjoyed by the working class.

War, bloody war, must be ended by the working class.

These are the principles and objects of the Socialist Party and we fearlessly proclaim them to our fellowmen.

We know our cause is just and that it must prevail.

With faith and hope and courage we hold our heads erect and with dauntless spirit marshal the working class for the march from Capitalism to Socialism, from Slavery to Freedom, from Barbarism to Civilization.

Suggested Reading

Many of the books recommended in the notes and suggested readings of Chapter 4 are also relevant to socialist agitation. In addition to the speech reproduced in this book, the Socialist Labor Party has published a number of other DeLeon speeches in pamphlet form, including *The Burning Question of Trades Unionism, Reform or Revolution*, and *Two Pages from Roman History*. The best biography of Debs is Ray Ginger, *The Bending Cross*, New Brunswick, N. J., 1949. The definitive biography of Henry George is C. A. Barker, *Henry George*, New York, 1955. There is no satisfactory biography of Haywood, but his autobiography is available under the title *Bill Haywood's Book*, New York, 1929. In addition to Commons and Kipnis, both of which have been cited earlier, the reader will find useful material in Howard H. Quint, *The Forging of American Socialism*, Columbia, S.C., 1953. A partisan analysis of IWW may be found in Fred Thompson, *The I.W.W., Its First Fifty Years*, Chicago, 1955.

chapter 6

the rhetoric of civil rights

Since the Supreme Court decision on public school segregation in 1954, the term *civil rights* has been used more and more in a highly specialized sense to refer to the struggle of Negroes and other minority groups to attain the full rights of American citizenship. Such limited usage is certainly within the meaning of the term, but it does violence to the long history of the struggle for greater freedom of the individual within Western civilization, and particularly within the framework of the Anglo-American tradition since the seventeenth century.

Although the beginnings of the concept of personal liberty can be traced to the Magna Charta in 1215, that document was primarily for feudal barons, and the late middle ages remained authoritarian and arbitrary. Serfdom lapsed more from the economic pressure of labor shortages brought on by plague than by any assertion of theoretical rights. A temporary period of baronial anarchy during the Wars of the Roses eventually produced a reaction in a period of dictatorial government under Henry VII. Henry VIII strengthened this power by acquiring for the crown the vast resources of the church, making it unnecessary for him to rely on Parliament for money or to submit to "redress of grievances" as a condition of Parliamentary grants.

Under the seventeenth-century Stuart monarchs, however, a long struggle for the enlargement of civil rights began, first between the King and Parliament, and in the late eighteenth and nineteenth centuries for the right of the people to control the legislatures in England, America, and the various countries of the British Empire. The first struggle was largely won by the Whig revolution of 1688-89; the second was established in principle by the end of the nineteenth century, but its application to all the people in both Britain and the United States continues to be a major concern today.

An important factor in the civil rights struggle is the canonization of historic documents which mark advances in human freedom. Although these documents were originally addressed to specific grievances and were often not intended to be applied to the masses of the people, the special status they have been given has caused more and more groups to demand that the rights stated should be applied on a broader basis. Thus the rights of feudal barons, set forth in the Magna Charta, became the basis for the seventeenth-century Petition of Right and Bill of Rights. The limited concept of freedom of speech for members of Parliament set forth in these documents became the basis of popular agitation for universal freedom of speech. John Locke's philosophical defense of the Revolution of 1688 became the grounds for the American Revolution. The Declaration of Independence and the American Bill of Rights in turn have been the basis of ever broader application of the principle that "all men are created equal."

Generally the demand for civil liberties has dealt with three major issues, with two more acquiring importance in recent years: (1) Freedom of belief and dissent; originally this was primarily a matter of religious belief, but it has become also a demand for the right of nonconformity in social and political views as well. (2) Freedom of speech and of the press; the right to disseminate and advocate views different from those held by those in power, or by the majority of the people; a serious conflict of values arises when writers and speakers advocate the adoption of a form of government which would restrict or impair these rights. (3) The right to vote and to be represented by persons chosen by free ballot, even if authorities outside consider the person chosen to be of unworthy character; the issue differs little whether the representative is John Wilkes[1] in the eighteenth century or Adam Clayton Powell in the twentieth. (4) In more recent years additional freedoms have been stated as corollaries of the older ones, chiefly through the extension of the right to "the pursuit of happiness" stated in the Declaration of Independence; freedom of movement and freedom of association are two of these. (5) Finally, in recent years major importance has been given to the right of equal opportunity in education and employment.

One of the most eloquent statements of the concept of civil liberty is to be found in the dissenting opinion of Justice Oliver Wendell Holmes in the case of Abrams vs. the United States, 1919:

[1] John Wilkes was barred from Parliament in 1764 partly on the grounds of having libeled the then Prime Minister Lord Bute, and partly on grounds of personal immorality. His constituents persisted in re-electing him, and eventually Parliament relented and seated him. For an account of agitational activity accompanying this case, see Henry Jephson, *The Platform: Its Rise and Progress*, Vol. I, New York, 1891, pp. 32–67.

Persecution for the expression of opinions seems to me perfectly logical. If you have no doubt of your premises or your power and want a certain result with all your heart you naturally express your wishes in law and sweep away all opposition. To allow opposition by speech seems to indicate that you think the speech impotent, as when a man says that he has squared the circle, or that you do not care whole-heartedly for the result, or that you doubt either your power or your premises. But when men have realized that time has upset many fighting faiths, they may come to believe even more than they believe the very foundations of their own conduct that the ultimate good desired is better reached by free trade in ideas—that the best test of truth is the power of the thought to get itself accepted in the competition of the market, and that truth is the only ground upon which their wishes safely can be carried out. That at any rate is the theory of our Constitution. It is an experiment, as all life is an experiment. Every year if not every day we have to wager our salvation upon some prophecy based upon imperfect knowledge. While that experiment is part of our system I think that we should be eternally vigilant against attempts to check the expresssion of opinions that we loathe and believe to be fraught with death, unless they so imminently threaten immediate interference with the lawful and pressing purposes of the law that an immediate check is required to save the country.[2]

Because the demand for civil rights is older than the United States and has appeared in various agitations since colonial days, it would be possible to select speeches on this issue from any period. But because the issue is of over-riding importance in contemporary society, all of the speeches have been selected from the twentieth century. The basic theme of most of these speeches is the dignity of the individual. The speeches are developed by showing the contrast between the ideals professed by society and the application of those ideals to specific situations. They are at the same time a challenge to the majority to put their ideals into practice, and a declaration by the minority of the goal of eventually asserting those rights if they are not freely granted.

Emma Goldman

Free Speech and Unpopular Ideas

In his incendiary pamphlet, *Revolutionäre Kriegwissenschaft*, Johann Most recommended to any anarchist who was arrested for revolutionary acts or words that

[2]As quoted by Henry Steele Commager and Allan Nevins, eds., *The Heritage of America*, Boston, 1951, pp. 1092–93.

he should "transform the prisoner's dock into a speaker's rostrum."[3] In doing so, he would not only have an opportunity to defend himself, but would gain an audience for his propaganda which would not otherwise be open to him.

Following this advice, anarchists Emma Goldman and Alexander Berkman decided to speak in their own defense at their 1917 trial on charges of conspiracy to induce men to refuse to register for the wartime draft. Both had been in the public eye since the Homestead strike of 1892, when Berkman had tried unsuccessfully to assassinate Henry Clay Frick, General Manager of Carnegie Steel Company. At the time of the 1917 trial Miss Goldman had been for some years the editor of the magazine *Mother Earth*. In 1917 her anarchism was much less violent than it had been in earlier years. She was more concerned with freedom of speech and with birth control than with overt revolutionary acts, and many who were associated with her during these years became founders and leading figures in the American Civil Liberties Union and the Planned Parenthood movement.

The speech reproduced here is from a text printed in *Mother Earth* in July, 1917, shortly after the end of the trial, in which both defendants were convicted. Another text, printed as a propaganda pamphlet, appears to be of a slightly later date and bears the marks of extensive revision.[4]

Gentlemen of the jury: On the day after our arrest it was given out by the Marshal's office and the District Attorney's office that the two "big fish" of the no-conscription activities were now in the hands of the authorities, that there would be no more troublemakers and dangerous disturbers, that the government will be able to go on in the highly democratic method of conscripting American manhood for European slaughter. It is a great pity, it seems to me, that the Marshal and the District Attorney have used such a flimsy net to make their catch. The moment they attempted to land the fish on shore the net broke. Indeed the net proved that it was not able and strong enough to hold the fish. The sensational arrest of the defendants and the raid of the defendants' offices would have satisfied the famous circus men, Barnum & Bailey. Imagine, if you can, a dozen stalwart warriors rushing up two flights of stairs to find the two defendants, Alexander Berkman and Emma Goldman, in their separate offices quietly seated at their desks, wielding not the gun or the bomb or the club or the sword, but only such a simple and insignificant thing as a pen. As a matter of fact two officers equipped with a warrant would have sufficed to arrest us two, for I take it that we are well known

[3]A copy of Most's pamphlet may be found in the Labadie Collection at the University of Michigan. The quotation is from page 59.

[4]The greater authenticity of the *Mother Earth* version has been established in an unpublished graduate paper by Elizabeth Berry, "Will the Real Emma Goldman Please Stand Up," University of California, Los Angeles, May, 1966.

to the police department and the police department will bear me out that at no time have we run away or attempted to run away, that at no time have we offered any resistance to an arrest, that at no time did we keep in hiding under the bed. We have always frankly and squarely faced the issue. But it was necessary to stage a sensational arrest so that Marshal McCarthy and the attorney should go down to posterity and receive immortality. It was necessary to raid offices of the *Blast*[5] and the No Conscription League and *Mother Earth,* although without a search warrant, which was never shown to us. I ask you, gentlemen of the jury, should it be customary from the point of view of law to discriminate in the case of people merely because they have opinions which do not appeal to you? What is a scrap of paper in the form of a search warrant, when it is a question of raiding the offices of Anarchists or arresting Anarchists? Would the gentlemen who came with Marshal McCarthy have dared to go into the offices of Morgan or of Rockefeller or any of these men without a search warrant? They never showed us the search warrant, although we asked them for it. Nevertheless, they turned our office into a battlefield, so that when they were through with it it looked like invaded Belgium, with only the distinction that the invaders were not Prussian barbarians but good patriots who were trying to make New York safe for democracy.

The first act of this marvelous comedy having been properly staged by carrying off the villains in a madly rushing automobile which came near crushing life in its way, merely because Marshal McCarthy said "I am the Marshal of the United States," he even reprimanding officers on the automobile should not have rushed at such violent speed—I say the first act having been finished by locking the villains up, the second act appeared on the scene. And the second act, gentlemen of the jury, consisted not in prosecution but in persecution. Here are two people arrested, known to the police department, having lived in New York City for nearly thirty years, never having offered resistance to an arrest, always facing the issue. And yet we were placed under $50,000 bail, although the principal witness in the Cruger[6] case is held only in $7,000 bail. Why were we placed under $50,000 bail? Because the District Attorney knew that it would be difficult to raise that bail and therefore out of personal spite made us stay in the Tombs instead of enjoying our liberty. And furthermore, not only did the District Attorney and the prosecution insist upon $50,000

---

[5]Berkman was editor of the *Blast* and shared an office with Emma Goldman.

[6]Ruth Cruger disappeared February 15, 1917. In June her body was found buried in the cellar of a shop run by Alfredo Cocchi, who meanwhile had escaped to Italy. The significance of the case was enhanced by a considerable body of evidence implicating New York police in widespread gambling and vice activities operated by Cocchi. It was also suggested that police had connived in his escape. In the month before the Goldman trial, New York papers had carried sensational stories almost daily concerning the case. *New York Times,* February-September, 1917, passim.

bail, but when we produced a man whose property is rated at $300,000 in this city his real estate was refused. Why? Because the District Attorney suddenly remembered that he needed 48 hours to look into the man's reputation—knowing perfectly well that we were to go on trial on Wednesday, and yet not permitting the defendant, Alexander Berkman, to get out, although we had relied on an authentic and absolutely secure bail. So that I say that the second act, gentlemen of the jury, demonstrated that it was not only to be a case of prosecution, that it was also to be a case of persecution.

And finally the third act which was played in this court and which you, gentlemen of the jury, witnessed last week. I may say here that it is to be regretted indeed that the District Attorney knows nothing of dramatic construction, otherwise he would have supplied himself with better dramatic material, he would have used better acts in the play to sustain the continuity of the comedy. But the District Attorney is not supposed to know anything about modern drama or the construction of modern drama.[7]

Now then you have already been told and I am sure you will be charged by His Honor that the indictment against us is, having conspired and having used overt acts to carry out the conspiracy to induce men of conscriptable age not to register. That is the indictment and you cannot and you may not render a verdict for anything else, no matter what material came up in this court during the last week or ten days. As to the conspiracy: imagine, if you please, people engaged along similar lines for nearly thirty years, always standing out against war, whether that war was in China or Japan or Russia or England or Germany or America, always insisting with the great essayist Carlyle, that all wars are wars among thieves who are too cowardly to fight and who therefore induce the young manhood of the whole world to do the fighting for them— that is our standing; we have proved it by evidence, we have proved it by witnesses, we have proved it by our own position, that always and forever we have stood up against war, because we say that the war going on in the world is for the further enslavement of the people, for the further placing of them under the yoke of a military tyranny; imagine also people who for thirty years in succession have stood out against militarism, who claim militarism is costly and useless and brutalizing to every country; imagine us standing for years, and especially since conscription was declared in England and the fight began in Australia and conscription was there defeated by the brave and determined and courageous position of the Australian people; imagine that since that time we have been against conscription, then say how there can possibly be a conspiracy when people merely continue in their work which they have carried on

[7]Miss Goldman devoted much of her time to delivering critical lectures on contemporary drama, particularly stressing the social message of Ibsen.

for thirty years and for which they have spoken in different meetings and by letters! What kind of conspiracy is that? Was there any need of a conspiracy if we really had wanted to tell young men not to register? I insist that the prosecution has failed utterly, has failed miserably to prove the charge on the indictment of a conspiracy.

As to the meeting of May 18th: it was dragged in here only for reasons known to the prosecution, otherwise I can't understand why that meeting played such an important part. No matter what we would have said at that meeting, no matter what language we would have used, that meeting cannot constitute an overt act, because although it is true that the draft law was passed on the 18th, it is equally true that it was not made a law until the President of the United States signed that law. And the President of the United States did not sign it until late that evening, at the time when we had the meeting and couldn't have any idea or knowledge as to whether he was going to sign it. So the meeting of the 18th is utterly irrelevant. But since the meeting came in it is necessary to emphasize one or two points. And I mean to do so, because it concerns the defendant Emma Goldman. The main thing upon which evidently the prosecution concentrated is that the reporter credited the defendant Emma Goldman with saying, "We believe in violence and we will use violence." Gentleman of the jury, if there were no other proof to absolutely discredit this particular line and sentence and expression, there would yet be the following reasons: In the first place, I have been on the public platform for 27 years and one of the things that I am particularly careful of in my speeches is that they shall be coherent and shall be logical. The speeches delivered on that evening, on May 18, absolutely excluded the necessity of using the expression, "We believe in violence and we will use violence." I couldn't have used it, as an experienced speaker, because it would merely have made the whole speech nonsensical, it would have dragged in something which was irrelevant to the body of the speech or material used. That is one of the reasons why I never at that meeting said, "We believe in violence and we will use violence."

I am a social student. It is my business in life to ascertain the cause of our social evils and of our social difficulties. As a student of social wrongs it is my business to diagnose a wrong. To simply condemn the man who has committed an act of political violence, in order to save my own skin, would be just as pardonable as it would be on the part of the physician who is called to diagnose a case, to condemn the patient because the patient had tuberculosis or cancer or any other disease. The honest, earnest, sincere physician diagnoses a case, he does not only prescribe medicine, he tries to find out the cause of the disease. And if the patient is at all capable as to means, he will tell the patient, "Get out of this putrid air, get out of the factory, get out of the place where your lungs are being infected." He will not merely give him medicines. He will tell him the cause of the disease. And that is precisely my position in regard to violence. That is what I have said on all platforms. I have attempted to explain the cause and the reason fo racts of political violence.

And what is the cause? Is it conditioned in the individual who com-attempted to explain the cause and the reason for acts of political violence. at the bottom is the culminating result of organized violence on top.[8] It is the result of violence which expresses itself in war, which expresses itself in capital punishment, which expresses itself in courts, which ex-presses itself in prisons, which expresses itself in kicking and hounding people for the only crime they are guilty of: of having been born poor. So that after all when we come to consider an act of political violence com-mitted by an individual, I take it, gentlemen of the jury, that you are con-versant with history and that you know that not only a stray Anarchist here and there, but rebels of every movement in Ireland, in France, in Russia, in Italy, in Spain, all over the world, even in passive India, the country which has the most wonderful civilization and rests upon passive resistance—even in that country, men were driven to acts of violence by organized violence on top. So, as I said in one of the evidences we have given, we say with the greatest psychologist living. Havelock Ellis, that an act of political violence committed by an individual is the result of social wrong and social injustice and political oppression.   Wherever there is political liberty—and I can demonstrate it in the Scandinavian countries: has there been any act of violence committed in Norway, in Sweden, in Denmark, in Holland—why are there no acts of violence there? Because the government doesn't only preach free speech and free press and assembly, but lives up to it. There was no need to be driven into acts of violence. So, gentlemen, I say with Havelock Ellis that the political offender or the "political criminal," as you choose to call him, is so not because of criminal tendency, not because of personal gain, not because of personal aggrandizement, but because he loves humanity too well; because he cannot face wrong and injustice and because he cannot enjoy his meal when he knows that America is getting rich on two million wage-slave children who are ground into dust and into money and power.

And so, gentlemen, I have explained the act. I have explained the act. Does that mean advocating the act? If that is your version—and I can't believe that it will be—I say, gentlemen of the jury, that you might as well condemn Jesus for having defended the prostitute Mary Mag-dalen, you might as well say that he advocated prostitution because he said to the mob on that occasion: "Let him among you that is without sin, cast the first stone." I refuse to cast the stone at the "political criminal," if he may be called so. I take his place with him because he

[8]"Violence at the top" represents a basic contention of all anarchists in this period, a point of view also shared by many other radical agitators.

has been driven to revolt, because his life-breath has been choked up. And if I am to pay with prison for that, if I am to pay with my life-breath for that, gentlemen of the jury, I shall be ready at any time to take the consequences. But I refuse to be tried on trumped-up charges and I refuse to be convicted by perjured testimony for something which I haven't said, when it had absolutely no relation whatever to the indictment as stated, that we conspired and agreed to conspire and used overt acts to tell people not to register.

Gentlemen of the jury, the meeting of May 18 was called for an express purpose and for that purpose only. It was called to voice the position of the conscientious objector who, as far as America is concerned, was a new type of humanity. Oh I know that we should be expected to call the conscientious objector, just as he is being called by the papers, a "slacker," a "coward," a "shirker." These are cheap names, gentlemen of the jury. To call a man a name proves nothing whatever. What is the conscientious objector? I am a conscientious objector. What is he? He is impelled by what President Wilson said in his speech on the 3rd of February, 1917; he is impelled by the force of righteous passion for justice, which is the bulwark and mainstay and basis of all our existence and of all our liberty. That is the force which impels the conscientious objector: a righteous passion for justice. The conscientious objector, rightly or wrongly—that is a thing which you will have to argue with him—does not believe in war, not because he is a coward or a shirker, not because he doesn't want to stand responsible, but because he insists that, belonging to the people whence he has come and to whom he owes life, it is his place to stand on the side of the people, for the people, and by the people and not on the side of the governing classes. And that is what we did at that particular meeting. We voiced the position of the conscientious objector. But I reiterate once more, so you may not overlook it: that whatever we said on the 18th of May has no bearing whatever on the indictment for conspiracy, because that meeting took place before the president signed that bill.

Gentlemen of the jury, when we examined talesmen we asked whether you would be prejudiced against us when it was proved that we were engaged in an agitation for unpopular ideas. You were instructed by the court to say "if they were within the law." But there was one thing I am sorry that the Court did not tell you. It is this: that there has never been any ideal— though ever so humane and peaceful—introduced for human betterment which in its place and in its time was considered within the law. I know that many of you believe in the teachings of Jesus. I want to call your attention to the fact that Jesus was put to death because he was not within the law. I know that all of you are Americans and patriots. Please bear in mind that those who fought and bled for whatever liberty you have, those who established the Declaration of Independence, those who established the constitutional right of free speech—that they were not within the law; that they were the Anarchists of their time; that they wrote a famous document known as the Declaration of Independence, a document indeed so great that it is evidently considered dangerous to this day, because a boy was given ninety days in a New York court for distributing a leaflet of quotations from the Declaration of Independence. They were not within the law. Those men were the rebels and the Anarchists. And what is more important, they not only believed in violence but they used violence when they threw the tea into Boston harbor.[9]

Furthermore, your country and in a measure my country—my country out of choice—is now allied with France. Need I call your attention to the fact that the French republic is due to the men who were not within the law? Why, friends, even the man who is responsible for the stirring music of the Marseillaise, which unfortunately has been deteriorating into a war tune—even Camille Desmoulins was not within the law, was considered a criminal. And finally, gentlemen, on the very day when we are tried for a conspiracy, when we are tried for overt acts, our city and its representatives were receiving with festivities and with music the Russian Commission. Every one of the Russian commissioners is what you would choose to call an ex-political criminal. Every one of them had been in exile or in prison. As a matter of fact, gentlemen, the tree of Russian liberty is watered with the blood of Russian martyrs.[10]

So no great idea in its beginning can ever be within the law. How can it be within the law? The law is stationary. The law is fixed. The law is a chariot wheel which binds us all regardless of conditions or circumstances or place or time.[11] The law does not even make an attempt to go into the complexity of the human soul which drives a man to despair or to insanity, out of hunger or out of indignation, into a political act. But progress is ever changing, progress is ever renewing, progress has nothing to do with fixity. And in its place and in its time every great ideal for human reconstruction, for a reconstruction of society and the regeneration of the race—every great idea was considered extralegal, illegal, in its time and place. And so I must refer to Havelock Ellis when he said that the political criminal is the hero and the martyr and the saint of the new era. Hence the country that locks up men and women who will stand up for an ideal—what chance is there for that country and for the future

[9]Note how the speaker uses stereotypes familiar to and admired by the audience to make her point. The fact that she was a professed atheist did not deter her from using religious references.

[10]A paraphrase of Jefferson's letter to William Stevens Smith, November 13, 1787: "The tree of liberty must be refreshed from time to time with the blood of patriots and tyrants. It is its natural manure." Julian P. Boyd, ed., The Papers of Thomas Jefferson, Vol. XII, Princeton, 1955, p. 356.

[11]The wording of this idea is clearer in the pamphlet version of the speech: "The law is stationary, fixed, mechanical, a chariot wheel which grinds all alike without regard to time, place, and conditions, without ever taking into account cause and effect, without ever going into the complexity of the human soul."

and for the young generation, a country that has not in her midst dangerous disturbers and troublemakers who can see further than their time and propagate a new idea?

Well, gentlemen, I take it that perhaps the prosecution will say that that means propagating dangerous and seditious ideas in this time of war and patriotism. Maybe it does, gentlemen of the jury. But that doesn't prove that we are responsible for the existence of such ideas. You might as well condemn the very stars that are hanging in the heavens eternally and inalienably and unchangeably for all time, as to accuse us or find us guilty because we propagate certain ideas. Gentlemen of the jury, I wish to say right here we respect your patriotism. We wouldn't, even if we could, want you to change one single iota of what patriotism means to you. But may there not be two kinds of patriotism, just as there are two interpretations of liberty, the kind of liberty which is real liberty in action, and the kind which has been placed on a document and is dug out once a year on the 4th of July and is not allowed to exist for the rest of the year? And so, gentlemen, I wish to emphasize this very important fact, because I know how you feel on the war, I know what patriotism means to you: that the mere accident of birth or the mere fact that you have taken out citizens' papers does not make a man necessarily a patriot. Who is the real patriot, or rather what is the kind of patriotism that we represent? The kind of patriotism we represent is the kind of patriotism which loves America with open eyes. Our relation toward America is the same as the relation of a man who loves a woman, who is enchanted by her beauty and yet who cannot be blind to her defects. And so I wish to state here, in my own behalf and in behalf of hundreds of thousands whom you decry and state to be antipatriotic, that we love America, we love her beauty, we love her riches, we love her mountains and her forests, and above all we love the people who have produced her wealth and riches, who have created all her beauty, we love the dreamers and the philosophers and the thinkers who are giving America liberty. But that must not make us blind to the social faults of America. That cannot make us deaf to the discords in America. That cannot compel us to be inarticulate to the terrible wrongs committed in the name of the country.

We simply insist, regardless of all protests to the contrary, that this war is not a war for democracy. If it were a war for the purpose of making democracy safe for the world, we would say that democracy must first be safe for America before it can be safe for the world. So in a measure I say, gentlemen, that we are greater patriots than those who shoot off firecrackers and say that democracy should be given to the world. By all means let us give democracy to the world. But for the present we are very poor in democracy. Free speech is suppressed. Free assemblies are broken up by uniformed gangsters, one after another. Women and girls at meetings are insulted by soldiers under this "democracy." And therefore we say that we are woefully poor in democracy at home. How can we be generous in giving democracy to the world? So we say, gentlemen of the jury, our crime if crime there be, is not having in any way conspired to tell young men not to register, or having committed overt acts. Our crime, if crime there be, consists in pointing out the real cause of the present war.

I wish to state to you here that whatever your verdict is going to be it cannot have a possible effect upon the tremendous storm brewing in the United States. And the storm has not been created by two people, Alexander Berkman and Emma Goldman. You credit us with too much power altogether. That storm was created by the conditions themselves, by the fact that the people before election were promised that they would be kept out of war and after election they were dragged into war. Gentlemen of the jury, your verdict cannot affect the growing discontent of the American people. Neither can it affect the conscientious objector to whom human life is sacred and who would rather be shot than take the life of another human being. Of course your verdict is going to affect us. It will affect us only temporarily. And it will affect us physically: it cannot affect our spirit, gentlemen of the jury, whether we are found guilty or whether we are placed in jail. Nothing will be changed in our spirit. Nothing will be changed in our ideas. For even if we were convicted and found guilty and the penalty were, to be placed against a wall and shot dead, I should nevertheless cry out with the great Luther: "Here I am and here I stand and I cannot do otherwise."

And so, gentlemen, in conclusion let me tell you that my co-defendant, Mr. Berkman, was right when he said the eyes of America are upon you. And they are upon you not because of sympathy for us or agreement with Anarchism. They are upon you because it must be decided sooner or later. Are we justified in telling people that we will give them democracy in Europe, when we have no democracy here? Shall free speech and free assemblage, shall criticism and opinion, which even the espionage bill did not include—shall that be destroyed? Shall it be a shadow of the past, the great historic American past? Shall it be trampled underfoot by any detective, any policeman, anyone, who decides upon it? Or shall free speech and free press and free assemblage continue to be the heritage of the American people? And so, gentlemen of the jury, whatever your verdict will be, as far as we are concerned, nothing will be changed. I have held ideas all my life. I have publicly held my ideas for 27 years. Nothing on earth would ever make me change my ideas except one thing; and that is, if you will prove to me that our position is wrong, untenable, or lacking in historic fact. But never would I change my ideas because I am found guilty. I must say in the great words of two great Americans, undoubtedly not unknown to you gentlemen of the jury, and that is Ralph Waldo Emerson and Henry David Thoreau: when Henry David Thoreau was placed in prison for refusing to pay taxes he was visited by Ralph Waldo Emerson and Emerson said: "David, what are you doing in jail?" and Thoreau said: "Ralph, what are you doing outside, when people are in jail for their ideals?" And so, gentlemen of the jury, I do not wish to influence you. I do not wish to appeal to your passions. I do not wish to influence you by the fact that I am a woman. I have no such desires and no such designs. I take it that you are sincere enough and honest enough and brave enough to render a verdict according to your convictions, beyond the shadow of a reasonable doubt.

Please forget that we are Anarchists. Forget that we said that we propagated violence.[12] Forget that something appeared in *Mother Earth* when I was thousands of miles away three years ago. Forget all that. And merely consider the evidence. Have we been engaged in a conspiracy? Has that conspiracy been proved; have we committed overt acts; have those overt acts been proved? We for the defense say they have not been proved. And therefore your verdict must be not guilty.

Roger Baldwin

On Being Sentenced as a Conscientious Objector

When James Farmer spoke at an American Civil Liberties Union banquet in Detroit honoring the 80th birthday of Roger Baldwin and the 44th anniversary of the founding of ACLU, he declared it was like old home week. At a meeting of the ACLU, he said, "I meet so many old friends, and it's the greatest collection of ex-jailbirds and fighters for conscience's sake that you will find any place in the country."[13] He was right, of course, for it is a tradition of the American Civil Liberties Union to risk imprisonment in order to test laws restricting freedom.

Although Roger Baldwin was one of the founders of the Union, he had been active in civil liberties conflicts for a number of years before its founding. He had been a friend of Emma Goldman and

[12]In the pamphlet version the wording is: "Forget that it is claimed that we propagated violence." Probably the *Mother Earth* wording was a slip of the tongue or a reporter's mistake, since it is out of harmony with her earlier argument that she had not advocated violence.
[13]Transcribed from a tape recording at the offices of the American Civil Liberties Union of Michigan.

had supported her efforts to maintain freedom for unpopular causes, and he had been active in the National Civil Liberties Bureau and the American Union Against Militarism, out of which the ACLU emerged. Moreover, like Farmer, he was no stranger to the insides of jails. In 1918, at the age of 34, he chose to stand on his long record of pacifism and refused to submit to a physical examination for the draft. Before he was sentenced to one year in the Federal Penitentiary at Atlanta, he spoke in court at some length explaining his reasons for refusal. It is this speech which is reproduced here.

At a later period Peggy Bacon (author and caricaturist for the *New Yorker*) described Roger Baldwin in these words: "Dusty hair, a bit bedraggled. Turnout clean but careless. Manner tumblingly hurried. Personality generous, self-disciplined, aristocratic, Galahadian, full of fervor and violent integrity, emotional, ethical, tirelessly seeking the Grail. A genuine article."[14] It is easy to visualize such a man giving the 1918 court speech. The address was not one of defense, for Baldwin freely admitted that he had violated the law. Neither was it exactly an explanation, for he granted that it was a foolish act in the climate of 1918. But it was a simple, straightforward statement of the views of a tiny minority. "They are not the views that work in the world today. . . . But I fully believe that they are the views which are going to guide in the future." The *New York Times* on the day following his sentencing chided him for "words chosen in haste," and hoped that "while serving his term in prison, he will reach a new and better conclusion." Baldwin's basic views did not change, but in later years he wrote, "I would, I think, if faced with the issue again, accept the compromise of civilian service provided for objectors in World War II."[15]

In his long career as director of the ACLU, as civil liberties adviser to General MacArthur in Japan, and as a consultant to the United Nations on civil liberties, Roger Baldwin has continually sought to enlarge the scope of human liberty. As he put it in his speech at the Detroit ACLU anniversary banquet in 1964, "We survived with integrity of purpose. We may have gone off the reservation once in a while; I suppose we did. We were under all kinds of pressure, but I think we kept the faith with the principles of the Bill of Rights for all comers without compromise. We're almost respectable."[16]

The text of the speech printed here was written out in Baldwin's cell one morning just before the trial and was read to Judge Julius M. Meyer before sentence was passed. Shortly after the trial, the speech was published in pamphlet form under the title, *The Individual and the State: The Problem as Presented by the Sentencing of Roger Baldwin.*[17] The statement forms a part of the record in Roger Baldwin's file in the Oral History Project of Columbia Uni-

[14]*Current Biography,* New York, 1940, p. 44.
[15]Karl Resek, *The Progressives,* Indianapolis, 1967, p. 378.
[16]See note 13.
[17]Published November, 1918.

versity, and has recently been included in a book by Karl Resek, *The Progressives,* based on that material. It is reproduced here with the permission of Roger Baldwin.

Your Honor, I presume that myself, and not the National Civil Liberties Bureau, is on trial before this court this morning. I do not object to the reading into this record of the letters which the Government's attorney has read. Some of them I did not write. They represent one side of a work which I have been conducting as the Executive Officer of that organization during the past year. Our work is backed up and supported both by those who call themselves Pro-War Liberals, who are supporters of the war, and by those who are so-called Pacifists.

I have not engaged in personal propaganda. I have not made public addresses, except upon the subject matter of this Bureau. I have not written articles, except upon the subject matter of the Bureau, and I have felt throughout that it was a work which could be supported genuinely and honestly by those who opposed the war in principle, and by those who were supporting the war. I believe that the examination of the records of the Bureau now being made by the Department of Justice will conclusively demonstrate that the work has been undertaken with that sole purpose in view, and that it has been in the interest of the solution of certain democratic problems that this country has to face during war time.

I will say, in that connection for instance, that although the Post Office censorship throughout the war has been intolerant, narrow, and stupid, but one little pamphlet which we have issued—and we have issued a great many of them—has been excluded from the mails, and that in this Court within the last two weeks an injunction was issued, requiring the Post-Master of New York to accept for mailing all the pamphlets of this Bureau. I think that demonstrates pretty clearly that where the law is narrowly interpreted, rigidly interpreted, arbitrarily interpreted, as it is in the Post-Office Department at Washington, no exception has been taken to the general matter which has been sent out by this organization.

I know that the Government's Attorney is merely attempting to put before this Court my state of mind in taking the position I have about this act—in coming here as its deliberate violator.

I want to read to the Court, if I may, for purposes of record, and for purposes of brevity too, a statement which I have prepared, and which I hope will get across a point of view which the United States Attorney does not consider logical, but which I trust, at least, with the premises I hold, is consistent.

I am before you as a deliberate violator of the draft act. On October 9, when ordered to take a physical examination, I notified my local board that I declined to do so, and instead presented myself to the United States

Attorney for prosecution. I submit herewith for the record the letter of explanation which I addressed to him at the time.

I refused to take bail, believing that I was not morally justified in procuring it, and being further opposed to the institution of bail on principle. I have therefore been lodged in the Tombs Prison since my arraignment on October 10. During that period I have been engaged daily at the Department of Justice offices in systematizing the files of the National Civil Liberties Bureau, of which I have been the director. These files had been voluntarily turned over to the Department for examination, and had, through much handling, become seriously disarranged. That work being completed, I am before you for sentence.

And, by the way, may I take this occasion, your honor— this is quite aside from the proceedings—to express my thanks for the courtesy of every officer of this court, and of the Department of Justice, through these trying weeks. It has been exceptional.

The compelling motive for refusing to comply with the draft act is my uncompromising opposition to the principle of conscription of life by the State for any purpose whatever, in time of war or peace. I not only refused to obey the present conscription law, but I would in future refuse to obey any similar statute which attempts to direct my choice of service and ideals. I regard the principle of conscription of life as a flat contradiction of all our cherished ideals of individual freedom, democratic liberty, and Christian teaching.

I am the more opposed to the present act, because it is for the purpose of conducting war. I am opposed to this and all other wars. I do not believe in the use of physical force as a method of achieving any end, however good.

The District Attorney calls your attention, your Honor, to the inconsistency in my statement to him that I would, under extreme emergencies, as a matter of protecting the life of any person, use physical force. I don't think that is an argument that can be used in support of the wholesale organization of men to achieve political purposes in nationalistic or domestic wars. I see no relationship at all between the two.

My opposition is not only to direct military service but to any service whatever designed to help prosecute the war. I could accept no service, therefore, under the present act, regardless of its character.

Holding such profound convictions, I determined, while the new act was pending, that it would be more honest to make my stand clear at the start and therefore concluded not even to register, but to present myself for prosecution. I therefore resigned my position as director of the National Civil Liberties Bureau so as to be free to follow that personal course of action. But on the day my resignation took effect (August 31) agents of the Department of Justice began an examination of the affairs of that organization, and I was constrained to withdraw my resignation and to register in order to stand by the work at a critical moment. With that obligation discharged, I resigned, and took the next occasion, the physical examination, to make my stand clear.

I realize that to some this refusal may seem a piece of wilful defiance. It might well be argued that any man holding my views might have avoided the issue by obeying the law, either on the chance of being rejected on physical grounds, or on the chance of the war stopping before a call to service. I answer that I am not seeking to evade the draft; that I scorn evasion, compromise, and gambling with moral issues. It may further be argued that the War Department's liberal provision for agricultural service on furlough for conscientious objectors would be open to me if I obey the law and go to camp, and that there can be no moral objection to farming, even in time of war. I answer first, that I am opposed to any service under conscription, regardless of whether that service is in itself morally objectionable; and second, that, even if that were not the case, and I were opposed only to war, I can make no moral distinction between the various services which assist in prosecuting the war—whether rendered in the trenches, in the purchase of bonds or thrift stamps at home, or in raising farm products under the lash of the draft act. All serve the same end—war. Of course all of us render involuntary assistance to the war in the processes of our daily living. I refer only to those direct services undertaken by choice.

I am fully aware that my position is extreme, that it is shared by comparatively few, and that in the present temper it is regarded either as unwarranted egotism or as a species of feeble-mindedness. I cannot, therefore, let this occasion pass without attempting to explain the foundations on which so extreme a view rests.

I have had an essentially American upbringing and background. Born in a suburban town of Boston, Massachusetts, of the stock of the first settlers, I was reared in the public schools and at Harvard College. Early my mind was caught by the age-old struggle for freedom; America meant to me a vital new experiment in free political institutions; personal freedom to choose one's way of life and service seemed the essence of the liberties brought by those who fled the mediaeval and modern tyrannies of the old world. But I rebelled at our whole autocratic industrial system —with its wreckage of poverty, disease, and crime, and childhood robbed of its right to free growth. So I took up social work upon leaving college, going to St. Louis as director of a settlement and instructor in sociology at Washington University. For ten years I have been professionally engaged in social work and political reform, local and national. That program of studied, directed social progress, step by step, by public agitation and legislation, seemed to me the practical way of effective service to gradually freeing the mass of folks from industrial and political bondage. At the same time I was attracted to the solutions of our social problems put forth by the radicals. I studied the programs of socialism, the IWW, European syndicalism, and anarchism. I attended their meetings, knew their leaders. Some of them became my close personal friends. Sympathizing with their general ideals of a free society, with much of their program, I yet could see no effective way of practical daily service. Some six years ago, however, I was so discouraged with social work and reform, so challenged by the sacrifices and idealism of some of my IWW friends, that I was on the point of getting out altogether, throwing respectability overboard and joining the IWW as a manual worker.

I thought better of it. My traditions were against it. It was more an emotional reaction than a practical form of service. But ever since, I have felt myself heart and soul with the worldwide radical movements for industrial and political freedom—wherever and however expressed—and more and more impatient with reform.

Personally, I share the extreme radical philosophy of the future society. I look forward to a social order without any external restraints upon the individual, save through public opinion and the opinion of friends and neighbors. I am not a member of any radical organization, nor do I wear any tag by which my views may be classified. I believe that all parts of the radical movement serve the common end—freedom of the individual from arbitrary external controls.[18]

When the war came to America, it was an immediate challenge to me to help protect those ideals of liberty which seemed to me not only the basis of the radical economic view, but of the radical political view of the founders of this Republic, and of the whole mediaeval struggle for religious freedom. Before the war was declared I severed all my connections in St. Louis, and offered my services to the American Union Against Miltarism to help fight conscription. Later, that work developed into the National Civil Liberties Bureau, organized to help maintain the rights of free speech and free press, and the Anglo-Saxon tradition of liberty of conscience, through liberal provisions for conscientious objectors. This work has been backed both by pro-war liberals and so-called pacifists. It is not anti-war in any sense. It seemed to me the one avenue of service open to me, consistent with my views, with the country's best interest, and with the preservation of the radical minority for the struggle after the war. Even if I were not a believer in radical theories and movements, I would justify the work I have done on the ground of American ideals and traditions alone—as do many of those who have been associated with me. They have stood for those enduring principles which the revolutionary demands of war have temporarily set aside. We have stood against hysteria, mob-violence, unwarranted prosecution, the sinister use of patriotism to cover attacks on radical and labor movements, and for the unabridged right of a fair trial under war statutes. We have tried to keep open those channels of expression which stand for the kind of world order for which the President is battling today against the tories and militarists.

[18]Baldwin's position is that of the anarchists, but without the overtones of violence.

Now comes the Government to take me from that service and to demand of me a service I cannot in conscience undertake. I refuse it simply for my own peace of mind and spirit, for the satisfaction of that inner demand more compelling than any consideration of punishment or the sacrifice of friendships and reputation. I seek no martyrdom, no publicity. I merely meet as squarely as I can the moral issue before me, regardless of consequences.

I realize that your Honor may virtually commit me at once to the military authorities, and that I may have merely taken a quicker and more inconvenient method of arriving at a military camp. I am prepared for that—for the inevitable pressure to take an easy way out by non-combatant service—with guard-house confinement—perhaps brutalities, which hundreds of others [sic] objectors have already suffered and are suffering today in camps. I am prepared for court martial and sentence to military prison, to follow the 200–300 objectors already sentenced to terms of 10–30 years for their loyalty to their ideals. I know that the way is easy for those who accept what to me is compromise, hard for those who refuse, as I must, any service whatever. And I know further, in military prison I shall refuse to conform to the rules for military salutes and the like, and will suffer solitary confinement on bread and water, shackled to the bars of a cell eight hours a day—as are men of like convictions at this moment.

I am not complaining for myself or others. I am merely advising the court that I understand full well the penalty of my heresy, and am prepared to pay it. The conflict with conscription is irreconcilable. Even the liberalism of the President and Secretary of War in dealing with objectors leads those of us who are "absolutists" to a punishment longer and severer than that of desperate criminals.

But I believe most of us are prepared even to die for our faith, just as our brothers in France are dying for theirs. To them we are comrades in spirit—we understand one another's motives, though our methods are wide apart. We both share deeply the common experience of living up to the truth as we see it, whatever the price.

Though at the moment I am of a tiny minority, I feel myself just one protest in a great revolt surging up from among the people—the struggle of the masses against the rule of the world by the few—profoundly intensified by the war. It is a struggle against the political state itself, against exploitation, militarism, imperialism, authority in all forms. It is a struggle to break in full force only after the war. Russia already stands in the vanguard, beset by her enemies in the camps of both belligerents—the Central Empires break asunder from within—the labor movement gathers revolutionary force in Britain—and in our own country the Nonpartisan League, radical labor, and the Socialist Party hold the germs of a new social order. Their protest is my protest. Mine is a personal protest at a particular law, but it is backed by all the aspirations and ideals of the struggle for a world freed of our manifold slaveries and tyrannies.

I ask the Court for no favor. I could do no other than what I have done, whatever the court's decree. I have no bitterness or hate in my heart for any man. Whatever the penalty, I shall endure it, firm in the faith, that whatever befalls me, the principles in which I believe will bring forth out of this misery and chaos, a world of brotherhood, harmony, and freedom for each to live the truth as he sees it.

I hope your Honor will not think that I have taken this occasion to make a speech for the sake of making a speech. I have read you what I have written in order that the future record for myself and for my friends may be perfectly clear, and in order to clear up some of the matters to which the District Attorney called your attention. I know that it is pretty nigh hopeless in times of war and hysteria to get across to any substantial body of people, the view of an out and out heretic like myself. I know that as far as my principles are concerned, they seem to be utterly impractical—mere moon-shine. They are not the views that work in the world today. I fully realize that. But I fully believe that they are the views which are going to guide in the future.

Having arrived at the state of mind in which those views mean the dearest things in life to me, I cannot consistently, with self-respect, do other than I have, namely, to deliberately violate an act which seems to me to be a denial of everything which ideally and in practice I hold sacred.

Louis E. Lomax

I Am Somebody

In the nearly two hundred years since the Declaration of Independence set forth the principle "that all men are created equal, that they are endowed by their Creator with certain unalienable Rights," every generation of Americans has seen at least one group forced to struggle for inclusion within the category of "all men." The poor and uneducated, the factory laborer, and successive waves of immigrants fought against oppression and discrimination throughout the nineteenth and early twentieth century. For the most part, the efforts of these groups have been successful.

The American black man, however, although his roots in America go back to the seventeenth century, has been systematically excluded from a major portion of the rights to which "all men" are entitled. Although there have been many voices of protest among Negroes from the time of Frederick Douglass to the present, the insistent clamor of sustained agitation for Negro rights is a phenomenon of the mid-twentieth century. Beginning with the restrained protests of men like Carl T. Rowan, Leroy Wilkins, and Benjamin E. Mays, the protest movement gathered momentum under the leadership of peaceful activists like Martin Luther King. In turn, King was overshadowed by new and more strident voices like Malcolm X and Stokely Carmichael.

One prominent leader who personifies the dilemma of responsible Negro leadership is Louis E. Lomax, teacher, author, lecturer, and television personality. Mr. Lomax was engaged in newspaper work from the time of his graduation from Paine College in 1942 until 1958. Since that time he has written two books, many articles, and has lectured to hundreds of audiences, black, white, and mixed. In addition he has been master of ceremonies on highly controversial television programs of WNTA-TV (New York) and KTTV (Los Angeles).

With white audiences, Lomax uses a technique which might be characterized as calculated antagonism. He seems to be seeking to force his listeners to reveal their deep-seated prejudices by exposing the rationalizations they use to cover their views. With Negro audiences he uses some of the same technique, but alternates it with appeals to pride, seeking to destroy false values while he bolsters the self-esteem of his listeners.

Lomax's delivery style also differs before different groups. Before educated white audiences he speaks with only a trace of southern speech. Before Negro audiences, especially in emotionally toned passages, he often lapses into a modified dialect of his native Georgia. Whether or not this is intentional is not apparent, but it has a favorable effect on Negro audiences, most of the members of which were born in the South.

The speech given here was delivered in 1963 to a predominantly Negro audience in Pacoima, a Negro community in the San Fernando Valley area of Los Angeles. The text is taken from a tape recording and accurately reflects audience responses on the occasions when they interrupted the speech. In addition, there were many shouted reactions ("that's right," "Amen," etc.), which could not be accurately indicated and have been omitted from the printed text. The theme of the speech, *I Am Somebody*, is from a poem by the Reverend William H. Borders.[19] The speech is reprinted by permission of the author, Louis E. Lomax.

[19]Roy L. Hill used the same theme and quoted the poem in a speech at Xavier University, February 15, 1961. Roy L. Hill, *Rhetoric of Racial Revolt*, Denver, 1964, pp. 333–44.

Tonight is the climax of a hectic, almost incredible week for me, which began last Monday night when I lectured in New York City. On Tuesday night I lectured in Brooklyn and took a plane for San Francisco. On Wednesday morning I delivered two lectures before high school students, did three radio programs, two television programs, and addressed a mass meeting on Wednesday night. On Thursday I gave four lectures to high school students and addressed a mass meeting in Oakland on Thursday night. On Friday I spoke at two colleges in Sacramento and addressed a rally Friday night, and on yesterday I spoke at a luncheon in Sacramento, last night at a rally in Stockton, this afternoon at four o'clock at a rally at Stanford University. So if I look dizzy it isn't because I have been eating mushrooms (*laughter*), it's because I have had a difficult week.

But I can think of no more fitting climax than to be here with you in the San Fernando Valley tonight. It's the first time (although I have been to California several times before; and I see some of my friends from Los Angeles, and some, both white and Negro from my days in Chicago; and I'm glad to see them all)—but I've never been to the San Fernando Valley before, and particularly have I not been to your city before. All during this tour this week I've been under the sponsorship of NAACP groups and under the sponsorship of CORE groups, but they have had their meetings at the universities and at the downtown hotels, and I have been surrounded around by what we call white groups; and so, I landed in Los Angeles this afternoon a bit weary of a lot of things. (*laughter*) And as we came with my dear personal friends, Ted and Gloria Larkin, along the freeway we were relaxing, and the closer we got—and finally they looked down and they said, "There it is, Louis." And we came around a bend, and sure enough there before me, its bespangled lights setting up a galaxy, there was the San Fernando Valley. And I said to myself and to them, "How great thou art! What a wonderful thing! And wouldn't it be great if I, black as I am, could go down in that valley and buy a home, anywhere." And we hit the railroad tracks. (*laughter*) And I knew at long last (*laughter*) I had made it.(*laughter*) For all intents and purposes I was back home in Valdosta, Georgia. (*laughter*) It's good to be here. (*laughter and applause*) But by the same token it is good to be with you—to be among friends, Negro and white.

But by the same token, when I hit the railroad tracks, it was just as if I had gone from one world into another. And this didn't happen, my friends, by accident. This happened and it is maintained by design. So whereas I can understand that you get all worked up about Birmingham, and you can talk about "down South," it's about time for you to get worried about "down North" and "down West," because you're in trouble too. (*laughter and applause*) And my cup has just about run over with these bourgeoisie Negroes on the West Coast who get their $35,000 and

$40,000 homes and move away from the black masses, and who try to pretend with their white liberal friends that while they are drinking integrated cocktails, that everything is approximately all right. (*applause*) Everything is not all right. Something is very, very wrong, not only in Birmingham, but it's wrong in New York, and it's wrong in San Francisco, and it's wrong here. And this is why I'm saying to you, don't tell me to go slow, because these kids are going to run over me if I slow down, so I've got to get out of their way. (*applause*) And let it be made crystal clear that this thing that I have called the Negro revolt in my book is not only a revolution, a rising up, and a revolt against segregation; but it is a revolution, a rising up, a revolt against the entrenched old guard leadership, whether it be Negro or white—that leadership which is unwilling to give the last full measure to set my eleven-year-old son free.[20]

Now, as the doctor said in welcoming me to the town (he was correct), in my book I have been at times critical of the NAACP. What they didn't say was that I have criticized Martin Luther King. I criticized CORE. I criticized the Urban League. In other words my book is an analytical book, and I criticized and I praised everybody I talked about. But may I go on record and let it be crystal clear that for the sake of the freedom of my son I would criticize God Almighty if I thought He was wrong. Nobody in our world today who is fighting for freedom and for justice and for equality is immune, including Louis Lomax. And this is why when you white liberals say, "Lomax, don't get so wild, slow down," you see, I'm speeding up because these young people have already begun to wonder whether I'm, instead of being an Uncle Tom, perhaps I'm a Doctor Thomas. (*laughter*) You see—(*applause*) And in order to keep them from running over me, I have to push you.

Now I want to get into some things tonight. We're going to have a kind of prayer meeting[21] about freedom. But before I get into the main body of what I want to talk about, I want to say a word of caution and alarm that I'm spreading—and I'm not alone in this—all over this nation where I speak. And I will be giving some 49 lectures between now and the middle of February in practically every major city of this country. And I'm prefacing all of my lectures with this remark: My beloved brothers and sisters, I am troubled by the rising tide of conservatism that is sweeping across this nation. I am not talking about politics—that is, Republicans versus Democrats. As far as I'm concerned, neither has set my people free. But I am disturbed by the anti-Negro, anti-Semitic, ungodly anti-American elements that have gathered around Senator Barry Goldwater. And every time you pick up a newspaper and you see all these folk coming out for Goldwater, if you take their names to the

[20]Lomax is describing a process that accelerated even more rapidly in the years following the speech. See Stokely Carmichael's speech which follows. Also compare Emma Goldman's observations on violence in the preceding speech.
[21]The meeting was held in a church.

NAACP and check them out you will find that these are people who have been hating Negroes for days. And if you take those who have been coming out for Goldwater (as we've done in New York) and take their names down to the Anti-Defamation League and check them out, you'll find out they've been hating and fighting Jews for centuries. Now this isn't a question of Republicans versus Democrats; this is a question of right versus wrong. And this is why I'm glad my own governor, who is a Republican, Governor Rockefeller, has gotten into the race; and I'm glad that Governor Scranton of Pennsylvania, a fine man, has gotten into the race; because if the Republicans can give us men like Scranton or Rockefeller, then between them and Kennedy next year,[22] we will have a choice. But I have said to Governor—to Senator Goldwater in a telegram exactly what I am saying to you. I charge him with being silent, with acquiescing in the support of known anti-Negro, anti-Jewish elements. I charge him with associating with those elements in the deep South which are determined to destroy all of our freedoms. I've challenged him to debate these issues. Other Negroes are going to do the same thing. And I have told the Republican National Committee (and I'm not alone) that if they don't stop Goldwater, we are going to stop the Republicans. (applause)

Let me make it very clear, I do not love Kennedy. I do not believe Kennedy has done what he should do, not only for my people, but on the whole, I think he has had a weak-kneed administration. But if the Republicans (slight applause)—if the Republicans go out and let conservatism win, and nominate Goldwater, then we have no alternative but to support Kennedy—not because Kennedy smells so sweet, but because Goldwater stinks so badly. (applause)

Now you're going to hear more of that as the days go on. But remember that the folk who back Goldwater are the folk who would return your world to seventeen hundred and thirty-two. They would have you pull out of the United Nations; have you invade Cuba; have you drop an atomic bomb, I imagine, on Vietnam; blow down the Berlin wall. But most of all Mr. Goldwater has made it clear that in terms of race relations he would leave it to the several states to settle the issue—which means Governor Wallace would determine what happens in Birmingham; and this is like having the devil to become the high priest of morality. Now that is said; you shall hear more of it in the days just ahead.

I then want to deal with three things—three things which I think need to be said and need to be cleared up, not only for the sake of Negroes, but for the sake of the white liberals who have joined us—and we welcome them in this struggle. Now I would warn you brethren before I start on these three things that I am not a preacher. You preachers have had your chance (laughter) at eleven o'clock this morning. Now you've been

[22]The speech was delivered before the death of President Kennedy.

preaching all day, theology. Now tonight I am going to preach some Negro-ology. We're going to get down to what it is that's got these little boys and these little girls hung up. See, I'm not worried about most of you, because most of you are either lost or you're found. (*laughter*) And most of you old folk Negroes—some of you if you could, you wouldn't move out of the Negro ghetto. Most of you are too lazy and too trifling to go out and register so you can vote. So I'm not worried about you. [*applause*] You see, and when the revolution starts, you're going to be one of the first folk on the list. I'm going to talk about tonight what has happened to these folk, and what's happening to these young folks, and what we must do about it if we're going to have a peaceful change from racialism to brotherhood in the United States, particularly in California.

Now I said—I suggested earlier—in the course of this one week I have addressed students in integrated—I guess you can call them integrated—schools throughout Northern California. And when I got to Sacramento (I guess it was something of an honor) Governor Brown sent his own private limousine over to where I was staying, with an invitation to me to come to his office and tell him what I've seen. So for two hours we talked, and he was all shook up (*stir*), by the time I left. And I suppose many of you to be in pretty much the same fix before the next thirty minutes will have rolled around. But a length of time has come now, and let's get some issues up on the table and let's talk about them; because we Negroes have been lying to ourselves and to white folks for a hundred years. And it's time for us to stand up like men and women and say it like it is. And that's what I'm going to do.

Now the first thing that must happen in this community, and it must happen all over the United States (and here's a role that you preachers that don't want to go to jail can play): we must tell our young people that they are somebody. We must tell them to wipe the stigma of inconsequentialness from their brow. You have been victimized for a hundred years by a system which taught you that not only were you inferior, but by a theology, Reverend, which for a long time at dead center said that you were a descendant of Ham who laughed at his father's nakedness; therefore you're supposed to clean babies and scrub floors for white folks, because they are your superiors. You've been victimized by an intellectual system which reeks back to some ungodly and unscientific thing (or really the thing was scientific, but their interpretation of it wasn't), a thing called the Linnaean web, based on the findings of Carl von Linnaeus. And they proceeded to argue that a man's ability to think can be determined by the shape and the size of his head. So they ran around with calipers and slide rules and yard sticks and tape measures, measuring black heads to see how long they were, and how wide they were. And they came up with the amazing conclusion: "Poor little black thing—he can't think." And so you put all this together, and the American white man had him quite a comfortable thing going for him for a hundred years.

He had him a ready source of menials, which his economic system said he must have. His conscience didn't bother him because his preacher told him on Sunday morning that God blessed him as he hung me from a tree and raped my mother and prosecuted my father. He didn't rest uneasy at night because in his concept of Jesus was the notion that Jesus was white and white is right and therefore he is right, and I'm black and therefore I'm wrong; so anything he does to me—it's all right, and he can sleep. He was buoyed up by an intellectual system, phony though it was, which told him that scientifically white men were superior to black men —that they could outthink us, that they could do anything but outfight us. (*laughter*) So there the thing moved.

And then of course as a result of this, you began to believe it. Most of you Negroes don't want to admit this, but most of the Negroes of the generation just ahead of me and part of them in my generation really believed what white people told us about ourselves. We went around straightening our hair, putting conk (and we still do it) in our hair, trying to be like what we thought beauty is. We spent a fortune on bleaching creams trying to change our complexions; and those Negroes who were lighter skinned than other Negroes walked around with their noses in the air saying, "Although I am colored, I am less colored than thou art." (*loud and prolonged laughter*) And we became—we became mesmerized and hypnotized by this whiteness. Everything we saw and everything we lived put us in this concept—of thinking less of ourselves. Examine the language of your society. Everything black is associated with something evil, isn't it? And everything white is associated with something good. To be kept out of an organization is to what?—be blackballed. To be put on a bad list is to be black-listed. On the day that something bad happens to you, you call it what?—a black day. You love cats, but the one cat you don't want to walk in front of you is a black cat. Anything involved with being black, we've associated it with being evil. By the same token, to tell a big lie is what?—a black lie. But if it's an innocent lie that doesn't really hurt anybody it's a white lie. (*laughter and applause*) Everything white in American society is associated with goodness, with happiness, with truth. And I don't want to get into a fight with you preachers, but if you go and look in your Sunday School classes on Sunday morning— I don't know what you do here, but when I grew up in Georgia they gave us little Sunday School cards. You got them, didn't you? And there on the front of my Sunday School card—and I remember very vividly (my Dad is a Baptist preacher) going to church, and they handed me this Sunday School card, and there was a picture of Jesus; and it was right after they had lynched a Negro outside Valdosta. And I looked, and here is this picture of Jesus. Look! blond hair, blue eyes, Nordic features, flowing robe, and sandals. And I said to Daddy—I said, "Daddy, this looks like Governor Talmadge to me." (*laughter*) He said, "Son, that isn't a real picture of your Lord." He said, "That's somebody's concept of your

Lord." I said, "Jesus didn't really look like this?" He said, "No." I said, "How did Jesus look?". And he did as he always did; he said, "That which you can find by reading I will never tell you. Go find it." And he led me to the Bible. He said, "Now the one physical description of Jesus —you'll find it somewhere in this book." And he just turned to the book of the Bible involved, and he made me read the whole book. This is the way he got me to read, you see (which was a good thing for me), until I found it. I finally came upon it, and do you know what it said? It said of Jesus (and this is the only physical description of Jesus)—it said, "And his hair was like sheep's wool." And if Jesus's hair was like sheep's wool, it means Jesus looked more like me than he does Norman Vincent Peale (*laughter and applause*).[23]

But you see what had happened to me is the same thing that happens to these young people. It is that we had been trapped. Look at what they go through—and I'm dwelling on this and I hope you're getting to it, because this is what's happening to your children, and I'm going in a moment to show you how this leads to them dropping out of school, and winding up in prison. So now you stay right here and watch what happens to them. They come up in this society—this white thing is borne in on their consciousness. Now they turn on television and everything you see is white. The whole image is white. You open up *Life, Look, Time* magazine; you see an article by me, but where they really make their money is from advertising, and you have yet to see anything but a white man, or a white woman in that ad. And then these little boys and girls go to school, right here, to start to learn to read. Have you looked at what they have to use to learn to read? Little Boy Blue isn't blue (*laughter*). Go look at a picture of Little Red Riding Hood. She isn't red. Go look at Little Miss Muffett. Go look at Mary, And I don't even have to describe the language. Everything in front of them is this white image. They open the history books; they salute the flag; and they start looking through the history book of America looking for them-selves, trying to find how they belong. How do they fit in what's going on in the San Fernando Valley? How do they fit with what's going on in the world? And they start turning the pages. They never see anything about themselves; they never see anything about their foreparents; they never see anything about their grandparents. The only thing they learn in fleeting is that once upon a time they were little happy black slaves, who enjoyed picking cotton and eating watermelon, and sang all night long. But there's not one positive thing in the whole history of American educa-tion that helps these young people develop a sense of dignity and a sense of worth.

[23]The point was sensible, but Lomax was wise not to give the Biblical reference. See Revelation 1:14.

Now brethren you say what difference does it make. It makes this difference. By the time these young people are in eighth and in ninth grade, with
what's going on in your world, they know that the world that's waiting for
the white boy in their class is not waiting for them. These girls know very
well that they are not going to wind up chief supervisor at the Bell Telephone Company. These boys know very well that their opportunities are
limited, and they get caught up by this white thing. And one of them will
say (as they say to me all over the country), "Give me one good reason why
I should stay in school." And you know what? It's hard to come up with a
good, honest-to-God reason—to explain to these young people why they
should stay in school. And I have come up with one reason, and I'm won-
dering tonight if I can get you to join me in that reason. And I believe we
could tell the young people in this choir and in this audience that they
should stay in school, because by the time they get out of school you and
I will have knocked down every barrier there is, and they can stand up
and be free men and free women. (*prolonged applause*) And by the same
token I'm saying to you young people tonight (and I want you to listen to
me), if I get my head kicked in for you; if I get bitten by a dog as I did
in Birmingham, Alabama, and knocked down by a water hose as I did in
Birmingham, Alabama; if I go through all this hell for you, when the job
comes you'd better be ready! (*applause*)

So I'm saying to you Negro young folk, quit doing the slop and doing
the twist. Fellows, don't worry about putting conk on your hair—you look
all right. Don't get worried about what's on top of your head: get worried
about what's inside of it! (*applause*) I want you young folks to stand up
and be somebody. I want you girls to go ahead and become typists and
stenographers. I want you to learn how to read and write and speak good,
clear English, so when I go down to the telephone company and run that
man out of his cotton-picking mind, you can do the job. (*applause*)

You see the Negro revolt works on two levels: with one fist we're going
to have to go out here and demonstrate, and yell and scream, because this
is the only way you're going to get anything; and on the other hand, Reverend, you're going to have to turn your church basement into a school-
room one day soon. You're going to have to take all these little boys and
girls in your church who get messed up in these so-called integrated
schools; being taught by white teachers who are afraid of Negroes, and
don't know anything about Negroes; being counselled by counsellors who
can't even save themselves, let alone save children; and you're going to
have to save these children, and you're going to have to take the basement
of a magnificent church like this, and bring in some typewriters, some calculating machines, and some adding machines, and get some teachers
white and black who know how to type, who know how to take shorthand,
who know how to count, and who know how to write English; and sit

these young people down and beat them over the head till they learn. (*applause*) And it's not enough for you preachers to stand up here and tell us to meet you somewhere in glory (*laughter and applause*), because I, for one, am unalterably convinced that there's no road to heaven that doesn't come through the San Fernando Valley first. And if I remember my New Testament correctly, Jesus said, "Whatsoever you bind on earth, that will I bind in heaven."[24] Well, if you make a mess of the San Fernando Valley they don't need you up there to mess that up. (*laughter and applause*) What I'm trying to say gentlemen, what I'm trying to say ministers, is this: the purpose of the gospel is to speak to the frustrations of the people. Jesus came to save those who were lost. The purpose of the gospel is to do more than to shout and to pray and say "amen": it's to make useful citizens out of the people. (*applause*)

So I want to see some of you preachers mix some Negro-ology with your theology, and tell your young black parishioners to stand up and be somebody. Tell them something about their own history and if they don't know it, and you don't know it, go out and read it, and come back and tell them, because until they know it they never will be anybody. Here I am living in America, having fought in two wars, paying more taxes than I can earn money; every time I look around a new burden is being put on my shoulders, and somebody's telling me that I can't go to the bathroom; I can't buy a hamburger; thou shalt not live here, thou shalt not go there; thou shalt not drive here; thou shalt not—and I'm walled in by this segregationalist nonsense. This white man is crazy. He may not know it, but I'm somebody. He doesn't know with whom he is about to tangle. Because, if the truth were told, I was somebody before I even got here. If you go back deeply enough into my African past—I don't know about you, but I can tell from the way I walk and the way I feel some mornings that my old folks way back in Africa were kings and princes. (*laughter and applause*) And when I dig back into my past, I find out that I was teaching mathematics and geometry, and plotting the course of the stars in the skies when the white man of Europe was still living in the caves of England and running from the Romans. I came to this country before he did, and I marched with Cortez right through here down into Mexico. When Governor Barnett was nothing but a wicked gleam in his great-grandfather's eye, I walked into the Mississippi Valley with the French. I'm somebody. And I came to this country, some slave, some free, but all black, and I was always somebody. When this country was ready to die, to break the chains of colonialism, I, Louis Lomax, black man, in Crispus Attucks, was the first man to die on Boston Commons to set these white folks free from England. I'm somebody. (*applause*) In Phyllis Wheatley I taught them how to write poetry. In Paul Lawrence Dunbar I taught them the rhythm of anguish. In Frederick Douglass I taught them the

[24]Matthew 18:18.

meaning of oratory. In Sojourner Truth I taught them the meaning of militancy. In Booker Washington I gave them one of the first philosophies of American education. In W. E. DuBois I said, "Look, Western man, you'd better use your head and think." In 1917, he said, "Nigger, go away. I don't want you in my war." And I said, "Move, white man; this is my country." And I ran over him and I died on Flanders Field, to make this world free and safe for democracy. And I came back with my head bloodied, but still held high. And in Jesse Owens I beat him running. In Marian Anderson I beat him singing. In Joe Louis I beat him fighting. In Jackie Robinson I beat him playing baseball. And in Charles Drew I took the blood from his veins and showed him how to make the blood bank. And in Ralph Bunche I'll run the world if you'll move over and get out of the way. (*applause*) I'm somebody."[25]

And this is why—this is why—this is why the ballgame is over. This is why the word "nigger"—you can forget it. If anybody's a nigger, he is. He created the word nigger. I didn't. He made the word nigger because he needed to have somebody he felt better than. He can forget it now, because God didn't make my sons and daughters to clean up his kitchen. And God didn't make my son so he could have chauffeurs and shoe-shine boys. But God made little black boys for the same reason he made little white boys: so they can grow up like men, and some of them can work in kitchens, and some of them can be President of the United States. And I shall not rest in peace till that day comes in glory. (*applause*) So then, number one, I'm saying to you Negroes, wake up. Get a grip on your own community. Keep your children in school. And when your children say, "Mamma, why should I study?", you say, "Baby, you study because I'm going to fight." (*applause*) And if the children will study and the parents will fight we're going to overcome just as sure as that light is bright.

The second thing I want to leave with you tonight—not only the notion that we must fall in love with ourselves, and have pride in our race, but I think we must develop a complete and total awareness, not only a sense of freedom, but a sense of responsibility. You see, freedom and responsibility are twins. You can't have one without the other. And this is why a moment ago I was saying to these young people, "Let me go yonder and fight while you stay here and go to school." And I would like to enlarge very, very briefly on that notion: to say to you members of the Negro community—and when I speak of the Negro community, when I use the word Negro, I mean everybody who is for me. Now you may be white, but as far as I'm concerned your heart is black, so you are colored. So that is that. (*laughter*) We in the Negro community have never taken full advantage of the opportunities which we've always had, and which are increasing day by day. And one of the reasons why men like myself find it

[25]For the most part Lomax cites the same names as are in the Borders poem, but his development is original and in many respects more eloquent than the poem.

so difficult when we sit down to tangle with the hierarchy of the white power structure (and we had this to come home to us in New York) is that they can look at us—and you see these white politicians—Let me tell you something. You have never in your life seen anybody as cold and as calculating as politicians. These men are playing, brethren, a ruthless game of power, a ruthless game of money. They don't hate you. They don't love white folks. They don't care. All they're concerned about is the perpetuation of themselves and their parties, in power, in money and in office. When we go to the bargaining table, and I'm sure that these people in the NAACP can back me up—when we go to the bargaining table to wrestle with these people, the first thing they throw in our face is this: How many divisions of voters do you have behind you? When you sit down with the mayor of this town, or any other mayor in the San Fernando Valley,[26] and you try to tell him what he must do—well, if you can't vote he musn't do anything if he doesn't want to do it. But when he looks up one day and all the church bells in Negro churches throughout this valley are pealing out (not the funeral dirge, but they're shouting for happiness)—when all you Negroes decide (and those of you who are not registered, that you're going to take off a half day from work, and look like you've been demonstrating for jobs, you're going to march down the middle of the street and line up at the polls) you'd be surprised how integrated this valley would get. I don't know how many Negroes there are in this valley, but I'd be willing to bet you that you could find 50,000 unregistered Negroes somewhere between here and Los Angeles. Don't you think so? I know. Now can you imagine what would happen in this valley if they looked up by the first of June next year, and you had put 50,000 of those Negroes on the books; and not only have they registered, but the fact, Reverend, that you led them, the fact, Reverend, that you were in front of the line and led your people to the polls, means you have leadership with your people. Then when you sit down with the mayor of the town and you say, "Come brethren, let us pray together," he will open up with, "Our Father who art in heaven." (*laughter and applause*) And the only way you can make him do it is to walk up from a source of great political strength rather than a source of great political weakness; and this is what you've been doing. So all of this campaign is not running and screaming in the streets. Part of it's living up to our responsibilities; and one of our responsibilities is to vote.

By the same token I think one of our responsibilities is to do everything we can, although we disavow and deny the concept of the Negro ghetto (because I think eventually in our world there must be no ghetto)—but to the degree that there is a Negro ghetto, part of our responsibility is in

---

[26]At the time of this speech, Lomax was not familiar with the vast extent of the city of Los Angeles, which includes Pacoima and most of the other communities of the San Fernando valley.

—it seems to me, to ourselves and to our community—is to live good lives, to live clean lives, to clean up our community. Maybe you have to live in a shack, but it can be a clean shack. You may not have but one shirt—I went all the way through Yale University for a Master's Degree on two shirts, because I washed one every night. We Negroes have come a long way, and like the children of Israel we are about to get to the site of the promised land. Don't get carried away now. The God that brought you safe thus far is going to take you on. Your job now is to move closer and closer together. Quit trying to be white! Be black, and be proud of it. Stick together! Put your arms around one another and learn to love one another. Quit killing one another! and get ready to fight the enemy. If your preacher is weak, stand behind him and make him strong.

You Negro men, stand behind your women like you're supposed to do. Take care of your homes, like you're supposed to take care of your homes. Don't leave all of your money in the dice game and in the liquor shop and at the corner bar. Bring it on home so your boy can have some shoes, and so he can stand up and be somebody in the community.

And you Negro women quit criticizing your Negro men, and saying we're no good. If we're weak, make us strong. If we are bad, save us from our sins. But most of all, look at Lomax and say, "He may be weak, but he's mine. He's mine. Whatever he is, he's mine. (*applause*) He's mine." If I fall, you fall, and if you pluck me up we're both going to walk to glory together.

You know why I'm disturbed, though. You have to be so careful, because when we say—we make it known to the white power structure that we're going to try to clean up and work on our community, then they try to take your remarks and twist them to mean something they shouldn't mean. Now that used to happen to me two or three times; so in case there are some reporters here, I'm glad this is being recorded, but I want to clear up a couple of things. The very fact that I say that we Negroes are going to clean up our communities and stand by our families does not mean that I am responsible for the Negro crime rate. And it does not mean that every time a Negro does something wrong somewhere, that I personally become responsible for what some crazy Negro does.

I was in San Francisco the other day, and a deranged, obviously deranged, Negro fellow walked in a church and assaulted a white woman. The next day, brethren, both San Francisco newspapers came out with editorials blaming the entire Negro community for what one deranged black man had done. The chief of police of San Francisco got on the telephone and called Nathaniel Burbridge, who is a professor at the University of California (he was a Negro), who was head of the San Francisco United Freedom Movement, and told Nat Burbridge that he should stop teaching school and personally lead the posse to find this Negro criminal. Now, had they known that criminal was a Catholic, do you think they would have called Cardinal MacIntyre or Cardinal Spellman to come and find him. If they had known that criminal was a Jew, do you think they would have dared pick up the phone and call the chairman of the board of rabbis for San Francisco, and suggest that he go out and find the criminal? Only to you—only to you does this happen. And it's happened to you right down in this valley hasn't it? One Negro does something and somebody tells you, you can't buy a house. You see, now I think we need to serve notice that we are not responsible for everything some crazy Negro does. I'm responsible for me. That's about all I can say grace over, as we used to say in Georgia. And I'm trying to say to you, be responsible for yourselves. But we're saying to them by the same token, if a Negro does a crime, catch him; put him in jail. And since you're so interested in catching criminals, for God's sake try to catch some of those who have been throwing sticks of dynamite in Birmingham, Alabama. (*applause*)

And of course, when you hear all this nonsense, and you hear it down in this neck of the woods, because I've seen some of your newspapers about the Negro crime rate—what they forget is the difference between a qualitative and a quantitative analysis of the Negro crime rate. It is true that the incidence of crime, and particularly theft, is higher in the Negro community than it is in the white community. But I wonder if they've ever taken a good look at what we Negroes steal. And I would like to suggest that if you were to add up all of the money stolen by Negroes in the San Fernando Valley last year, it would be about 39 dollars less than Billie Sol Estes got in one fell swoop. What they don't talk about is the fact that United States Steel, U.S. Rubber, General Electric, General Dynamics, Con Ed, every major pharmaceutical firm, every major public utility, every major industry, almost, in this country—in the past eight years, they all have been indicted for frauding and theft from the government. There isn't a Negro on the board of directors. There is a nationwide crime wave. But when something happens down here, then they ask you to go out and catch the criminal. Well it's not our job. We're not members of the FBI. Let the FBI go and get the criminals. But by the same token, and you must always learn these distinctions, it is a responsibility of ours to, within our powers, keep our communities clean, keep our communities committed to justice, to righteousness.

Finally, then, my beloved, I would say this: not only must you give your children the sense of pride and development of your race for yourselves, not only must you develop a sense of responsibility, therefore, about your community, but most of all—and sometimes when I look at my own life I think that this is what God has sent me here to say—most of all, we of today, black and white, must accept the terrible burden of saving Western civilization from itself. I don't know how much you read. I don't know how much you understand of what you see on television. And I can fully understand it, if after a long and hard and busy day you would rather not be burdened down with the ultimate meaning of Vietnam,

Berlin, Cuba, Africa, Asia. But it so happens, my friends, that in the past six months, I first spent a month in Cuba, and I'm now fresh back from Germany, where I looked at conditions in both East and West Germany. And I came home convinced that we've lost Cuba. We've lost Cuba because, not because they love Communism, but because they hate us. And they hate us because we went in there and talked about being white. And because we were white, we lived apart. And between our whiteness and imposing our white supremacy notion through a mulatto ruling class —between that and the greed, we not only turned Cuba against us, but we've set the stage to lose all the Carribean, all of Latin and South America if we're not careful.

Then I looked at Germany, particularly East Germany and West Germany—West Berlin; and at night I walked around talking to the Germans, and I'm saying to them: "Where were you when Hitler did this thing?" Nobody knew anything. I couldn't find a German who ever saw Hitler, who knew anything about anything. I said to one German couple, "How old were you when all this happened?" They said, "Oh, we were eighteen." I said, "Well, don't you remember Izzie Goldstein and Abe who used to live here? Didn't you miss them one day?" "Yes." "Well, didn't it occur to you to ask where they went?" "No." Nobody knows anything. Yet six million people died in gas ovens. God knows how many hundreds of thousands died on the battlefields. And yet, in Germany today nobody knows anything, nobody is responsible for anything. But the Germans said to me, "You really want to see something? Come on, we'll show you something." And they took me down and showed me the autobahn, which is their freeway, and God knows it is a beautiful freeway. And they said, "Look at our buildings. Look what we've done, how we've lifted ourselves up with your help during the war." And I looked, and God knows: magnificent skyscrapers. West Berlin is one of the most beautiful cities I've ever been in in my life. And finally I looked at one of the supreme persons in charge of the American occupation troops, and I said, "Man, look! I see the economic miracle of West Germany. Where is the moral miracle? Have these people changed?" The answer is no. The feeling against Jews there is as high as it ever was, but they're just quiet about it. And if you want to find out what they really think—and there may be some young men in here tonight who know more about this than I do—but you should look at those poor little black boys in the American uniform, the uniform of the American Army, who fly into Germany—and they are the occupation troops. And they come on leave into Berlin and go into a tavern; and day after day they are beaten and kicked and thrown out—their heads running with blood—black American soldiers. And we are supposed to be running the country.

Now what am I trying to say—see if I can pull it together for you—I'm saying, right before your eyes we're losing the world. I'm saying we lost Cuba out of a combination of white supremacy and greed. I'm saying that we went to war, destroyed Hitler because of his notion of Aryan supremacy, and we have allowed an economic miracle to occur, and we're proud of it, but we have not accomplished a moral miracle. And the reason why—and this is why we lost Cuba—and the reason why there has been no moral miracle in West Germany is because deep in the heart of America we have the same anti-Jewish, anti-Negro attitudes one finds in Germany. And so how can the pot call the kettle white? (*delayed laughter and applause*)

And the only moral movement moving in Western civilization today is your movement for freedom. Nowhere else in Western civilization is the free wind of liberalism. Nowhere else can you hear the voice of protest, the voice of pain, and the voice of anguish, crying aloud for freedom, for justice. Where else is it? Everything else is dead. Everything else is silent. But for the voice of the Negro, Western civilization is like ancient Rome. And you can almost stand on one of the seven hills, Reverend, and wait to see the columns fall. Decay, rot, immorality, homosexuality, all kinds of deviates running the streets, the institutions crumbling right before your eyes; and the only light, the only voice that's being sounded is the voice of men like Martin Luther King. His dream ricocheting across the world. The only voice is the quiet, scholarly, soft, yet dynamic Roy Wilkins, hammering away, hamering away, hammering away. The only voice is the quiet scholarly voice of an NAACP lawyer in a courtroom in Mississippi saying, "It says this in the book." We're not only out to save ourselves, but we're out to save Western civilization. For if Western civilization is to be saved, the thing you white folks call the "nigger" is going to have to save it, because you are lost. We must save you. The integration of the Negro is the setting free of the Jew. The enfranchisement of the Negro is the ending of discrimination against the Catholic. And if a Negro can get into a washroom, it will mean that for the first time in his life the White Anglo-Saxon Protestant can walk the streets of the world as a free man. And this is why tonight I commend unto you the struggle for freedom. I invite you to join with the forces of the world (not only of America, but of the world) in the denunciation of justice [*sic*], in the search of God through freedom, through liberty.

Just outside my home in Valdosta, some 30 miles I drove down the road one day, one comes to an old rickety bridge, way out in the woods all by itself. And there's a sign at the entrance as you come to that bridge. And the sign says, "Capacity load, 5,000 pounds, law rigidly enforced." And I remember driving up to this bridge, and I read the sign, and I chuckled to myself. I said, "Now here I am 30 miles from nowhere. Who in the world is going to enforce the law on this bridge?" Then I drove on the bridge. I got the answer. The bridge began to sway, began to rock, began to reel. And it became clear to me that that bridge didn't need a policeman standing there. (*slight laughter*) The bridge was its own law. And if you got on that bridge with more than 5,000 pounds you'd wind up in the river. In a very real sense the American Negro is the bridge Western civilization must cross if it is to save itself and set up a firm communication with the rest of the world. And at the entrance to that bridge, which is my body and that of my son, your body and that of your daughter, there is a sign saying, "Justice, freedom, now! law rigidly enforced."

We don't have any guns. We don't have any ammunition. Despite the lies you tell, we don't even have razors. (*slight laughter*) We don't have any money. You have the hydrogen bomb, the atomic bomb; all the artillery is on your side, and we have nothing; but here we are. I'm the bridge you must cross, Western civilization, before you can win back Asia. And there's no point in trying to stop Madame Nhu until you do something about Barry Goldwater. And there's no point in trying to invade Havana until you invade Birmingham. And there's no point in blowing down the Berlin Wall until you get Negroes across the railroad tracks in Pacoima, because they're all tied together. (*applause*) And so it is— my body—it stretches out, and this man must cross it, and the law is rigidly enforced. If he gets on me and he tramples me, I'm going to shake, and I'm going to rattle, and I'm going to make noise, and this whole thing is going to go plunging down into the sea.

But by the same token, this which makes me the bridge makes me the salvation. For history hath brought me forth then, for this hour. So then up ye mighty race. Join hands of one accord. Let us then, who love freedom, forget our ethnic and our religious origins. And let us commit ourselves to the task of liberating our sons and our daughters and ourselves from second-class citizenship. Let us kneel in, stand in, vote in, study in, do what we must, but make our world that which it must be. And it's only after we will have done this that we can link arms—Catholic and Protestant, Jew and Gentile, black and white—and march through the San Fernando Valley singing, "Free at last, Free at last, Thank God Almighty, Free at last." (*long applause*)

Stokely Carmichael

Black Power

To one who has studied the history of agitational movements, the recent developments indicating a profound division among leaders of the civil rights movement should not come as a surprise. The Chartist leaders of 1840 had divided into advocates of moral force and advocates of physical force. The anarchists of 1886 were the physical force faction of the socialist movement. The twentieth-century split between communists and social democrats is another example of the same phenomenon. In each case the physical force faction insisted that although they expected violence to come, they believed that it would be initiated by the oppressors, and when it did come they intended to be ready to reply in kind.

The black power movement is the physical force faction of the civil rights crusade. Like their predecessors in other agitational groups, black power leaders are vague about both their ends and their means. Although their speeches contain threatening language like that in the final sentence of Stokely Carmichael's Berkeley speech, there is little indication that CORE or SNCC leaders have any intention of initiating violent revolutionary action. Rather they seem to be seeking a political, economic, and social base of power from which to negotiate with the white community. At the same time, black power leaders reserve the right to meet violence with violence when others strike the first blow.

To Roy Wilkins of the NAACP, Whitney Young of the Urban League, and Martin Luther King of the Southern Christian Leadership Conference, black power looks like a regression to separatism and segregation. Speaking at Los Angeles, Roy Wilkins stated the NAACP position: "Negroes are Americans, citizens of the United States; their identity is here, as Americans. Separation isn't going to get us very far." On the other hand black power leaders in a private position paper quoted by the *New York Times*, August 5, 1966, asserted that, "We are now aware that the NAACP has grown reactionary . . . and stands as one of the main roadblocks to black freedom."

Stokely Carmichael was born in Trinidad in 1941 and moved to New York City eleven years later. Thus, like most of the black power leaders (Adam Clayton Powell is a notable exception), he is a young man. With the impatience of youth he rejects any advice to go slow. The organization he headed in 1966–67, the Student Nonviolent Coordinating Committee, originally got its inspiration from leaders like James Farmer and Martin Luther King, both of whom have cooperated with white people and solicited their aid, and both of whom have organized their campaigns around nonviolent resistance to segregation and suppression. But since Carmichael succeeded in ousting the moderate leader John Lewis in the spring of 1966, SNCC has asserted that black demonstrators will henceforth resist violence when it is invoked against them. White liberals, formerly welcomed by SNCC chapters, will now be barred from any policy-making role in the organization, although they may be given subordinate roles. As Carmichael noted in the Berkeley speech, whites must work in their own communities to change white attitudes.

The Berkeley Black Power Conference of November 1966 was not directly related to the Free Speech Movement of 1964–65, but many white students and nonstudent supporters of the FSM attended Carmichael's speech and applauded its sentiments. Also in evidence were members of the Berkeley Vietnam Day Committee. But the conference was organized and structured by Negroes, and like other meetings addressed by Stokely Carmichael during this period, it was directed to the attainment and use of black power as an independent factor, cooperating with, but not subsidiary to, white organizations with similar goals.

The text of the speech is from a tape recording. It has been transcribed exactly as delivered, and is reproduced here with the permission of the Student Nonviolent Coordinating Committee, Atlanta, Georgia.

(*applause*) Thank you very much. It's a privilege and an honor to be in the white intellectual ghetto of the West. (*laughter*) We wanted to do a couple of things before we started. The first is that, based on the fact that SNCC through the articulation of its program by its chairman has been able to win elections in Georgia, Alabama, Maryland—and our appearance here will win an election in California—in 1968 I'm going to run for President of the United States. (*cheers and applause*) I just can't make it, because I wasn't born in the United States; that's the only thing holding me back. (*laughter*)

We wanted to say that this is a student conference, as it should be, held on a campus, and that we're not ever to be caught up in the intellectual masturbation of the question of black power. That's a function of the people who are advertisers who call themselves reporters. (*applause*) Oh. For my members and friends of the press, my self-appointed white critics, I was reading Mr. Bernard Shaw two days ago, and I came across a very important quote, which I think is most apropos to you. He says, "All criticism is an autobiography." Dig yourself. (*applause and cheers*) OK. The philosophers Camus and Sartre raise the question whether or not a man can condemn himself. The black existentialist philosopher who is pragmatic, Frantz Fanon,[27] answered the question. He said that man could not. Camus and Sartre say not. We in SNCC tend to agree with Camus and Sartre that a man cannot condemn himself. Were he to condemn himself, he would then have to inflict punishment upon himself. An example would be the Nazis. Any prisoner—any of the Nazi prisoners who admitted after he was caught and incarcerated that he committed crimes, that he killed all the many people that he killed, he committed suicide. The only ones who were able to stay alive were the ones who never admitted that they committed a crime against people—that is, the

[27]Fanon was a West Indian whose works have been published in French. Best known is *Les Damnés de la Terre*, Paris, 1961. There is an English translation by Constance Farrington: *The Wretched of the Earth*, New York, 1963.

ones who rationalized that Jews were not human beings and deserved to be killed, or that they were only following orders.

On a more immediate scene the officials and the population—the white population in Nashoba County, Mississippi (that's where Philadelphia is) could not, could not condemn Rainey, his deputies, and the other fourteen men who killed three human beings. They could not because they elected Mr. Rainey to do precisely what he did; and that for them to condemn him would be for them to condemn themselves. In a much larger view SNCC says that white America cannot condemn herself, and since we are liberals, we have done it. You stand condemned. Now a number of things that arise from that answer of how do you condemn yourselves: It seems to me that the institutions that function in this country are clearly racist, and that they're built upon racism, and the question then is how can black people inside of this country move; and then how can white people who say they're not part of those institutions begin to move; and how then do we begin to clear away the obstacles that we have in this society, to make us live like human beings? How can we begin to build institutions that will allow people to relate with each other as human beings? This country has never done that, especially around the country [question] of white or black.

Now several people have been upset because we've said that integration was irrelevant when initiated by blacks, and that in fact it was a subterfuge, an insidious subterfuge for the maintenance of white supremacy. Now we maintain that in the past six years or so this country has been feeding us a thalidomide drug of integration, and that some Negroes have been walking down a dream street talking about sitting next to white people, and that that does not begin to solve the problem; that when we went to Mississippi we did not go to sit next to Ross Barnett, we did not go to sit next to Jim Clark, we went to get them out of our way; and that people ought to understand that; that we were never fighting for the right to integrate; we were fighting against white supremacy. (*applause*)

Now then in order to understand white supremacy we must dismiss the fallacious notion that white people can give anybody their freedom. No man can give anybody his freedom. A man is born free. You may enslave a man after he is born free, and that is in fact what this country does. It enslaves blacks after they're born. So that the only act white people can do is stop denying black people their freedom. That is, they must stop *denying* freedom; they never give it to anyone.

Now we want to take that to its logical extension, so that we could understand then what its relevancy would be in terms of new civil rights bills. I maintain that every civil rights bill in this country was passed for white people, not for black people. (*applause*) For example, I am black. I know that. I also know that while I am black I am a human being. Therefore I have the right to go into any public place. White people didn't know that. Every time I tried to go into a place they stopped me.

So some boys had to write a bill to tell that white man, "He's a human being; don't stop him." That bill was for the white man, not for me. I knew it all the time. (*applause*) I knew it all the time. I knew that I could vote and that that wasn't a privilege: it was my right. Every time I tried I was shot, killed, or jailed, beaten or economically deprived. So somebody had to write a bill for white people to tell them, "When a black man comes to vote, don't bother him." That bill again was for white people, not for black people. So that when you talk about open occupancy, I know I can live any place I want to live. It is white people across this country who are incapable of allowing me to live where I want to live. You need a civil rights bill, not me. I know I can live where I want to live. (*applause and cheers*) So that the failure to pass a civil rights bill isn't *because* of black power; isn't *because* of the Student Non-violent Coordinating Committee; it's not *because* of the rebellions that are occurring in the major cities; it is incapability of whites to deal with their own problems inside their own communities—that is the problem of the failure of the civil rights bill. (*applause*)

And so in a larger sense we must then ask, how is it that black people move? And what do we do? But the question in a greater sense is how can white people who are the majority and who are responsible for making democracy work, make it work. They have miserably failed to this point. They have never made democracy work, be it inside the United States, Vietnam, South Africa, the Philippines, South America, Puerto Rico, wherever America has been. She has not been able to make democracy work. (*applause*) So that in a larger sense, we not only condemn the country for what it has done internally, but we must condemn it for what it does externally. We see this country trying to rule the world, and someone must stand up and start articulating that this country is not God, and that it cannot rule the world. (*applause*)

Now then before we move on we ought to develop the white supremacy attitude, that we are either conscious or subconscious of, and how they run rampant through the society today. For example, the missionaries were sent to Africa. They went with the attitude that blacks were automatically inferior. As a matter of fact that's the first act the missionaries did, you know, when they got to Africa, was to make us cover up our bodies, because they said it got them excited. (*laughter*) We couldn't go bare-breasted any more because they got excited. Now when the missionaries came to civilize us, because we were uncivilized, to educate us because we were uneducated, and give us some literate studies because we were illiterate, they charged a price. The missionaries came with the Bible, and we had the land; when they left, they had the land, and we still had the Bible. (*applause*) And that has been the rationalization for Western civilization as it moves across the world and stealing and plundering and raping everybody in its path. Their one rationalization is that the rest of the world is uncivilized and they are in fact civilized;

and they are un-civ-i-lized. (*applause*) And that runs on today, you see, because what we have today is what we call "modern day missionaries," and they come into our ghettos—they—Head Start, Upward Lift, Bootstrap, and Upward Bound is into white society.

Because they don't want to face the real problem, because a man is poor for one reason and one reason only, because he does not have money, period. If you want to get rid of poverty, you give people money, period. And you ought not to tell me about people who don't work, and you can't give people money without working. Because if that were true, you'd have to start stopping Rockefeller, Bobby Kennedy, Lyndon Baines Johnson, Lady Bird Johnson, the whole of Standard Oil, the Gulf Corp, all of them, including probably a large number of the board of trustees of this University. (*applause and cheers*)

So the question then, clearly is not, whether or not one can work; it's who has power—who has power to make his or her acts legitimate? That is all. And in this country that power is invested in the hands of white people. And they make their acts legitimate. It is now therefore for black people to make *our* acts legitimate. (*applause*)

Now we are engaged in a psychological struggle in this country, and that is whether or not black people have the right to use the words they want to use without white people giving their sanction to it. (*applause*) And we maintain that whether they like it or not, we're going to use the word "black power" and let them address themselves to that. (*applause*) But we are not going to wait for white people to sanction black power. We're tired waiting; every time black people move in this country, they're forced to defend their position before they move. It's time that the people who are supposed to be defending their position do that; that's white people. So they ought to start defending themselves as to why they have oppressed and exploited us. Now it is clear that when this country started to move in terms of slavery, the reason for a man being picked as a slave was one reason—because of the color of his skin. If one was black, one was automatically inferior, inhuman, and therefore fit for slavery, so that the question of whether or not we are individually suppressed is nonsensical, and it's a downright lie. We are oppressed as a *group* because we are black, not because we are lazy, not because we are apathetic, not because we're stupid, not because we smell, not because we eat watermelon and have good rhythm. (*applause*) We are oppressed because we are black.

And in order to get out of that oppression one must wield the group power that one has, not the individual power, which this country then sets the criteria under which a man may come into it. That is what is called in this country integration. You do what I tell you to do and we'll let you sit at the table with us. And that we are saying that we have to be opposed to that. We must now set a criteria, and that if there's going to be any integration it's going to be a two-way thing. If you believe

in integration, you can come live in Watts, send your children to the
ghetto schools. Let's talk about that. If you believe in integration, then
we're going to start adopting us some white people to live in our neigh-
borhoods. (*applause*) So it is clear that this question is not one of integration or segregation. Integration is a man's ability to want to move in
there by himself. If someone wants to live in a white neighborhood and
he is black, that is his choice. It should be his right. It is not because
white people will not allow him. Or vice versa if a black man wants to
live in the slums that should be his right. Black people will let him; that is
the difference. And it's a difference in which this country makes a number
of logical mistakes when they begin to try to criticize the program articu-
lated by SNCC.

Now we maintain that we cannot afford to be concerned about 6 per
cent of the children in this country, black children, who you allow to come
into white schools. We have 94 per cent who still live in shacks. We are
going to be concerned about those 94 per cent. You ought to be concerned
about them too. The question is are we willing to be concerned about
those 94 per cent. Are we willing to be concerned about the black people
who will never get to Berkeley, never get to Harvard, and cannot get an
education, so you'll never get a chance to rub shoulders with them, and
say, "Why, he's almost as good as we are; he's not like the others"? So
the question is how can white society begin to move to see black people
as human beings. I am black, therefore I am. Not that I am black and I
must go to college to prove myself. I am black, therefore I am. And don't
deprive me of anything and say to me that you must go to college before
you gain access to X, Y, and Z. It is only a rationalization for one's suppression.

The political parties of this country do not meet the needs of the
people on a day to day basis. The question is how can we build new
political institutions that will become the political expressions of people
on a day to day basis. The question is how can you build political institutions that will begin to meet the needs of Oakland, California? And
the need of Oakland, California, is not 1,000 policemen with submachine
guns. They don't need that. They need that least of all. (*applause*) The
question is how can we build institutions where those people can begin
to function on a day to day basis, where they can get decent jobs, where
they can have decent houses, and where they can begin to participate in
the policy and make the decisions that affect their lives. That's what they
need, not Gestapo troops, because this is not 1942, and if you play like
Nazis, we're playing back with you this time around. Give ears to that.
(*applause*)

The question then is how can white people move to start making the
major institutions that they have in this country function the way it is
supposed to function. That is the real question; and can white people
move inside their own community and start tearing down racism where

in fact it does exist, where it exists. It is you who live in Cicero and stopped us from living there. It is white people who stopped us from moving
into Granada. It is white people who make sure that we live in the
ghettos of this country. It is white institutions that do that. They must
change. In order, in order for America to really live on a basic principle
of human relationships a new society must be born. Racism must die,
and the economic exploitation of this—of nonwhite people around the
world must also die. Must also die. (*applause and cheers*)

Now there are several programs that we have in the South among some
poor white communities. We're trying to organize poor whites on a base
where they can begin to move around the question of economic exploitation and political disfranchisement. We know we've heard the theory
several times. But few people are willing to go into this. The question is,
can the white activist not try to be a Pepsi generation who comes alive
in the black community, but can he be a man who's willing to move into
the white community and start organizing where the organization is
needed? (*applause*) Can he do that? The question is, can white society
or the white activist disassociate himself with two clowns who waste time
parrying with each other rather than talking about the problems that are
facing people in this state? Can you disassociate yourself with those
clowns and start to build new institutions that will eliminate all idiots
like them? (*applause and cheers*) And the question is if we are going
to do that, then where do we start and how do we start? We maintain
that we must start doing that inside the white community. Our own
personal position politically is that we don't think the Democratic Party
represents the needs of black people. We know it don't. (*applause*) And
that if in fact white people really believe that, the question is, if they're
going to move inside that structure, how are they, how are they going
to organize around a concept of whiteness based on true brotherhood
and based on stopping economic exploitation so that there will be a
coalition base for black people to hook up with? You cannot form a
coalition based on national sentiment. That is not a coalition. If you
need a coalition to redress [*sic*] itself to real changes in this country,
white people must start building those institutions inside the white community. And that is the real question, I think, facing the white activist
today. Can they in fact begin to move into and tear down the institutions
which have put us all in the trick bag that we have been into for the
last hundred years.

I don't think that we should follow what many people say, that we
should fight to be leaders of tomorrow. Frederick Douglass said that the
youth should fight to be leaders today. God knows we need to be leaders
today, because the men who run this country are sick. (*applause and
cheers*) Are sick. So that, can we in a larger sense begin now today to
start building those institutions and to fight to articulate our position,
to fight to be able to control our universities (we need to be able to do

that), to fight to control the basic institutions which perpetuate racism by destroying them and building new ones. That's the real question that faces us today, and it is a dilemma, because most of us do not know how to work.

And that the excuse that most white activists find is to run into the black community. Now we've maintained that we cannot have white people working in the black community, and we've made it on psychological grounds. The fact is that all black people question whether or not they are equal to whites, because every time they start to do something white people are around showing them how to do it. If we are going to eliminate that for the generation that comes after us, then black people must be seen in positions of power, doing and articulating for themselves. (*applause*) For themselves. That is not to say that one is a reverse racist; it is to say that one is moving in a healthy ground; it is to say what the philosopher Sartre says; one is becoming an antiracist racist. And this country can't understand that. Maybe it's because it's all caught up in racism. I think what you have in SNCC is an antiracist racism. We are against racists. Now if everybody who's white see themselves as a racist and then see us against them, they're speaking from their own guilt position, not ours. (*applause*)

Now then the question is how can we move to begin to change what's going on in this country. I maintain, as we have in SNCC, that the war in Vietnam is an illegal and immoral war. (*applause*) And the question is what can we do to stop that war? What can we do to stop the people, who in the name of our country, are killing babies, women, and children? What can we do to stop that? I maintain that we do not have the power in our hands to change that institution, to begin to recreate it so that they learn to leave the Vietnamese people alone, and that the only power we have is the power to say, "Hell, no!" to the draft. We have to say (*applause*)—we have to say to ourselves that there is a higher law than the law of a racist named McNamara; there is a higher law than the law of a fool named Rusk; and there's a higher law than the law of a buffoon named Johnson. It's the law of each of us. (*loud and prolonged applause and cheers*) The law of each of us. It is the law of each of us saying that they will not allow them to make us hired killers. We will stand pat. We will not kill anybody that they say kill, and if we decide to kill, we're going to decide who we're going to kill. (*applause*) And this country will only be able to stop the war in Vietnam when the young men who are made to fight it begin to say, "Hell, no, we ain't going." (*applause*)

Now there's a failure because the peace movement has been unable to get off the college campuses where everybody has a 2S and not going to get drafted anyway. And the question is how can you move out of that into the white ghettos of this country and begin to articulate a position for those white students who do not want to go. We cannot do that.

It is sometimes ironic that many of the peace groups have begun to call us violent and say they can no longer support us, and we are in fact the most militant organization for peace or civil rights or human rights against the war in Vietnam in this country today. There isn't one organization that has begun to meet our stand on the war in Vietnam. We not only say we are against the war in Vietnam; we are against the draft. We are against the draft. No man has the right to take a man for two years and train him to be a killer. A man should decide what he wants to do with his life. (*applause*)

So the question then is—it becomes crystal clear for black people, because we can easily say that anyone fighting in the war in Vietnam is nothing but a black mercenary, and that's all he is; anytime a black man leaves the country where he can't vote to supposedly deliver the vote to somebody else, he's a black mercenary. (*applause*) Anytime a black man leaves this country, gets shot in Vietnam on foreign ground, and returns home and you won't give him a burial place in his own homeland, he's a black mercenary. (*applause*) He's a black mercenary. And that even if I were to believe the lies of Johnson, if I were to believe his lies that we're fighting to give democracy to the people in Vietnam, as a black man living in this country, I wouldn't fight to give this to anybody. I wouldn't give it to anybody. (*applause*) So that we have to use our bodies and our minds in the only way that we see fit. We must begin like the philosopher Camus to come alive by saying, "No." That is the only action by which we begin to come alive, and we have to say no to many things in this country.

This country is a nation of thieves. It stole everything it has, beginning with black people, beginning with black people. (*applause*) And the question is how can we move to start changing this country from what it is, a nation of thieves. This country cannot justify any longer its existence. We have become the policemen of the world. The marines are at our disposal to always bring democracy, and if the Vietnamese don't want democracy, well then we'll just wipe them to hell out, because they don't deserve to live if they won't have our way of life. (*applause*)

There is then in a larger sense, what do you do on your University campus? Do you raise questions about the hundred black students who were kicked off campus a couple of weeks ago?[28] (A VOICE: "*Eight hundred.*") Eight hundred? And how does that question begin to move? Do you begin to relate to people outside of the ivory tower and university walls? Do you think you're capable of building those human relationships as the country now stands? You're fooling yourself. It is impossible for white and black people to talk about building a relationship based

[28]The reference is not to university students. A group of Negro high-school students from Oakland were invited to leave the Berkeley campus shortly before Carmichael spoke.

on humanity when the country is the way it is, when the institutions are clearly against us.

We have taken all the myths of this country and we have found them to be nothing but downright lies. This country told us that if we work-ed hard we would succeed, and if that were true we would own this country lock, stock, and barrel. (*applause and cheers*) Lock, stock, and barrel. It is we who have picked the cotton for nothing; it is we who are the maids in the kitchens of liberal white people; it is we who are the janitors, the porters, the elevator men; it is we who sweep up your college floors; yes, it is we who are the hardest workers and the lowest paid— and the lowest paid. And that it is nonsensical for people to start talking about human relationships until they are willing to build new institutions. Black people are economically insecure. White liberals are economically secure. Can you begin to build an economic coalition? Are the liberals willing to share their salaries with the economically insecure black people they so much love? Then if you're not, are you willing to start building new institutions which will provide economic security for black people? That's the question that we want to deal with. That's the question that we want to deal with. (*applause*)

We have to seriously examine the history that we have been told, but we have something more to do than that. American students are perhaps the most politically unsophisticated students in the world. (*applause*) In the world. Across every country of the world, while we were growing up, students were leading the major revolutions of their countries. We have not been able to do that. They have been politically aware of their exis-tence. In South America our neighbors down below the border have one every 24 hours just to remind us that they are politically aware. (*applause*) And that we have been unable to grasp it because we've always moved in the field of morality and love while people have been politically jiving with our lives. And the question is how do we now move politically and stop trying to move morally. You can't move morally against a man like Brown and Reagan. You've got to move politically to cut them out of business. (*applause*) You've got to move politically. You can't move morally against Lyndon Baines Johnson because he is an immoral man. He doesn't know what it's all about. So you've got to move politically. (*applause*) You've got to move politically.

And that we have to begin to develop a political sophistication which is not to be a parrot: ("The two party system is the best system in the world.")[29] (*applause*) There is a difference between being a parrot and being politically sophisticated. We have to raise questions about whether or not we do need new types of political institutions in this country, and we in SNCC maintain that we need them now. We need new political

[29]Carmichael spoke this quotation in imitation of a parrot voice.

institutions in this country. (*applause*) Any time—any time Lyndon Baines Johnson can head a party which has in it Bobby Kennedy, Wayne Morse, Eastland, Wallace, and all those other supposed-to-be-liberal cats, there's something wrong with that party. They're moving politically, not morally. And that if that party refuses to seat black people from Mississippi and goes ahead and seats racists like Eastland and his clique, it's clear to me that they're moving politically, and that one cannot begin to talk morality to people like that. We must begin to think politically and see if we can have the power to impose and keep the moral values that we hold high.

We must question the values of this society, and I maintain that black people are the best people to do that, because we have been excluded from that society, and the question is, we ought to think whether or not we want to become a part of that society. That's what we want. (*applause*) And that is precisely what it seems to me that the Student Nonviolent Coordinating Committee is doing. We are raising questions about this country. I do not want to be a part of the American pie. The American pie means raping South Africa, beating Vietnam, beating South America, raping the Philippines, raping every country you've been in, I don't want any of your blood money. I don't want it, don't want to be part of that system. And the question is how do we raise those questions. (*applause*) How do we raise them. . . (*phrase covered by applause*) How do we begin to raise them? (*continued applause*)

We have grown up and we are the generation that has found this country to be a world power, that has found this country to be the wealthiest country in world. We must question how she got her wealth. That's what we're questioning. And whether or not we want this country to continue being the wealthiest country in the world at the price of raping everybody else across the world. That's what we must begin to question. And that because black people are saying we do not now want to become a part of you, we are called reverse racists. Ain't that a gas? (*applause*)

Now then we want to touch on nonviolence because we see that again as the failure of white society to make nonviolence work. I was always surprised at Quakers who came to Alabama and counseled me to be nonviolent, but didn't have the guts to start talking to James Clark to be nonviolent. That is where nonviolence needs to be preached—to Jim Clark, not to black people. They have already been nonviolent too many years. (*applause*) The question is, can white people conduct their nonviolent schools in Cicero where they belong to be conducted, not among black people in Mississippi? Can they conduct it among the white people in Granada? Six foot two men who kick little black children, can you conduct nonviolent schools there? That is the question that we must raise, not that you conduct nonviolence among black people. Can you name me one black man today who has killed anybody white and is

still alive? Even after rebellion, when some black brothers throw bricks
and bottles, ten thousands of them have to pay the price, because when
the white policeman comes in anybody who's black is arrested, because
we all look alike. (*applause*)

So that we have to raise those questions, we the youth of this country
must begin to raise those questions. And we must begin to move to build
new institutions that will speak to the needs of people who need it. We
are going to have to speak to change the foreign policy of this country.
One of the problems with the peace movement is that it is too caught up
in Vietnam, and that if we pulled out the troops from Vietnam this week,
next week you'd have to get another peace movement for Santo Domingo.
And the question is, how do you begin to articulate needs to change the
foreign policy of this country, a policy that is decided upon race, a
policy in which decisions are made upon getting economic wealth at any
price, at any price. Now we articulate that we have to hook up with
black people around the world; and that hookup is not only psychological,
but becomes very real. If South America today were to rebel, and black
people were to shoot the hell out of all the white people there, as they
should, as they should, Standard Oil would crumble tomorrow. (*applause*)
If South Africa were to go today, Chase Manhattan Bank would crumble
tomorrow. (*applause*) If Zimbabwe, which is called Rhodesia by white
people, were to go tomorrow, General Electric would cave in on the
east coast. The question is how do we stop those institutions that are
so willing to fight against Communist aggression but close their eyes
against racist oppression. That is the question that you raise. Can this
country do that? Now many people talk about pulling out of Vietnam,
what will happen? If we pull out of Vietnam, there will be one less
aggressor in there; we won't be there. We won't be there. And so the
question is how do we articulate those positions?

And we cannot begin to articulate them from the same assumptions that
the people in the country speak, because they speak from different assumptions than I assume the youth in this country are talking about. That we're
not talking about a policy of aid or sending peace corps people in to teach
people how to read and write and build houses while we steal their raw
materials from them. Is that what we're talking about? Because that's
all we do. What underdeveloped countries need is information about
how to become industrialized, so they can keep their raw materials where
they have it, produce them, and sell it to this country for the price it's
supposed to pay, not that we produce it and keep selling it back to them
for a profit and keep sending our modern-day missionaries there, calling
them the sons of Kennedy. (*applause*) And that if the youth are going to
participate in that program, how do you raise those questions where you
begin to control that peace corps program? How do you begin to raise
them?

How do you raise the questions of poverty? The assumption for this country is that if someone is poor, they are poor because of their own individual blight, or they weren't born on the right side of town, they had too many children, they went in the army too early, their father was a drunk, they didn't care about school, they made a mistake. That's a lot of nonsense. Poverty is well calculated in this country. It is well calculated, and the reason why the poverty program won't work is because the calculators of poverty are administering it. That's why it won't work (*applause*)

So how can we, as the youth in this country, move to start carrying those things out? We must move into the white community. We are in the black community. We have developed a movement in the black community. The challenge is that the white activist has failed miserably to develop the movement inside of his community. And the question is, can we find white people who are going to have the courage to go into white communities and start organizing them. Can we find them? Are they here? And are they willing to do that? Those are the questions that we must raise for the white activist.

And we're never going to get caught up in questions about power. This country knows what power is. It knows it very well. And it knows what black power is because it deprived black people of it for four hundred years. So it knows what black power is. But the question is why do white people in this country associate black power with violence. The question is because of their own inability to deal with blackness. If we had said "Negro power" nobody would get scared. (*laughter*) Everybody would support it. If we said power for colored people, everybody'd be for that, But it is the word black—it is the word black that bothers people in this country, and that's their problem, not mine. (*applause*) Their problem.

Now there's one more thing they lie, and then we want to move on very quickly, and that is the lie that says anything black is bad. Now you're all a college and university crowd. You've taken your basic logic course. You know about a major premise, minor premise. So people have been telling you anything all black is bad. Let's make that our major premise. Major premise: Anything all black is bad. Minor premise or particular premise: I am all black. Therefore. . . (*delayed applause and laughter*) I'm never going to be put in that bag; I'm all black and I'm all good. (*applause*) Anything all black is not necessarily bad. Anything all black is only bad when you use force to keep whites out. Now that's what white people have done in this country, and they're projecting their same fears and guilt on us, and we won't have it. We won't have it. (*applause*) Let them handle their own affairs and their own guilt. Let them find their own psychologists. We refuse to be the therapy for white society any longer. We have gone mad trying to do it. We have gone stark, raving mad trying to do it.

I look at Dr. King on television every single day. And I say to myself,

"Now there is a man who's desperately needed in this country. There is a man full of love. There is a man full of mercy. There is a man full of compassion." But every time I see Lyndon on television, I say, "Martin, baby, you got a long way to go." (*applause*)

So that the question stands as to what we are willing to do. Are we willing to say no, to withdraw from their system, and begin within our community to start to function and to build new institutions that will speak to our needs. In Lowndes County we developed something, the Lowndes County Freedom Organization. It is a political party. The Alabama law says that if you have a party you must have an emblem. We chose for the emblem a black panther, a beautiful black animal, which symbolizes the strength and dignity of black people, an animal that never strikes back until he's backed so far into the wall he's got nothing to do but spring out. And when he springs he does not stop. (*applause*)

Now there's a party in Alabama called the Alabama Democratic Party. It is all white. It has as its emblem a white rooster, and the words, "White Supremacy for the Right." Now the gentlemen of the press, because they're advertisers, and because most of them are white, and because they're produced by white institutions, never calls [*sic*] the Lowndes County Freedom Organization by its name. But rather they call it the Black Panther Party. Our question is, why don't they call the Alabama Democratic Party the White Cock Party? (*applause*) It is clear to me that that just points out America's problem with sex and color, not our problem. (*applause*) Not our problem. And it is how white America is going to deal with those problems of sex and color.

If we were to be real and to be honest, we would have to admit, we would have to admit, that most people in this country see things black and white. We would have to do that. All of us do. We live in a country that's geared that way. White people would have to admit that they are afraid to go into a black ghetto at night. They are afraid. That's a fact. They're afraid because they'd be "beat up," "lynched," "looted," "cut up," etc. It happens to black people inside the ghetto every day, incidentally. Now white people are afraid of that. So you get a man to do it for you—a policeman. Now you figure his mentality, where he's afraid of black people. The first time a black man jumps, that white man's going to shoot him. He's going to shoot him. Police brutality is going to exist on that level, because of the incapability of that white man to see black people come together and to live in the conditions.

This country is too hypocritical, and we cannot adjust ourselves to its hypocrisy. The only time I hear people talk about nonviolence is when black people move to defend themselves against white people. Black people cut themselves every night in the ghetto—don't anybody talk about nonviolence. Lyndon Baines Johnson is busy bombing the hell out of Vietnam—don't nobody talk about nonviolence. White people beat up black people every day—don't nobody talk about nonviolence. But as soon as black people start to move, the double standard comes into being. You can't defend yourself. That's what you're saying. Because you show me a man who would advocate aggressive violence that would be able to live in this country. Show him to me. The double standard's again come into itself. Isn't it ludicrous and hypocritical for the political chameleon who calls himself a Vice President in this country (*laughter*) to stand up before this country and say, "Looting never got anybody anywhere." (*laughter and applause*) Isn't it hypocritical for Lyndon to talk about looting, that you can't accomplish anything by looting, and you must accomplish it by the legal ways? What does he know about legality? Ask Ho Chi Min; he'll tell you. (*applause*)

So that in conclusion, we want to say that number one, it is clear to me that we have to wage a psychological battle on the right for black people to define their own terms, define themselves as they see fit, and organize themselves as they see fit. Now the question is how is the white community going to begin to allow for that organizing, because once they start to do that they will also allow for the organizing that they want to do inside their community. It doesn't make a difference, because we're going to organize our way anyway. We're going to do it. The question is how we're going to facilitate those matters, whether it's going to be done with a thousand policemen with submachine guns, or whether or not it's going to be done in a context where it's allowed to be done by white people warding off those policemen. That is the question.

And the question is, how are white people who call themselves activists ready to start to move into the white communities on two counts, on building new political institutions to destroy the old ones that we have, and to move around the concept of white youth refusing to go into the army? So that we can start then to build a new world. It is ironic to talk about civilization in this country. This country is uncivilized. It needs to be civilized. It needs to be civilized. (*applause*) And that we must begin to raise those questions of civilization, what it is, who do it. And so we must urge you to fight now to be the leaders of today, not tomorrow. We've got to be the leaders of today. This country, this country is a nation of thieves. It stands on the brink of becoming a nation of murderers. We must stop it. We must stop it. (*applause*) We must stop it.

And then therefore in a larger sense, this is a question of black people. We are on the move for our liberation. We have been tired of trying to prove things to white people. We are tired of trying to explain to white people that we're not going to hurt them. We are concerned with getting the things we want, the things that we have to have, to be able to function. The question is can white people allow for that in this country. The question is, will white people overcome their racism and allow for that to happen in this country. If that does not happen, brothers and sisters, we have no choice but to say very clearly, "Move over, or we're going to move over you." (*loud and prolonged applause*)

Suggested Reading

In addition to the readings suggested in Chapter 1, there is a vast literature dealing with civil liberties. A few which might prove profitable include W. O. Douglas, *The Anatomy of Liberty*, New York, 1963; Sidney Hook, *The Paradoxes of Freedom*, Berkeley, Calif., 1962; Milton R. Konvitz, ed., *Aspects of Liberty*, Ithaca, N.Y., 1958; L. J. Barker and T. W. Barker, Jr., *Freedoms, Courts, Politics*, Englewood Cliffs, N.J., 1965; Irving Brant, *The Bill of Rights: Its Origin and Meaning*, Indianapolis, 1965. Sidney Hook's book incorporates his lectures at the University of California, Berkeley, in the Jefferson Memorial Lecture Series. *Aspects of Liberty* is an anthology of essays dealing with intellectual, moral, and legal aspects of civil liberties. In addition to these, the reports of a nationwide survey for *Newsweek* by William Brink and Lou Harris would be of interest. Brink and Harris report their findings under the title, *The Negro Revolution in America*, New York, 1964. Topics covered include: What Negroes want; why and how they are fighting; whom they support; what whites think of them and their demands. For specific civil liberties problems consult the American Civil Liberties Union, *Review of the Year*, New York, 1920.

For other materials dealing with the Negro drive for equality, see Louis Lomax, *The Negro Revolt*, New York, 1963; Martin Luther King, Jr., *Why We Can't Wait*, New York, 1964; Roy L. Hill, *The Rhetoric of Racial Revolt*, Denver, 1964; C. Eric Lincoln, *The Black Muslims in America*, Boston, 1962.

chapter 7

the rhetoric of anti-communism

The messages of the left and the right may differ markedly, but their rhetorical methods are strikingly similar. Both are convinced that a gigantic conspiracy exists to create or to perpetuate an intolerable evil; both are frustrated by the indifference of many people to their messages; both are convinced of the absolute rectitude of their own positions and the absolute evil of their opponents'; both believe that an extremely simple solution will solve an extremely complex problem; both seek to establish freedom for themselves and their associates without too much concern for the rights of others to equal freedom. Agitators on the left seek the freedom to interfere with social and business activity of which they disapprove; agitators on the right protest the regulation of business, taxation for the general welfare, and interference with their right to associate only with people exactly like themselves. To spokesmen of the left, liberals seem to support the oppressive status quo; to those of the right liberals are scarcely distinguishable from communists.

In wartime agitation increases at both ends of the political spectrum. If national danger is acute, as in 1941–45, or if victory is easy, as in 1898, the tensions are slight and easily surmounted. But in frustrating and little understood wars such as the Korean conflict, or the even less clearly defined Vietnam war, the pressure from radical agitators of both left and right grows rapidly.

Successful revolutions also breed fear and counteragitation at the opposite end of the political value scale. Because revolutions of the left

152

are more common in today's society, most of these counteragitations originate in right-wing groups and reflect the fear of radical change which the revolutions would produce. Reactions like this have produced the Alien and Sedition Acts of 1798, southern black codes after the reconstruction era, anti-Communist agitation after the Russian revolution, and the McCarthy era after the Chinese revolution.

In right-wing rhetoric, every move to modify society in the slighest particular is a revolutionary plot. The Communists have infiltrated the churches with the insidious doctrine of the social gospel; social scientists at the universities have doctored their data in order to impose revolutionary change and pervert the minds of the young; left-wing politicians posing as moderates have seized control of the Democratic Party and are trying to do the same to the Republicans. The most extreme reactionary spokesmen assert that liberals are poisoning their water with fluorides, imprisoning conservatives in mental hospitals, and removing their power to resist by trying to control the sale of firearms. Once the possibility of conspiracy is accepted no extension of the concept is too preposterous.

The spokesmen of the radical right are seldom personally oppressed by the evils they protest. Malcolm X could tell an audience of Detroit Negroes, "If you're black, you were born in jail," and his listeners would instantly identify with his idea. The threat to an audience listening to Senator McCarthy at a $100-a-plate dinner is more remote. Similarly a well-fed audience at Knott's Berry Farm could hardly feel physically threatened as they listened to Billy James Hargis. The threat is psychological rather than physical. It is their comfortable stereotype of life as it was, their value system, that the enemy seeks to destroy. Once that is gone, the speakers argue, the whole American way of life will follow, and Communist tyranny will be imposed.

But even though the threat seems remote or even unreal to outsiders, right-wing audiences listen attentively and approvingly to speeches like those reproduced here. Because feeling is intense, speakers use little restraint in language. Nothing is relative; there are only absolutes. Thus the language of the right blends with that of the left. The objects of the attack are different but the methods vary little. There are different conventions as to what language is permissible or appropriate to the audience, but within those conventions, the limit of intensity is reached.

The intensity of feeling and the audience's acceptance of the premises allow the speakers to use loose arrangement, touching on audience emotions and value systems, rather than arguing a case. When evidence is presented, the audience is likely to be uncritical about both its source and its relevance. If the evidence agrees with the listeners' point of view, it is accepted as proof. The speeches of the right and those of the left also frequently use the same support techniques.

Joseph R. McCarthy

The Red-Tinted Washington Crowd

More than any other figure at mid-century, Senator Joseph McCarthy was the spokesman for and the idol of the right wing of American political thought. His future course was scarcely foreshadowed in his first campaign for the Senate in 1946. Indeed his campaign resembled, in form if not in content, those waged in Wisconsin for half a century by the La-Follette dynasty which he succeeded. The younger Robert LaFollette, confident of victory against an unknown, had stayed at his desk in Washington until too late, and McCarthy's intensive grass roots, man-of-the-people campaign broke the LaFollette hold on the state. The new senator went to Washington without a clear program, and none emerged during the first year or two of his term. The Communist issue was yet to be discovered and exploited.

On February 9, 1950, Senator McCarthy made a speech in Wheeling, West Virginia, in which he charged that the Department of State was riddled with Communists, and that the Secretary of State (and McCarthy) knew who they were. Variant versions of his speeches reported that there were 205, 81, and 57 Communists in the State Department. Also it was never clear whether his charges referred to "card-carrying Communists," or to Communist sympathizers, or just to security risks. His critics charged that the confusion was intentional.

Almost at once McCarthy became a national figure. Each time he spoke his bulging briefcase became his trademark. "I have here a copy . . .," he would say, reaching into the briefcase and waving a sheaf of papers before his audience. Since no immediate answer was possible, the technique was effective and any challenge to the content of the papers virtually impossible.

McCarthy's opponents declared that the briefcase was filled with statements taken out of context, cropped photographs, distortions and misrepresentations. If so, he was not the first agitator or politician to use such methods. Moreover, the Hiss case, the aggressive actions of the Soviet Union, the rise of Communist China, and the Korean war had created fear and tension in American society and many were ready to listen to anti-Communist agitation. McCarthy's partisans dismissed attacks upon him as the work of a fanatical Communist conspiracy which was, in their view, rapidly taking over the federal government, the Democratic Party, the liberal wing of the Republican Party, and even the churches. McCarthyism became a counteragitation of formidable proportions, and McCarthy himself for three years intimidated not only President Truman and his administration, but President Eisenhower and his administration as well.

The speech presented here was delivered to a Republican campaign meeting at Appleton, Wisconsin, on the night before the 1952 election. It was broadcast nationally as the final word in a series of rhetorical exchanges between McCarthy and Adlai Stevenson and his supporters. The text is from a tape-recording of the radio broadcast, transcribed exactly as delivered. It is reproduced here with the permission of Mrs. G. J. Minetti, Senator McCarthy's wife at the time of his death.

Thank you very much, Steve Miller, and good evening to my friends and neighbors in my home town of Appleton, Wisconsin, and to the millions of Americans across the land who are listening to this radio broadcast.

First, from the bottom of my heart, let me thank my people of Wisconsin who gave me such a fine go-ahead vote on September 9th. Especially, especially do I thank the tens of thousands of Democrats who crossed into the Republican column and gave me their support. Now they were not voting for McCarthy as an individual; they were voting against the evil which besets this nation. They were voting against the evil of wars that we're afraid to win, corruption and Communism in Washington.[1] Now those Democrats have proved what I have long maintained, and that is, that the millions of loyal Americans who have long voted the Democratic ticket, that they are not Democrats first. They are Americans first, and Democrats and Republicans second.

Now I know, I know that those Democrats tomorrow will vote for America if the raw, harsh facts are laid bare before them. Now the duty, the duty to give the American people the facts, regardless of how unpleasant those facts may be—it is the duty of those of us who knew the people of America sent them to Washington to stand guard on the watch towers of this nation.

Over the past months and years, I have been devoting every effort of mind and body to paint the picture as it is so that an informed people can take action, as I am sure they will take action tomorrow when you elect General Eisenhower and give him Republican senators and house members. (*applause*)

This task, this task has taken me far from Wisconsin. It's been a long, long rough road. And it's good my friends, very good, very good to be back here with you tonight at home. Thank you. (*applause*)

[1]The Republican platform in 1952 was reduced to the slogan, "The three K's, Korea, Korruption, Kommunism."

Tonight I also want to tell you, the people of Wisconsin, how grateful I am that you were so patient with me in allowing me to spend so much time outside of the State of Wisconsin, in other states. I have been absent so much, relying upon the fact that you the people here in Wisconsin know where I stand, and how I stand, despite the greatest smear in the history of the state. I shall be very, very thankful, not only for your votes tomorrow, but also for anything you can do to get out and make sure that we have the largest vote we've ever had in the State of Wisconsin.

And just one more, one more brief message particularly to my Wisconsin audience. Last night, last night Wisconsin saw and heard a new low in campaign degeneracy and dishonesty. A man named Ed Morgan appeared with the Democrat candidate over state television and radio hookups. He falsely posed as a spokesman for the FBI. He is doing the same tonight, and here's the ad, my good friends, which appeared in your local paper. "FBI"—(where is it now? Here we are.) "FBI man answers Joe McCarthy." Well I knew something about this man; so I wired J. Edgar Hoover, and said. "Mr. Hoover, is this an FBI man, or is he a faker?" And I got a wire back about an hour ago, and he says that this man has had no connection whatsoever with the FBI—for over five years, and that he has no authority whatsoever to speak for the FBI, and I hand this wire to the press so they may see it. (*applause*)

Who is this (*over applause*)—who is this carpetbagger who's out here trying to tell you how to vote? He is a lawyer, he is a lawyer for the notoriously inefficient OPS.[2] He was the assistant chief counsel for the Pearl Harbor investigation. He wrote the infamous Pearl Harbor report. He also headed the staff of the unlamented Tydings Committee, and wrote the whitewash report clearing all those I named before that committee. And as you know, fifteen of those who were cleared by that report have since been removed from government because of either disloyalty or security reasons, and last night, last night he told the American people and again tonight—he said McCarthy just testified as a character witness for Earl Browder. Let's quickly examine this deliberate falsehood. Earl Browder was charged with having been in contempt of the Tydings Committee, for having failed to cooperate with them. I was called to testify and under oath gave the court the complete story of how Browder, the top Communist, under Morgan's and Tydings' coaching, cooperated whole-heartedly with them in whitewashing Browder's Communist friends. The court agreed with me and said he cooperated so fully he could not have been in contempt of that committee, although I said of course I have nothing but complete contempt for it myself.

But here in Wisconsin, but here in Wisconsin you see this last minute attempt to dredge up Tydings' right-hand man and bring him into this

[2]Office of Price Stabilization

state, and falsely pose as an FBI man. You wonder how low, how low they can conceivably get.

Now a week ago tonight in Chicago on a nationwide television and radio broadcast I attempted to pull together all the loose ends in the history of a man who wants to be President on the Democrat ticket. Yesterday, the Stevenson camp made what they called an answer to that history. A fantastic lying spree if I ever heard one. Now Stevenson has previously asked—asked the American people to judge him by the advisors that he personally selected. To that I said okay Adlai, let's do that, and I gave the history of those advisors. They made answer to that; let's look at their answers briefly tonight if we may.

Now one of the advisors selected by the Democrat candidate to help him to do his thinking and writing is Bernard De Voto. In Chicago I read some of De Voto's writings in which he ridiculed the FBI as a bunch of "college trained flatfeet." In the same article, which I hold in my hand, nothing secret about it, he urges that no one give the FBI information on Communists in government. Now, after I exposed him here is what he said. He said "Anyone who has read my writings," De Voto's, "knows that I am one of the most anti-Communist writers." I am not going to answer him. I am going to call upon a great witness to answer him. One of the greatest Americans I know next to Doug MacArthur and Eisenhower, J. Edgar Hoover, head of the FBI. I hold in my hand a letter which Hoover wrote. Keep in mind he wrote this before this campaign started. J. Edgar Hoover was not taking part in the campaign. Here's what he said. He said, "I have Mr., I've read Mr. Bernard De Voto's article, 'Due Notice to the FBI,' which appears in the October 1949 issue of *Harper's Magazine*. I do not care to dignify Mr. De Voto's compilation of half-truths, inaccuracies, distortions, and misrepresentations with even a denial or an explanation." Then J. Edgar Hoover goes on in this article to point out that "if De Voto's advice," his advice to withhold information from the FBI, information about Communists, if that "were followed it would be a great service to the Communist Party, and a grave threat to the security of this nation." Now there is nothing secret about this my friends. It's all down here in black and white. It is a cold, printed record and it cannot be erased by their shouting. And if anyone in my audience tonight, my radio audience tonight, questions the accuracy of this, I suggest that before you vote tomorrow you go to the public library, pick up *Harper's*, which normally I wouldn't recommend for reading (*laughter*), pick up *Harper's* for October 1949.[3] Turn to the article "Due Notice to the FBI," by Stevenson's advisor, and then get the following issue which contains

[3]It is hardly to be imagined that any substantial number of McCarthy's listeners would bother to look up the articles, but the reader of the speech would profit by testing McCarthy's conclusions by following his advice.

the letter from J. Edgar Hoover. To Hoover—. Now I ask the American people, especially the good loyal Democrats, when you go to the polls tomorrow remember that Stevenson said, "Judge me by the advisors whom I select." Then keep in mind that he selected as a top advisor a man who says, "If you know about Communists, don't tell the FBI." Now my good friends, what will his job be if a calamity does occur tomorrow and if Stevenson were elected? What job would he have? Would he perhaps have the job as head of the FBI? Who knows?

In Chicago I also called attention to the fact that another of the three men whom Stevenson selected as his advisors and speech writers, had urged that Communists be allowed to teach your children. His answer was—(listen to this. Here is the number one man of the camp.) When I said he urged that Communists be allowed to teach your children, his answer was, he said, "McCarthy was correct in quoting me about the fact that I felt that Communists have the right to teach in the Universities." But he said that "McCarthy took it out of context." He said, "He left out this phrase." Listen to the phrase that was left out. "So long as they do not disqualify themselves by intellectual distortions in the classroom." Do you know what that means? I don't. (*laughter and applause*) As anyone knows, a Communist teacher must be intellectually distorted, or he wouldn't be a Communist. (*laughter and applause*) We also know, we also know that a Communist teacher cannot know freedom of thought, nor freedom of expression. Unless he follows the Communist Party line laid down in Moscow, he is kicked out of the Party. Now in view of the fact—in view of the fact that we are a nation of God-fearing people, regardless of whether we are Jewish, Catholic, or Protestant, I also quoted Stevenson's top advisor's statement about religion. Here is the exact quote taken from the *Saturday Review*, the date May 24 of this year. The whole, let me quote it. "The whole record of history gives proof that a belief in God," here's a quote from Stevenson's man. "The whole record of history gives proof that a belief in God has created human vanity as over-weening and human arrogance as intolerable as the vanity and the arrogance of the Communists." This was taken from a review of Whittaker Chambers' book called *Witness*. Now some of you may have read it. You will recall that the theme of that book was that belief in God is the hope of our civilization. This idea was then ridiculed by Stevenson's advisor.[4] And what answer do they give to this? The answer which they gave was, they say "Oh, McCarthy took this out of context." Now of course I didn't quote the entire article. But if any of you care to read it before you vote tomorrow, go to your public library. Get the librarian. You can do it, it's there. Get the librarian to give you the *Saturday Review* of May 24, and then turn to page 40 and see whether this was taken out of context. But Stevenson says, "Judge me by the advisors whom I select." (*applause*)

[4]Arthur Schlesinger, Jr., later an adviser and speech writer for John F. Kennedy.

I fervently hope—I fervently hope and pray that the American people take his advice and do that tomorrow. (*stir*)

Now let's move on rapidly to the third of the three speech writers, an advisor picked by the Democrat candidate himself. They weren't foisted upon him. He said those are my men, those are the men I want as my braintrust. The third man, James Wechsler.[5] When Wechsler was confronted with the cold proof which I gave in Chicago, that he and his wife were members of the Communist League, what was his answer? He couldn't deny it. But he said, "Oh yes, but," he said, "I have reformed since then." Now my good friends, in that answer he doesn't state when, where, why, or how he reformed. He now edits a New York paper, which editorially in many respects follows the Communist Party line right down to the last period.

There you have the picture my good friends. There you have the picture of the braintrust that will be running Washington if the American people make a mistake tomorrow. And it isn't a pleasant picture—a picture of a man who says I want to be a President on the Democrat ticket, a man who says, "Judge me by the advisors whom I select." And we find that one of the advisors says "don't tell the FBI about Communists. Keep that information from the FBI." The second writer advises letting Communists teach your children—pervert and twist and distort their minds—ridicules the American belief in religion. And the third man. Third man Wechsler says, "Oh yes I belonged to the Communist League but I have reformed." (*stir*)

Now my good friends I do not tell you tonight. I do not tell you that Schlesinger, Stevenson's number one man, number one braintrust, I don't tell you he's a Communist. I have no information on that point. But I do know that if he were a Communist he would also ridicule religion.[6] He would also advise that Communists be allowed to teach your children. He didn't make any Communists unhappy when he did that.

I do not tell you that De Voto, the number two man in the Stevenson braintrust is a Communist. But I do know that if he were a Communist, he would also advise the American people not to give the information about his fellow Communists to the FBI.

I don't know; I don't know whether Wechsler, the number three man in the Stevenson braintrust is a Communist. We do know, however, that he has publicly admitted that both he and his wife belonged to the Communist League. We know of course that he claims that he dropped out, but with no outward sign, no outward sign of any change in the path he has followed. We of course also know that Communists don't mind lying, and if a Communist were caught red-handed as a member of the Com-

---

[5]James A. Wechsler was editor of the *New York Post*, 1946–1949.

[6]McCarthy avoids the logical fallacy by refusing to state the conclusion: "I don't tell you he's a Communist." But the listener is invited to complete the fallacy for himself.

munist League, he would naturally do as Wechsler does—claim that he had reformed.

The Communists, Communists you know don't wear, they don't wear their party membership on their coatsleeves. They work, the only time they can work, effectively, is secretly in the dark recesses.

And there my good friends you have the picture of his three-man braintrust. There you have the answers he gave. If we, the American people, make the ghastly mistake of selecting this man as President, they will still be his braintrust. As I have often said to my good friends who have said that Stevenson is Truman's puppet. I say that is not true. That is not true. Truman, I think, essentially, while a cheap little politician, is a loyal American. (*uproar and applause*) It took Truman— I shouldn't say it took Truman—it took the Acheson, Lattimore crowd a long time to surround Truman with a type of people who could control his thinking and pull the strings. But with Stevenson you have an infinitely more dangerous picture. Here you have a man, who picks as his top advisors the type of men whom I have named—men my good friends, were the left—if that were possible—who were at the left of the Achesons, the Lattimores, and the rest of that red-tinted crowd in Washington. They say vote for Stevenson— you'll get a change. You'll get a change my friends, but a change for the worse, infinitely for the worse.

Now in Chicago, in Chicago two nights ago, the Democrat candidate made this statement, and I quote his exact words. He said, "We are far from where we seek to go." A revealing and shocking statement. We are still far from where we seek to go. Now where do we want to go? Not where the American people want to go my friends. We don't want to be led by a braintrust that says, "Communists should teach your children"— a braintrust that ridicules religion—that says to the American people, "Don't tell the great FBI about Communists"—a braintrust, one third of which says, "Yes, I was caught red-handed as a member of the Communist League."

So I have been fighting night and day, for months and years, to expose and get Communists, and Communist-line thinkers out of positions of power in Washington. Tomorrow, you the American people will either get rid of the Communists and fellow travelers, or you will vote more of them into power. There's no middle ground tomorrow my good friends. Either you get more of it, or you get less of it. Now if you want a real change. If you want to get rid of the Communists and the corrupt mess in Washington, your task is to work all day tomorrow to make sure that we elect Eisenhower and a Republican Senate and a Republican Congress. That you can do. (*tumultuous applause*)

I especially call upon the loyal—I especially call upon the loyal Democrats of this nation. I don't call upon them to desert their party. But I call upon them to realize at long last that they have no party in Washington, and that the only way that they can regain control of that once great political party, and then scrub and flush and wash clean the foul mess that is Washington, is to elect General Eisenhower and give him a Senate and a House that will work with him. (*great applause*)

I think my good Democrat friends could pay a great service to the nation if tomorrow they would all be guests of the Republican Party. The way some of them do. (*applause*)

Over the past weeks you have heard over and over like a broken record, the admonition of the Acheson, Truman, Stevenson team. You've all heard it. "Vote for us because you ain't ever had it so good." And when General Eisenhower exposed the fact that the Stevenson team were asking for votes on the basis of war prosperity, the usual answer—Stevenson bled and screamed that Eisenhower was helping Moscow. Just how telling the truth and giving the American people the facts helps Moscow I still don't know.

Now let's, let's examine this campaign slogan of the Truman-Acheson-Stevenson camp. The slogan, "Vote for us because you ain't ever had it so good." I hold in my hand an issue of the CIO news, and no one has ever claimed that this is a Republican propaganda sheet, I don't believe. The date is significant, April 17, 1950.[7] That's just two months and one week before the Korean War. Let me quote from this CIO report. They say "more than four million persons are totally unemployed, and an additional six to eight million are working only part time. The unemployment figure is about a million higher than it was a year ago, and about two million higher than two years ago. And there is nothing at present to indicate that the situation will improve noticeably in the future." End of quote. Now with unemployment increasing at the rate of one million a year according to one of our great labor organizations, this meant of course that we were heading right smack into a depression. Well then what happened? About that time—about that time Acheson made his famous, or perhaps I should say infamous, public statement that South Korea lies outside of our line of defense, that we would not fight if the Communists decided to take over South Korea.[8] Now this was a most

[7]In the tape-recording from which the speech was transcribed, McCarthy misstated the date as 1952, an obvious slip of the tongue. However, it should be noted that McCarthy omitted one significant statement from the CIO editorial: "We don't intend to infer that there's a depression just around the corner or that the present unemployment situation is one which is rapidly pushing the nation toward a crisis." *CIO News*, April 17, 1950, p. 4.

[8]Acheson's statement was widely interpreted to mean what McCarthy says it meant. Actually, however, it drew a line through the island chain from Japan to the Philippines, and left the status of Korea ambiguous. It was never specifically excluded from American protection.

fantastic, a most unbelievable invitation for the Communists to take over South Korea. And when the Communists accepted the invitation, as they were bound to do, and moved into South Korea, then we landed our fighting men in Korea and have sent them engaging in a war in one of the most unfavorable spots on Earth, most unfavorable from the standpoint of winning a decisive victory. Now add those three things together, my good friends, tomorrow when you go to the polls. Add those three things together. They are not accidental. Number one: 10 to 12 million, fully or partially unemployed. Number two: Acheson says to the Communists, come on boys, take over South Korea. We won't interfere. And number three: the Communists accept the invitation and we move in. And since then, over a million Koreans and over 120,000 American boys have consecrated the hills and valleys of Korea with their blood. Now American mothers—American mothers—the mothers of the boys who died in Korea, must wonder why Acheson issued the public invitation for the Communist to take over—the invitation which brought on that war. There are only two alternatives. Either he as he said then believed that we would not interfere if the Communists took over. And if that's true this poses another question. What caused him and Truman to change their minds, if you call them that? And above all. And above all, why should we notify the Communists that they would have free wheeling in South Korea? The second alternative is that he knew the plan all along. The plan was to put American boys into Korea if the Communists accepted the invitation. If so, then why invite the Communists in? But what does, what does the Democrat candidate say about this? He says, "Oh it's a thrilling program, a thrilling program." Certainly, certainly Adlai it is not thrilling to the mothers and wives of the young men who have died in this war—a war which according to the administration we dare not win for fear of making the Communist Russia mad. Thrilling? Thrilling perhaps to red Russia who without losing one drop of blood has watched the destruction of the cream of our armed forces, the decimation of our air force, and the squandering of billions and billions of dollars.

Well, if you the American people agree with the Democrat candidate that it's a "thrilling program" you can decide to have more of it tomorrow. If, however, you are sick way down deep inside at the deliberate sell-out of America, a sell-out according to the plans, to the careful plans of the red-printed-tinted crowd who have been so bad for America and so good for Communist Russia—if you believe that, then you the American people can call for a new day of decency and honesty, a day of bright sunlight where there has been hopelessness and darkness. You can do it tomorrow by voting for Eisenhower and a Republican Senate and Congress. You can say to all of Hiss's friends in Washington and in Springfield, we are at long last through with you gentlemen, we are through with you forever, lock, stock, and barrel. (*Loud applause and cheers*)

Christ Was a Reactionary

Billy James Hargis, organizer and driving force within the Christian Crusade movement, was born in 1925 in Texarkana, Texas. He is the joint product of a small town environment, the depression, and God-fearing hard-working parents, who believed firmly in the American dream. His education was undiluted by liberal influences. Academically deficient for admission to Texas Christian University, he entered Ozark Bible College at Bentonville, Arkansas, completing his theological studies in a year and a half and being ordained to the ministry in the Christian Church at the age of eighteen.[9]

In less than five years, disturbed by what he considered to be indifference to the Communist menace in American churches, he began to preach against Communist and liberal influences, utilizing not only his pulpit, but the radio as well. Soon these activities absorbed most of his time, and he resigned his pulpit to devote full time to the organization which eventually developed into a nation-wide movement under the name Christian Crusade.

Hargis is constantly traveling to address anti-Communist rallies in cities throughout the country. From time to time he conducts leadership schools, not only at the national headquarters at Tulsa, but at such distant points as Miami and Los Angeles. At a typical school held at Tulsa in February of 1967, featured speakers, in addition to Hargis' staff, included such nationally known figures as General Edwin Walker, Ezra Taft Benson, Congressman Albert Watson, and John Unger, Sr., National Commander of Disabled American Veterans.[10]

Local rallies addressed by Hargis usually feature short appearances by or introductions of local leaders, but the major participation is by members of his personal staff. An important part of such a meeting is the raising of money to combat the menace of Com-

[9]For background material on Billy James Hargis, I am indebted to Dale Leathers, whose Ph.D. thesis at the University of Minnesota, 1965, included Hargis in *A Descriptive Study of Revolutionary Reaction of the 1960's: The Rhetoric of Salvation*.

[10]Program of the Sixth Annual Leadership School, Tulsa, February 20-24, 1967. Other widely known figures listed in Hargis' advisory board include T. Coleman Andrews, Eisenhower's Director of Internal Revenue; Colonel Curtis Dall, onetime son-in-law of Franklin D. Roosevelt; Walter Knott, of Knott's Berry Farm; Clarence E. Manion, former Dean of Notre Dame Law School; and Major General C. A. Willoughby, Chief of Intelligence to General MacArthur during World War II and the Korean War.

munism and the more subtle insidious influence of liberalism in both politics and religion. His audiences are composed almost exclusively of those committed to the aims he espouses.

To Hargis the central issue of the twentieth century is a fight between those who are trying to preserve the fundamental values of America, and those who seek to subvert those values. As he told Dale Leathers in an interview at Tulsa, "The only thing I will assume is, one, that America is right, that this country is right, and second, that God is right."[11] Presumably Hargis, by careful study of the Bible, knows exactly what God wants. His opponents, by neglecting the Bible are undermining fundamental Christian values, which, in essence, are also fundamental American values. Because liberal leaders have no faith, they are leading the country into evil ways, and a righteous God will have no choice but to punish not only the leaders, but also those who follow them.[12] Christian Crusade offers the alternative to both the religious and the political heresies, and an opportunity to turn aside God's wrath.

The speech produced here, typical of those being given by Hargis at the time, was delivered at Long Beach Municipal Auditorium, February 12, 1967. It was recorded by Ronald Garr and transcribed exactly as delivered, except for a portion of the first and last sections of the speech. The content of the omitted portions is indicated in the text, and the title has been supplied by inference from one of the statements in the text. The speech is printed here with the permission of Billy James Hargis.

[The first twenty-three minutes of Dr. Hargis' speech at Long Beach was a low keyed warm-up of his audience. He included greetings to members of his audience, personalized versions of stock stories, a reference to his appearance the night before on the Joe Pyne Show, notice of radio stations where his regular broadcasts are carried, and other matters of interest to his highly partisan audience. Following this informal introduction, the body of the speech was presented in a much more dynamic delivery often rising to a rapid and forceful crescendo. The text begins at the end of the informal section.]

Now this afternoon rather than delivering you some sort of pat speech, I'm just going to talk about several issues that I feel are very interesting and issues that I think you'd like to think along and about.

The sixteenth chapter of Matthew, the first three verses. "The Pharisees also with the Sadducees came, and tempting, desired Jesus that he would show them a sign from Heaven." Of course they were always trying to trap him too. They were always trying to discredit him. You know, my

11Leathers, *op. cit.*, p. 130 (see note 9).
12To Hargis, faith is a source of certain knowledge, superior even to empirical fact.

friends, Christ was a reactionary, and all the apostles were reactionaries. The church has always been a reactionary institution. God help the church when it goes to sleep in society and no longer reacts to evil. That's what's happening.

Today's modernistic, liberal church is wedding the state; it's marrying the state. Consequently it's no longer a reactionary institution. It doesn't stand for any convictions; it has no convictions. Why the majority of our churches have even compromised on the matter of morals. They now talk of the new morality. There are no moral restraints. There are no moral guidelines. There are no Bible teachings on morality according to these liberal clergymen. They say that anything is moral until it hurts some-body. If it doesn't hurt anyone, it's not immoral, or amoral. Well of course the church is not resisting; the church is not reacting. It's compromised on even moral convictions. It's compromised with atheism even on its supernatural beliefs. Atheism says that the virgin birth of Christ was impossible. The majority of your clergymen today go along with the atheists and the agnostics and say that Christ was not virgin-born. And now there are some among the churchmen who are saying that God is dead. This is complete compromise.

I still contend that all the problems we have in America today could be solved if every preacher in the United States would preach the Bible that he on his knees at ordination swore that he would uphold. (*Applause, covering next phrase*) If they were merely preaching the Bible, we'd have no difficulty at all. (*continued applause*) The reason we have Com-munism internally, the reason you have Berkeleys, the reason you have demonstrations such as you had on Sunset Strip last night is because of a moral breakdown in the land, a lessening of conviction, a lessening of moral conviction, especially. This is due to the preachers who have made peace with the world. They've compromised with the world; they've appeased the world. They no longer stand.

That's the reason that I said on the Pyne program, and I say it again here tonight, that one of my main goals in life is to get you out of these denominations that are in the National Council of Churches, that have compromised the faith, denied the God of our fathers (*applause*), and get you into Bible believing churches. (*continued applause*) Why should you as a political conservative attend a liberal church? It's most inconsistent. I don't know of any political liberals that inconsistent. Show me a political liberal, one that supports Hubert Horatio and mop-headed Bobby, and I guarantee you that he'll go to a liberal church. A man that's a liberal politically wouldn't think of attending a theologically orthodox church. At least they're more consistent than we are. But how many conservatives today are financing and underwriting liberal churches. It doesn't make sense. You should put your money and your influence in a church where the preacher will take a stand for Christ against Communism. And if you can't find a church like that in your neighborhood, keep looking until you find one. And if you can't find one ultimately, start one. Your support and your influence should be in a church that takes a stand for Christ and against Communism. Your support and your influence should be in a church that has nothing to do with the National Council of Churches.

You talk about revival, and these preachers are saying we need revival, and what we've got to have is revival. How in the world can you have revival until you convert your preachers? What if you do revive the laymen? What are they going to be fed? They'll be starved to death the first Sunday they're in church. The first Sunday they go to church and the preacher preaches on the gospel according to Martin Luther King, you've destroyed it all. That's our problem; they're preaching the gospel accordinging to Martin Luther King, instead of the gospel according to Matthew, Mark, Luke, and John. They've compromised with the world; they're at peace with the world. They don't want to disturb their relationship with the world, and especially with the organized society.

And so my friends, the church of Jesus Christ had better be reactionary. I don't really get mad if they call me a reactionary. They called Christ a rabble rouser. Did you know that? On the night of his betrayal the only charge they brought against Jesus that was accurate was when they said he stirs up the people, and thank God he did that. He stirred up the people against the corrupt state and against the corrupt religious system of his day. He would not compromise with Rome and he would not compromise with the apostate church of his time. Jesus stood out as a sore thumb. He wouldn't join the Pharisee camp; he wouldn't join the Sadducee camp. He stood alone but he stood with God. And he taught us that alone with God we are a majority. Do you believe that? Do you believe that? (*applause*)

So we read here where . . . oh, this is interesting. Here was the first ecumenical move. The Pharisees were extreme radicals. They believed that unless you went to their church, that unless you agreed with their theological interpretations, you were absolutely lost. Unless you observed their ritual, unless you towed their line, unless you accepted their dictates, theological dictates, you were absolutely done in. The Sadducees on the other hand were liberals. They didn't believe in resurrection after death. They didn't believe in any of the orthodox teachings of Judaism.

These people hated each other, but they hated Christ more than they hated each other. Isn't this interesting? They hated each other. They couldn't cooperate with each other but they came together in some sort of a temporary ecumenical movement in their determination to destroy Christ. Because Christ opposed both—both alternatives or both extremes. Christ opposed this false Phariseeism, but he also opposed this liberal Sadduceeism. And so Christ came among them; they joined together; they sought to destroy him; they tempted him, desiring him to perform a miracle so they could repudiate him, castigate him.

Verse 2, he answered and said; he didn't do what they said. Why should I? Why should you? Last night if I had just answered yes or no they would have torn me apart on that program. I decided in the first two minutes that that program—that they—that its intent was to destroy me in this community. So I took the bull by the horns. I grabbed the initiative. I got off the defensive and got on the offensive. And that's what the church of Jesus Christ ought to do. (*applause*)

So you're a member of a conservative organization. Why should you apologize for it? I guarantee you I will not be a member of any organization that I have to apologize for being a member of that organization. You should be proud of your affiliation. You should be proud of your fundamental concepts. You should be proud of your orthodox beliefs. You should be proud of your stand for Christ against Communism. You should get on the offensive and let the world know that God's on the throne. He's not dead, and that you're God's representative, and you are absolutely on the forefront in the fight for Christ against Communism. (*applause*)

That's the reason we talk about leadership. We don't want people in the ranks; we want people in the leadership position. We want you to influence your community. Don't let your community influence you. You influence the community! Today the liberal church, the National Council of Churches' affiliated denominations have let the world influence them. They are being completely influenced by the world, by the political system especially. I don't intend to let the world influence me. I intend to influence the world. I'm a leader, not a follower. Christians should be leaders, not followers. I am more than a conqueror through Jesus Christ who strengthens me, the scripture says. You are a leader in Christ; you're not a follower. There's only one person above you and that is the person of Jesus Christ himself. The apostle Paul says in the scriptures, my friends, that you're a priest in the sight of God. You're a priest in the sight of God. You can go directly to God in prayer. You can get your orders through your understanding of the scriptures, your discerning of the scriptures and the leadership of the Holy Spirit. So, therefore, take a place of leadership.

There are two ways to betray your country. One way is by actually joining in with the conspirators, to destroy it, like the Communist or the extreme left liberals. You can participate in a conspiracy designed to destroy your country. That's one way to destroy it. But there's a second way. The second way is called silence. When in your heart you know that you should be shouting from the rooftops, "Repent!" when you should be exposing the enemies of God's church, when you should be defending God's truth and you refuse to do it because of cowardice or timidity or any other reason— that, my friends, is just as bad as the man who actually participates knowingly in a conspiracy. You destroy the work of Christ by a conspiracy of silence.

Thanks be to God that you people here this afternoon, that most of you, at least those of you who are supporters of Christian Crusade, you distinguish yourself by standing out in your communities as leaders. You talked when you should talk. You have been willing to bare your breasts to the bullets of the enemy, to stand up for Christ and against Communism. You've stood for your convictions. It's hurt you financially. Some of you have lost positions as did Bill Manahan. Some of you have suffered socially. Some of you have been looked down upon and been referred to as extremists and kooks and everything else. But you stood. Having done all, stand, the scripture says. And having done all, stand! I will never apologize that I believe Jesus Christ is the hope of the world, and that I believe that America is God's greatest nation under the living sun. I don't apologize for that. (*applause*)

We can win if we make up our minds to victory. If we want victory, we can have victory. People went around with their faces down saying we lost in 1964. You remember what I said, and I say it again; we did not lose. It was the first time in my life that 27,000,000 Americans stood up and were counted for conservative candidates. That was the greatest victory I ever saw for conservatives. (*applause*) If we could just have encouraged those people to reach one more person, to go on out and win one more person, we would have had a greater victory than we had in 1966. Listen my friends, we won a victory in November, 1966. We have in the House of Representatives today in Washington, D.C., a conservative, a conservative coalition made up of conservative Democrats and conservative Republicans. This is the first time this has happened for years. You have a conservative coalition in the House of Representatives today. And you have a conservative coalition in the Senate if you go out and whip these liberal Senators when they come up for re-election in 1968. (*applause*)

Now look, they have taken away my tax exempt status because I backed prayer and Bible reading on a voluntary basis in public schools; so they've taken the muzzle off of me. I can now say whatever I want to say, so I'm serving notice this afternoon. I am glad I'm living in 1967, and I'm going to do everything in my power to defeat Lyndon B. Johnson and Hubert Horatio Humphrey in 1968. (*applause*) So L.B.J. had better start campaigning; I am. (*laughter*) The campaign has already started. I haven't got money enough for buttons but I'm already campaigning. Ladies and gentlemen, I am out to defeat every candidate that runs for office from state to national, Republican or Democrat. I'm after these liberals who are soft on Communism, these liberals who preach the welfare state instead of the free enterprise concept, these liberals who contend God is dead. I say that it's high time that we wrestle control of our state governments and national government from these liberals that are destroying us from within and put it in the hands of men like Ronald Reagan who love their country and will stand up for their country. (*applause*)

Now we've got to get back to this text. So Christ was the reactionary spiritual influence of his time. He didn't toe the mark. He didn't accept the jurisdiction of the liberals or the extreme Pharisees who felt they alone had the keys to the Kingdom. Christ stood up; he opposed. His whole ministry was one of opposition. Christ opposed. Christ stood upon his convictions. And it was because he was a reactionary they railroaded him to the cross. You and I know that God willed the death of Christ because without the shedding of blood there is no remission of sin. God looked down through the centuries, saw the sin of man, and He knew the only way that man could ever be saved was for Christ to die for us. So God permitted, God allowed this horrible crucifixion of His only be-gotten son.

The people who were responsible were those, especially, apostate religious leaders of his time. Remember it wasn't the Romans that rail-roaded Him to the cross. Oh, they drove the nails in His hands. And it was a Roman citizen that thrust the spear in His side. But He was brought to Golgotha Summit and bound to the cross by an apostate clergy, a clergy who had made its peace with the world, a clergy who had wed-ded the Roman Empire, and a clergy that didn't want a disturbing influ-ence in its midst, raising up the people, rousing up the people in protest to its false leadership. So the clergy saw to it that the crowd that said, "Hosanna, blessed be the name of God," on Sunday, the next Friday the same throats, the same hypocritical throats cried, "Crucify!" Who did it? Who manipulated this fickle crowd, caused them to crucify the Lord of glory? The apostate clergy of his day. It was the chief priests, the clergy, the priests who railroaded and manipulated Him to the cross, thinking that the grave, the Tomb of Joseph of Arimathea would hold Him. But thanks be to God, there has never been a tomb dug that could hold the Son of God. He came forth from the grave. And He triumphed and in time those chief priests were forgotten. The names of the priests who caused the crowd to say, "Crucify Him," have been buried in the sands of time. Today we only remember the reactionary. We only remember the one who was opposed, the one who was killed because of His opposi-tion to an apostate religious system of His time, the name of Jesus Christ.

I tell you quite frankly, my friends, I think this conservative element in America, these anti-Communists who are called by their opponents right-wingers, extremists, this little conservative minority in this nation that have not bowed the knee to Baal, that have stood for their convic-tions, that have suffered financial hardship, that have suffered social op-position in order to stand for their convictions, I believe that that little remnant of conservatives in America is God's leaven that leaveneth the

lump. I believe it's God's people, it's God's chosen ones for this generation, this time, and with the help of God we're going to see the greatest
victory for conservatism that we ever dreamed of in 1968. (*applause*)

So Christ answered and said, refusing to let them call the tune, He
said when it's evening you say it will be fair weather, for the skies—
(how many of you have ever forecast the weather that way?) In the
evening when you have a beautiful sunset, you say chances are it's going
to be a beautiful day tomorrow. Any of you fellows that fish, you know
that that's about the only forecast that we have. We go out on a lake,
when we've only got a day or two, and we look very carefully at the
sunset in the western sky. If it's beautiful, we're assured that tomorrow
we're going to have a good day. We'll get out on the lake early. We'll
have a wonderful time. Christ says that you look at the morning sunset;
he says if in early morning the sun looks like setting instead of rising, if
the eastern sky looks like a sunset in the western sky then you know it's
going to be foul weather today. He says you can discern the face of the
sky. You can tell by the sunset in the west or the sunrise in the east what
the weather is going to be in the next few hours. But notice this, "Oh,
ye hypocrites, you can discern the face of the sky but you cannot discern
the signs of the times."

Now that's what's wrong with the laymen that stay in the National
Council of Churches; that's what's wrong with Americans who continue to
support these soft-on-Communism liberals. They cannot discern the sign
of the times. They're not knowledgeable. They haven't been awakened.
That's where we come in. We have to awaken them. We have to make
them knowledgeable. That's why we use radio. That's why we use mass
publication. That's why we use rallies like this. We have five teams on the
road conducting these rallies each month to try to reach the people.
You're not going to save this country by sitting behind a lovely desk
someplace. You're going to have to go out on the highways and byways
and compel them with the truth, not with force but with the naked presentation of facts; because Jesus said, "Ye shall know the truth, and the
truth shall make you free." We have to get the facts out. That's what
we're dedicated to. We're dedicated to getting the truth out concerning
the enemy and the mistakes of our mistaken liberal opponents, and the
end results of these tragic mistakes, the tragic results I should say, of
their mistakes.

We have to learn to discern. We have to teach others to discern. Now
we pick up the newspaper. You saw that program last night. That attorney
from Chicago, Illinois—quite frankly he hurt his cause much more than
he helped it. That man inferred that it was Jesus Christ and Christians
who had brought Adolf Hitler on the stage. Now ladies and gentlemen,
this is, this is terrible; this is blasphemy, Adolf Hitler in the first place
politically was a socialist. He wasn't an anti-Communist. He wasn't a
free-enterpriser conservative. In the first place, Adolf Hitler was a socia-

list. His party was National Socialism. These men even refused to define the meaning of Naziism. I say Nazism, but they didn't like that so I'll speak correctly—for their sake. Naziism simply means National Socialism. Hitler was a socialist. Hitler was a left-winger. Mussolini was a socialist. Mussolini's philosophy was a welfare-state philosophy, very much akin to the philosophy of the administration in Washington, if you want to know the truth of the matter. Government controls—government interference in the lives of individuals, but allowing certain companies to be privately owned, socialism to a point—this was Mussolini's system. It wouldn't surprise me if he hadn't called it the Great Society. (*applause and laughter*)

Adolph Hitler was a socialist. He was not a Christian; he was an atheist. I remember speaking in Bodlingen, which is outside of Stuttgart in West Germany, after the war; and I spoke at a Lutheran nunnery, where they were training nuns for the Lutheran Church. And the head sister told me a story that Hitler had come into their convent early in the war, and she was telling me what a hypocrite he was. She said as he walked into the convent they had a table there with Bibles, little New Testaments, and gospel tracts. This Lutheran church in West Germany is quite evangelical, not quite so staid and formal as we are accustomed to here, but quite an evangelical group, quite concerned with the winning of souls. And he saw this tables of Bibles; and she said, "I saw him back up to the table and put one in his pocket; I saw him. I was standing where I could see him." And of course, they hadn't invited Hitler to speak. He was the head of the state; he demanded to speak; so they brought the people in the convent together to hear Hitler speak. And Hitler at one dramatic point in his message reached in and pulled out this Bible he had stolen. And he said, "You can see, sisters, I carry the word of God with me all the time."

Now ladies and gentlemen, that's pretty hypocritical, isn't it? But I think it's also hypocritical for a liberal politician, who no longer believes that God is alive and who no longer believes in the diety of Christ— I think it's equally hypocritical for him to take an oath of allegiance or take an oath of office with his hand on the Bible. To me one's just as bad as the other. (*applause*) I think it's also hypocritical for a preacher in the National Council of Churches, who no longer believes in the virgin birth of Christ, the blood atonement of Christ, the bodily resurrection of Christ, the second coming of Christ, the inspiration of the scriptures, I think it's equally hypocritical for him to stand up on Sunday morning and quote the Apostles' Creed. If he doesn't believe in the Apostles' Creed, he shouldn't quote the Apostles' Creed. His mistake is just as great as Hitler's mistake, and perhaps more so.

Hitler was an atheist; he was an agnostic; he did not believe in God; he was a socialist. But more than that he was in cahoots with Stalin and Communism, and these liberals' minds and their memories are very short. They have forgotten that Germany and Russia were allied until just a short time before the United States got into the war. The Russians and Germans were allied; Stalin and Hitler had a pact to control the world. They were both Marxists. They were both socialists. They were both welfare staters. And it was only when these thieves started fussing and fighting that the break came.

These liberal friends in this country—they would have you to believe that Nazism was like the conservative movement in America today, that it was anti-Communist, free enterprise, and Christian. I ask that man one question: Are you saying that Christ is responsible for Adolph Hitler? And isn't it strange that these liberals, when they talk about the killing of the 6,000,000 Jews and the 2,000,000 Catholics—isn't it strange that they never mention the 20,000,000 Christians and Jews that have been killed under Stalin and Mao Tse Tung and the Communist dictators around the world? (*applause*) What about the people that Castro kills today in Cuba? What about the Christians that are being killed still in China? What about the religious Tibetans that were liquidated? The male population was almost liquidated by Mao Tse Tung and his hordes. Why do the liberals have such short memories? They vividly remember the atrocities under Hitler, but they are blinded to the massacre of the millions of human beings by these godless Communists. Could it be that they have a certain affinity with Communism, a certain sympathy for Communism, and that therefore they pursue their blindness? They refuse to face realities that Communism has killed more people than Hitler ever dreamed of? That Communist dictators have grabbed more land surface than Hitler ever dreamed of in his heyday? How is it that they're so blind?

Ladies and gentlemen, the scripture has an answer. The scripture says that in the latter times (if you haven't read this scripture lately, you should)—1st Timothy, chapter four, verses one and two—"Now the spirit speaketh expressly that in the latter times some shall depart from the faith." Now he's talking about so-called preachers, ministers. You can't depart from something that you were not originally a part of. Today the people that are attacking the existence of God are ministers. Thomas J. J. Altiser, who started this blasphemous cult called the Christian Atheistic Society with the philosophy that God is dead, teaches ministers of the Methodist denomination at Emory University at Atlanta, Georgia. "Some shall depart from the faith, giving heed to seducing spirits." This means evil spirits, anti-Christ spirits, Satanic spirits.

Ladies and gentlemen, I contend that any senator, any senator, that voted against prayer and Bible reading on a voluntary basis in public schools last September, when they had a chance to vote for or against the Dirksen Amendment—I contend that those senators that voted against these spiritual traditions—they were not being led by the Spirit of God. They were being led by seducing spirits, but not the spirit of God. I guarantee you the Spirit of God will not lead any man to vote against prayer and Bible reading on a voluntary basis in education. (*applause*) And I further say, ladies and gentlemen, that any senator that voted against prayer and Bible reading on a voluntary basis, when that man comes up for re-election, I contend that Christians ought to go all out to defeat him and keep him from returning to the United States Senate. (*applause*)

May I remind you there were only three Republican senators in all America who voted against our spiritual tradition. Three! Javits, who now wants to be vice-president on the Republican ticket in 1968. Over my dead body he'll be vice-president of the United States in 1968! (*applause*) Javits, Clifford Case, and Kuchel of California. You ought to dedicate yourselves between now and the time that Kuchel comes up for re-election to drive that man out of the United States Senate. (*applause*) Now my beloved friends, only three Republicans, twenty, thirty Democrats, Teddy Kennedy voted against it, Bobby Kennedy voted against it, J. William Fulbright voted against it, Wayne Morse voted against it. They all, all these liberals, the liberal spokesmen who claim to believe in democracy, but they voted against something the people wanted—prayer and Bible reading on a voluntary basis in public schools. There have been three national polls that had asked Mr. and Mrs. John Doe, "Do you favor the Dirksen Amendment? Do you favor prayer and Bible reading?" And in the three national polls 85 per cent of the people favored it. But the liberals didn't care what the majority wanted. They don't believe in democracy. They lie through their teeth when they say they believe in democracy. They do not believe in majority rule. Here was a case where the people's voice was heard. They favored prayer and Bible reading. But no liberal could bring himself to vote for our spiritual traditions. So irregardless of the people's wants they voted against it. Hypocrites? Yes, they're hypocrites. It seems to me that these faithful that are always calling others hatemongers, it seems to me that they must be pretty expert in the subject or they wouldn't recognize one when they saw one. Shakespeare would say, "Methinks they protest too much."

All right, "led by seducing spirits and doctrines of devils." Now here is the reason for all this inconsistency. In the latter times these apostate state leaders (that is, they who have turned their backs on the traditions of their Christian society), the apostate religious leaders who have turned their backs on the con—their orthodox religious concepts, "speaking lies in hyprocrisy, having their conscience seared with a hot iron." Your conscience is not a valuable guide. Did you know that? The apostle Paul said that he killed early Christians out of a good conscience. You can mesmerize your conscience. You can absolutely brainwash your conscience. You can sear your conscience. Your conscience is not necessarily the voice of God within you unless you have the Holy Ghost living and abiding within you.

No my friends, this is an age of utter hypocrisy. Men talk of democracy and they practice dictatorship. Men talk of academic freedom and they practice the worst kind of dictatorship. The Johnson-Humphrey administration claim they believe in letting the voice of the Communists be heard, and they do not believe in one viewpoint. The National Council of Churches went before the Senate and lobbied, actively lobbied to destroy prayer and Bible reading and the government didn't say a word about that. But because I got a million signatures on petitions to uphold prayer and Bible reading, on that legal technicality they revoked the tax exempt status of Christian Crusade. The National Council of Churches lobbied to get the Voting Rights Bill passed, to get the Civil Rights Bill passed. They lobbied to repeal the McCarren-Walter immigration act. They lobbied to cut off financial appropriations to the House Committee on Unamerican Activities, the responsible committee of Congress whose job is to protect the internal security of the United States. There's nothing wrong with that, because that's in keeping with the American Civil Liberties Union far out left-wing philosophy; that's in keeping with the Americans for Democratic Action far out liberal philosophy; that's in keeping with Hubert Horatio, Bobby Kennedy, Johnson's far out left-wing liberal philosophy. In other words, you can lobby as a tax exempt foundation or church organization providing you're in step. But I got a million signatures to ask Congress to amend the Constitution to allow prayer and on that legal technicality they have revoked the tax exempt status of Christian Crusade.

Now ladies and gentlemen, I want to tell you something. They may have thought that I would lie down and take it, but I don't intend to. I'm suing the government. I'm appealing this, and I'm prepared to keep this in court the rest of my life until this issue is solved. (*applause covering next sentence*) Can the conservatives be allowed freedom of speech in the United States of America? (*continued applause*)

Now if you don't think that's something, you know what they did to me two weeks ago, don't you? Did you read about it in the Los Angeles paper last Saturday? Oh, it's just like Ma Perkins; every installment's different. Now they have come back and they say, "Well, now since we have held that Christian Crusade was not a religious corporation, because you influenced a political decision—." Now remember the only specific piece of legislation by name and bill number that was presented against me and Christian Crusade as evidence was the Becker Amendment. Now let me repeat that. When we asked them to prove the charge that I had influenced legislation. Since the days of the Magna Carta, you had a right to know the basis of their opposition or the basis of their charge. What piece of legislation did I influence? Give me the name. Give me the bill number. Let's not deal in generalities.

So the Internal Revenue, the Infernal Revenue Service as I prefer to think of it, came back and said, that we had supported the Becker Amendment, which we had, to allow prayer and Bible reading. This is the only specific charge they brought against me by name and by bill number in Congress. So on the basis of that technicality they revoked my tax exempt status—which means, ladies and gentlemen, if they get by with that, every preacher in California that backed prayer and Bible reading on a voluntary basis in public schools from a pulpit is in danger of losing your tax exempt status. Now they have come back in the last month since January 1 and they have said since I was not religious according to their feelings (I was political, not religious), therefore, the Internal Revenue Service does not consider me, Billy James Hargis, as a preacher of the Gospel since the day I started to work for Christian Crusade. Now the Constitution of the United States says that Congress can make no law concerning the establishment of a religion or the free exercise thereof. And that same paragraph of the Constitution says that they cannot prevent freedom of speech, not even from the pulpit.

Every minister in America is furnished a house by the church he works for—parsonage we call them, we Protestants call them—some call them manse. But a house is furnished. The house doesn't belong to the preacher. It belongs to the church. Betty and I did not have a house. We rented an apartment. But as our children came along, our four children, Christian Crusade bought a parsonage and we have lived rent free just like every pastor in America is furnished a rent free parsonage as a part of his salary. Your church furnishes your pastor a rent free parsonage. Now the government says since Christian Crusade is political, not religious, I have got to pay income tax on that parsonage all these years that I lived in it! Now ladies and gentlemen, many of you here . . . those of you here today who have been in our home, you know that you couldn't rent—that you couldn't rent that house in the city of Tulsa for $125 dollars a month. We would be lucky to get $125 a month for rent. Do you know what the government has charged me for that house? They have charged me $300 a month to live in that house. They arbitrarily set it. They have charged me $300 a month, which is income. Now get this. Not satisfied with that, the automobile that I drive across the United States raising money for Christian Crusade—they have now said that I should not be allowed a car, and they're charging me $150 a month for the privilege of riding across America to raise money to keep Christian Crusade broadcasts on the air.

In the first place, I don't even have that kind of money. I couldn't even pay one year, let alone seven. So I decided that I've had it. They're persecuting Christian Crusade. They're harassing us. They're trying to destroy us. They're determined to make this—take this work off the radio, to stop these publications, to prevent these rallies. They're doing every uncivil, unconstitutional, unfair thing that Johnson can think of to accomplish this. You know, Hubert Horatio Humphrey promised me that he would do this. Before the elections in 1964 in a speech in New York

City he said, and referring to me and another, "We will take care of those noisy anti-Communists once we are elected."

Now ladies and gentlemen, I am suing the Internal Revenue Service of the United States government. (*applause*) So my friends, this is our story, we are suing. It was announced last week that we have filed a suit against Internal Revenue Service. And we're going to take this all the way to the Supreme Court if necessary. And I tell you quite frankly, you people that belong to fundamental Bible-believing churches that are not in the National Council of Churches, they've got your number too. And if they can declare that I'm not a minister because I'm not a member of an affiliated denomination with the National Council of Churches and therefore I'm not allowed ordinary ministerial considerations in the filing of my income tax, then this thing will ultimately get down to you too on the same basis.

You know, quite frankly my friends, I've been in this fight for twenty years. I get tired, very tired. Last night Santa Barbara, this afternoon here, tonight Pomona, tomorrow night Santa Maria, Tuesday night Fresno, Wednesday night Salinas, Thursday night San Jose, Friday night San Francisco, Saturday night Tulsa, preach in the pulpit Sunday morning when we start the leadership school. No day off, week after week, not one day. I see my wife and four children luckily ten days a month. And now I have to get out and raise the money to, to try and get the freedom of speech, not only for me but every independent preacher by resisting this action of the Internal Revenue Service against Christian Crusade and against me personally. My friends, when you find somebody that'll stand up and fight for your freeeedom, you should not only pray for them but you ought to back them to the very hilt. What if I didn't stand up? It would get your church, get to your church much quicker. It would affect your minister much quicker. It would affect you much quicker. Actually, when you're supporting these conservative causes that are putting up a fight, you are investing in your own freedom. Sooner or later they'll touch you my friends. They'll touch anybody that resists this liberal establishment. You too will have a day of harassment and opposition and persecution unless you support those people that are willing to stand up.

Betty and I look at it like this, we have passed the point of no return. I've never been to Niagara Falls as much as I have traveled around this country. I have never been there, but a friend of mine who did take the time to stop off in Buffalo and see it, says that there's a sign up the river. People that go boating in the river above the falls—there is a sign up the river on the banks, a big sign that says, "The point of no return." That when you get to that point you're in a current and you can't reverse if you want to. I don't believe that America has approached the point of no return. I believe that we can return. I believe that we can recapture the machinery of government and I believe that we can establish churches that will do more for God than any church system or church organization in the history of America did. I don't think we've passed the point of no return. I think we can reverse this trend.

I want you to know this. I don't want your support if you think we're going to lose. If you think we're defeated, I don't want your support. You support me if you want to win. You support me if you want to save this country and reverse this trend and build Bible churches and build Christian-oriented schools. We haven't passed the point of no return. If we would have passed the point of no return, Christ would have already come and raptured his church and the world would have gone to Hell. But we haven't passed the point of no return; we have a chance. We have the greatest chance we've ever had politically in 1968. And if you change the situation politically you're going to help it spiritually. You know that don't you? We haven't passed the point of no return. But have you? That's the question. Have you given up? Have you permitted Satan to sing his siren song of defeatism until you believe it's too late? Is all the fight gone? Have you lost your will to win?

The liberals have lost their will to win. Ladies and gentlemen, we should turn our military loose in South Vietnam, let those boys win that war and come home to live at peace with their families. (*applause*) And had not this liberal-oriented administration not lost the will to win, this would already have been accomplished. Listen, if we can't, if we're not, if we're not military equals to North Vietnam what makes you think we could win a war against Russia or China? No it isn't that we're not military equals; we're far superior militarily, economically, spiritually. It means that our liberal friends are afraid. They're afraid of their shadows. They talk of nuclear fallout. They talk of nuclear energy. They talk of atomic war. They talk of—they're afraid! They have no God in Heaven. They depend on their own strength and knowledge and they're afraid! They live in mortal fear! But my God is not dead and I'm not afraid! God is alive and God is still concerned with nations and especially, in my, in my opinion, is he concerned about the greatest Christian nation in the world, the United States of America! (*applause*)

I haven't lost the will to win. I haven't passed the point of no return. I'm going to win that lawsuit against the Internal Revenue Service. I'm going to win. I'm going to appeal, appeal, appeal until they'll be sorry they ever heard of Christian Crusade or Billy James Hargis. I'm not about to give up!

[For the next five minutes of his speech, Dr. Hargis appealed to the audience, invoking religious and patriotic values, to live up to "your responsibility to God, your obligation to God," and to give to Christian Crusade to the point of "sacrifice." He concluded this section with a prayer in which he told God and his audience that "unless each of us work as if everything depends upon us and trust God as if everything depends upon

Him, we shall not win the victory we seek." At the end of the prayer, with no break of any kind he went into the mechanics of taking the offering. "Now the ushers will come immediately and give you an envelope . . . . " For about fifteen minutes more, Hargis continued to talk, sometimes informally, sometimes in dialogue with his audience, sometimes passionately. During all of this time the offering was being taken.]

Suggested Reading

Objective analyses of right-wing movements are not easy to find, since most books on right-wing activity are written either by extreme partisans or violent opponents. Richard Rovere's *Senator Joe McCarthy*, New York, 1959, is a good example of a hostile biography of the Senator, as is an earlier study by Jack Anderson and Ronald W. May, *McCarthy: the Man, the Senator, the "Ism,"* Boston, 1952. The opposite bias is expressed in McCarthy's own book, *McCarthyism, the Fight for America*, New York, 1952. Similarly Arnold Forster and Benjamin R. Epstein, *Danger on the Right*, New York, 1964, deal with later right-wing figures in an atmosphere of alarm rather than of objectivity. On the other hand right wingers Fred Schwarz, *You Can Trust the Communists*, Englewood Cliffs, N.J., 1960; and Robert Welch, *May God Forgive Us*, Chicago, 1954, are obviously interpreting data from a vantage point on the right.

Probably complete objectivity on such an explosive contemporary subject is unattainable. The closest approach to it would come in such studies as Norman F. Furniss, *The Fundamentalist Controversy*, New Haven, 1954; and Ph.D. theses such as Arthur L. Peterson, *McCarthyism: Its Ideology and Foundations*, University of Minnesota, 1964; and Dale Leathers, *A Descriptive Study of Revolutionary Reaction of the 1960's: The Rhetoric of Salvation*, University of Minnesota, 1965. The complete record of the Senate hearings involving Senator McCarthy's charges may be found in *Special Investigation on Charges and Counter-charges Involving: Secretary of the Army Robert T. Stevens, John G. Adams, H. Struve Hensel, and Senator Joe McCarthy, Roy M. Cohn, and Francis P. Carr*, 2 vols., Washington, D.C., 1954, 2,937 pages. The text of a documentary film dealing with the hearings may be found in Emile De Antonio and Daniel Talbot, *Point of Order!* New York, 1964. This volume, only 108 pages long, contains only a small part of the original hearings.

Index